Beginning Game Programming with Flash®

Lakshmi Prayaga
&
Hamsa Suri

THOMSON
COURSE TECHNOLOGY
Professional ■ Technical ■ Reference

ISBN-10: 1-59863-398-8
ISBN-13: 978-1-59863-398-6
Library of Congress Catalog Card Number: 2007923319
Printed in the United States of America
08 09 10 11 12 TW 10 9 8 7 6 5 4 3 2 1

THOMSON
COURSE TECHNOLOGY
Professional ■ Technical ■ Reference

Thomson Course Technology PTR,
a division of Thomson Learning Inc.
25 Thomson Place
Boston, MA 02210
http://www.courseptr.com

Publisher and General Manager, Thomson Course Technology PTR:
Stacy L. Hiquet

Associate Director of Marketing:
Sarah O'Donnell

Manager of Editorial Services:
Heather Talbot

Marketing Manager:
Jordan Casey

Senior Acquisitions Editor:
Emi Smith

Project Editor:
Dan Foster, Scribe Tribe

Technical Reviewers:
Erik Larson and Rex Cason

PTR Editorial Services Coordinator:
Erin Johnson

Copy Editor:
Laura Gabler

Interior Layout Tech:
ICC Macmillan Inc.

Cover Designer:
Mike Tanamachi

CD-ROM Producer:
Brandon Penticuff

Indexer:
Larry Sweazy

Proofreader:
Gene Redding

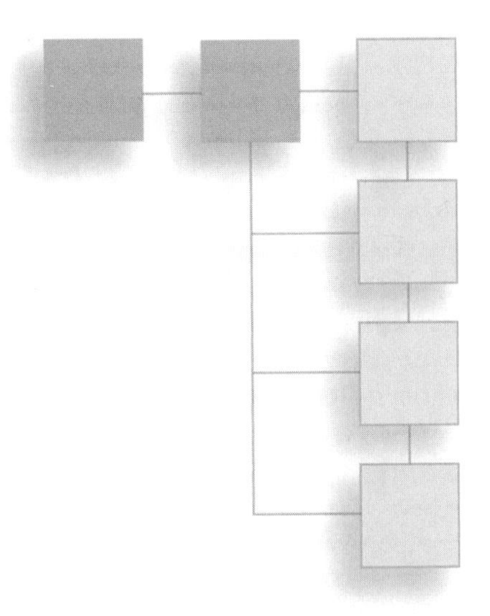

Acknowledgments

Thanks to Jay Shankar for helping us with the game design for the games in this book. Jay Shankar is a software designer and has been working with Flash for the past few years.

To Vinay Suri, a high-school student in California who helped us with graphics for the games. Vinay is interested in computer graphics art and animations.

To Dr. Chandra Prayaga, associate professor at the University of West Florida Physics Department, for helping us with chapters that required concepts in physics.

To Laura Gabler, for copyediting and addressing formatting issues in an extremely efficient manner and for providing corrections in record time.

Last, but not least, we thank some of our students. Thanks to Erik Larson and Rex Cason—graduate students in the Computer Science Department at the University of West Florida—for technical edits of the content, and thanks to George Trice—an undergraduate student majoring in Digital Art at the University of West Florida—for the screen shots for all the games in the book.

About the Authors

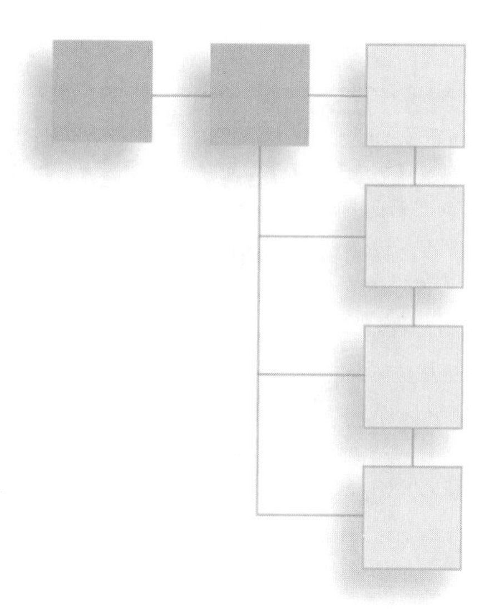

Dr. Lakshmi Prayaga is a faculty member in the Computer Science Department at the University of West Florida. She has a doctoral degree (Ed.D.) from the University of West Florida, a master's degree in Software Engineering from the University of West Florida, a master's degree in Business Administration from the Alabama A&M University in Huntsville, and a master's degree in Philosophy from Bangalore University, India. Her research interests lie in gaming as an instructional strategy and the role of technology in education and Web applications. Currently she is very active in design and implementation of games in K-12 and higher educational settings. In collaboration with the Escambia County School District, Dr. Prayaga recently received a Mathematics and Science partnership award from the Florida Department of Education for designing games for middle schools to teach mathematics for 7th- and 8th-grade students. The games will be implemented in the Fall of 2007. Her hobbies include cooking, traveling, and shopping. She is very proud of her husband, who is very patient and encouraging.

Hamsa Suri is a software engineer in California. She has a master's degree in Computer Science from the University of Manchester, England. She has worked on several big development projects for companies located in the Bay Area, Georgia, and Florida. She is also a faculty member at the University of Phoenix, teaching postgraduate courses online in Computer Science, Business, and Technology. She is a proud mother of two children and has a very supporting husband. She enjoys spending time with her family and getting involved in their numerous activities.

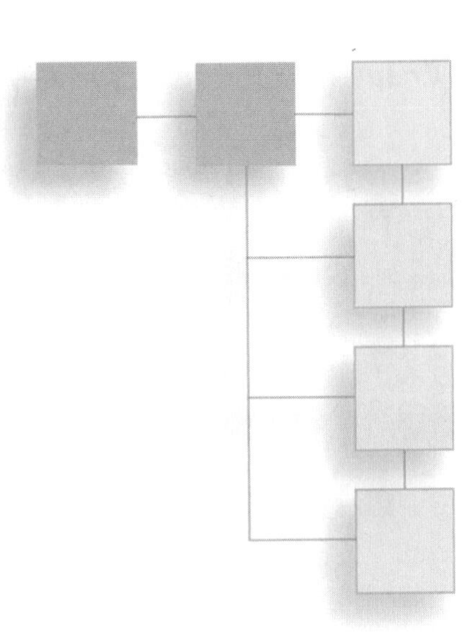

Contents

Chapter 1 **Introduction to Flash** **1**

What Is Flash? 1

The Four Parts of a Flash Document 2

The Stage 2

The Timeline 4

Flash Tools and Panels 5

Flash Symbols 9

Review Questions 11

Chapter 2 **Introduction to ActionScript** **13**

What Is ActionScript? 13

Variables, Data Types, and Assignments 14

Keyframe Code 14

Explanation 16

Expressions 17

Visual Built-In Classes 18

Movie Clips 18

Buttons 19

Text Field 20

Activities for Frame 2 28

Activities for Frame 3 35

Summary 41

Review Questions 41

Chapter 3 Interactivity—Adventure Game (Treasure Hunt) 43

Basic Software-Engineering Principles 43
Introduction to Game Design 44
  Importance of a Storyboard 44
  Functions 45
  Built-In Functions in Flash 46
  Events and Event Handlers 48
Sample Adventure Game 49
  Creating the Movie Clip for the Program 49
  Creating the Button for the Program 49
  Activities for Layer 1, Frame 1 51
  Activities for Layer 1, Frame 2 53
  Activities for Layer 1, Frame 3 55
  Activities for Layer 1, Frame 4 56
  Activities for Layer 1, Frame 5 58
  Activities for Layer 1, Frame 6 60
Summary 62
Review Questions 62
Project 62

Chapter 4 Animations 65

Introduction to Animation and Visual Effects 65
Types of Animation 66
  Tweened Animation 66
  Cel Animation (Traditional Frame by Frame) 72
  Other Visual Effects 74
Summary 88
Review Questions 90
Projects 90

Chapter 5 Game Development 93

The Game Plan 93
  Phase One: Design Phase 94
  Phase Two: Game Development and Coding 103
  Code Used in the Game 103
  Phase Three: Testing Your Flash Movie 114
  Some Common Errors to Watch Out For 114
Summary 115
Review Questions 115
Project 115

Chapter 6 Arrays and Movie Clip Methods 117
Let's Make a Game! 117
Arrays. 118
Arrays in ActionScript. 119
Drag and Drop Methods 120
startDrag() 120
stopDrag() 120
Linkage Identifier. 120
Explanation of the Code. 122
Loops 123
Picture Puzzle Game. 123
Summary 138
End-of-Chapter Exercises 138
Project 139

Chapter 7 Loops and Arrays in Flash: Simple Simon Game 141
What Are Loops? 141
for Loops. 142
while Loops 142
do. . .while Loops 143
What Are Arrays? 143
Creating an Array. 144
Array Methods. 145
Simple Simon Piano Game. 149
Creation of the Simple Simon Game 150
Game Logic Explanation. 152
Summary 160
Review Questions 160
Project 161

Chapter 8 High Scores Game 163
What Is a SharedObject? 163
Uses of a SharedObject. 163
Summary 182
Review Questions 182
Project 182

Chapter 9 Math and Physics for Games **183**
Realistic Movement 183
How Do Objects Move on the Stage? 184
Summary 215
End-of-Chapter Exercises 216
Programming Exercises 216

Chapter 10 Project: A Quiz Using Snakes and Ladders **217**
Elements of a Quiz 217
Story Line 218
Storyboard 219
Game Development 220
Summary 241
Project 242

Index **243**

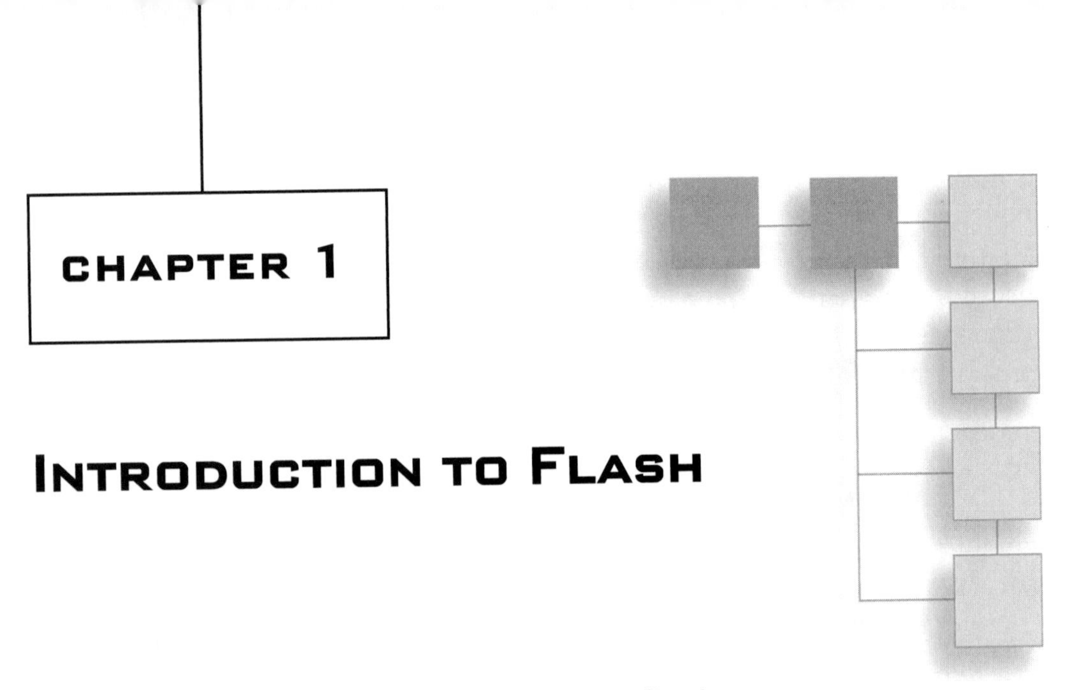

Chapter 1

Introduction to Flash

- Understand what Flash is and learn its applications
- Use the Flash authoring environment
- Use the Flash stage
- Use the Flash Timeline
- Recognize the difference between a key frame and blank key frame
- Know the Flash panels
- Know the different types of symbols in Flash

What Is Flash?

Flash is a high-impact, dynamic, and robust 2D designing and authoring tool widely used by designers and developers around the world to create presentations, games, and other content that enables user interaction. Flash projects or applications include simple animations, video content, complex presentations, applications, and much more. The terms *Flash document* and *Flash movie* are used synonymously throughout this book.

Flash allows you to create media-rich applications by integrating and authoring different media elements such as pictures, sound, video, and special effects. Flash is most widely used to create content for delivery over the Internet due to its small file sizes, which are achieved through Flash's extensive use of *vector graphics.* Vector graphics consume significantly less memory than bitmap graphics because they are represented by mathematical formulas instead of large data sets. Bitmap graphics are larger because each individual pixel in the image requires a separate piece of data to represent it.

There are two options for embedding graphics in a Flash project. If you are artistic, you can use the Flash authoring environment and create the required graphics. On the other hand, if you are a hard-core developer, you can import graphics elements such as .jpg, .png, or .gif files created with other graphics packages such as Adobe Photoshop, or you can download images from the Internet into your Flash document. Once you have the graphics files, you can organize the images on the Flash stage and, in conjunction with the Timeline, create your Flash movie. The stage and Timeline will be discussed in the next section of the chapter.

A Flash file is saved with an extension of .fla, which is the extension of the source file. When this Flash document is ready for export to the Web, it is exported as a .swf compressed file. To run the .swf file, the client machine must have Flash Player. To obtain the best performance, Adobe recommends the most current version of Internet Explorer (IE) and Flash Player. At the time of this writing, the current versions are IE 7 and Flash Player 9. Flash Player can be downloaded freely from the Adobe Web site: http://labs.adobe.com/technologies/flashplayer9/.

The Four Parts of a Flash Document

The Flash authoring environment includes four main parts: the *stage,* where you include all the graphics and text and any other elements you want the user to see or interact with; the *Timeline,* which you use to organize your game assets (graphics, sound files, and the speed for those graphics); the *tools and panels,* which provide you with the means to create your game assets; and finally, the *symbols,* which are the buttons, movie clips, and graphics that provide the required interactivity to the user.

The Stage

The Flash stage is similar to a dais (a raised platform) on which actors appear to perform a show. In Flash, the stage is a rectangular area. The stage is set to default dimensions of 550 × 400 pixels with a white background where you place your graphics, videos, buttons, and so on, which will be rendered at run time. Objects placed within the boundaries of the stage are the only objects visible to the player at run time. The gray area surrounding the stage is called the *work area*. Objects placed on this area are not visible to the user or the person playing the game.

Open Flash on your computer if you have not already done so, and refer to Figure 1.1 to identify the stage, the work area, the toolbar, the library, and the Timeline. Also, take note that any tabbed window can be "undocked" and repositioned. This is useful because it can increase productivity.

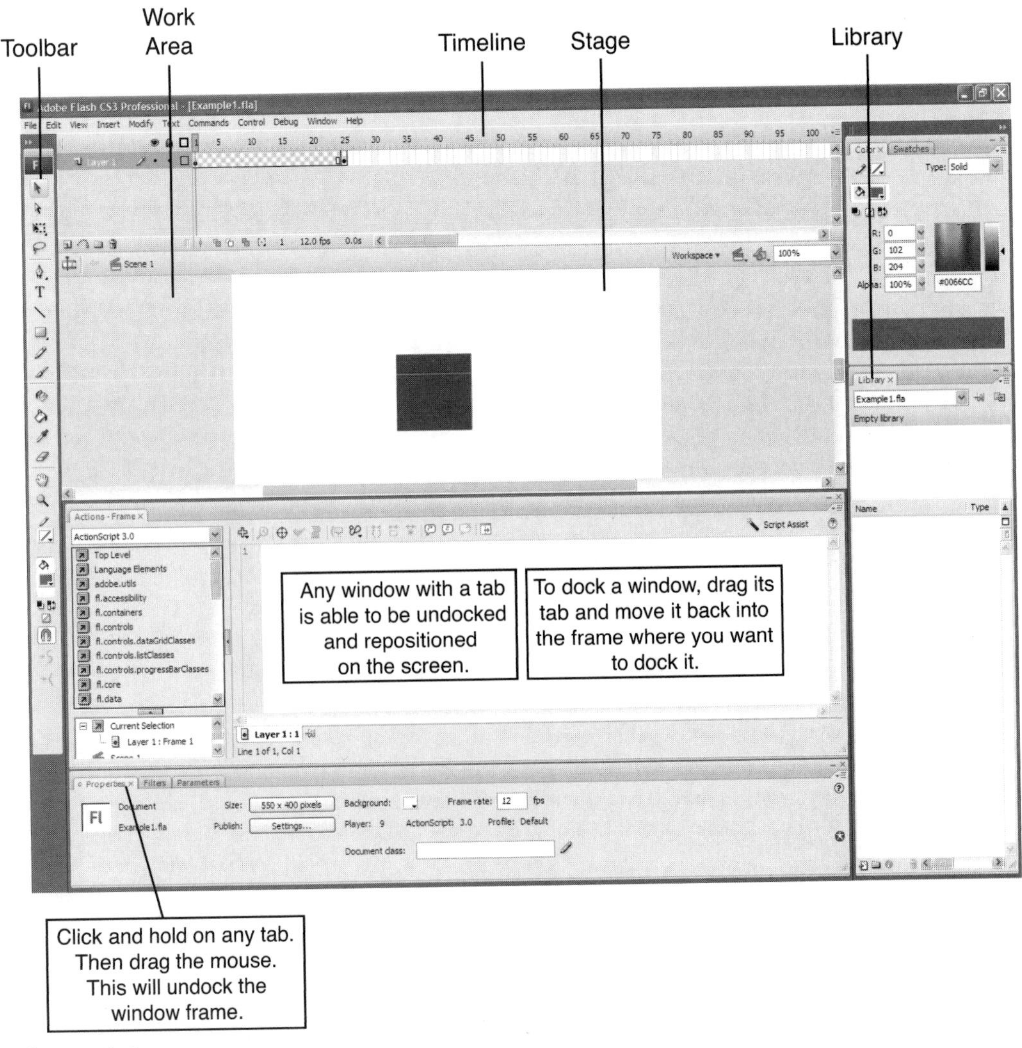

Toolbar
Work Area
Timeline
Stage
Library
Any window with a tab is able to be undocked and repositioned on the screen.
To dock a window, drag its tab and move it back into the frame where you want to dock it.
Click and hold on any tab. Then drag the mouse. This will undock the window frame.

Figure 1.1
The stage and work area.

The Timeline

The Timeline basically consists of a playhead that indicates the current position in a Flash movie, multiple layers for organizing your graphics and other game assets, a large number of empty frames, the current frame, the frame rate, and the elapsed time (see Figure 1.2). The Timeline allows you to arrange and program your game assets in the layers and frames to follow the game design. Game design is discussed in Chapter 3.

Flash has two different types of keyframes: a blank keyframe and a keyframe. A blank keyframe removes everything on the stage and gives you a blank stage—a clean slate with which to start afresh. A keyframe, on the other hand, copies everything on the stage from the previous frames up to that point, including any ActionScript code.

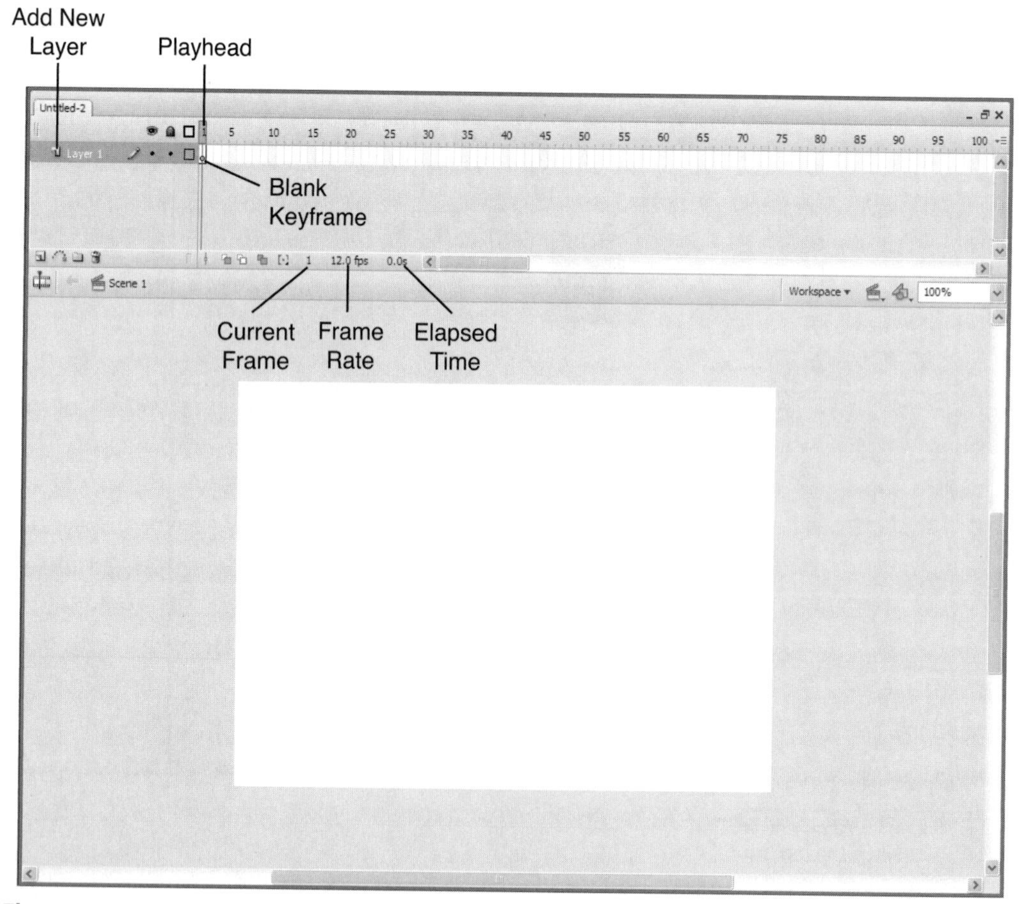

Figure 1.2
The Timeline.

By default, a new Flash document has a blank keyframe on layer 1. A blank keyframe is required to place any content on the stage. By default, content added on the stage in a specific frame is visible throughout the movie and extends over several frames unless a blank keyframe is added to a frame. A blank keyframe deletes everything on the stage when the Flash movie enters that specific frame. To add a blank keyframe to any frame, right-click on the frame and choose Insert Blank Keyframe or press F7. Exercise 1.1 illustrates the use of a blank keyframe.

Exercise 1.1

1. If you have not opened Flash yet, go ahead and open a new Flash document. If you just opened the Flash program, you will see the different types of documents that can be opened. Choose Flash File to open a new Flash document. If you already have been working in Flash, then simply choose File, New to open a new document.

2. Locate the toolbox (see Figure 1.5) or if you don't see it, click on Window from the main menu and choose the Tools option. Use the Oval tool in the toolbox and draw a circle on the stage. To draw a circle, first click on the Rectangle tool and hold your mouse on it. Then, from the drop-down menu, choose the Oval tool and draw a circle on the stage. Your screen should look similar to Figure 1.3.

3. Click on frame 19, and you should still see the circle on the stage. Everything from frame 1 was copied to frame 19.

4. Click on frame 20 and press F7. If you look at the stage now, you'll see that nothing is on it. The blank frame removes everything on the stage, so when the movie advances to this frame, it is empty.

5. At this point, something new can be added to this frame. Use the Rectangle tool and draw a rectangle on the stage. Your screen should now be similar to Figure 1.4.

6. Play the movie by pressing Ctrl+Enter. You should see the movie begin with the circle, and when the Timeline reaches frame 20, you should see the square. (Because the default frame rate is set to 12 frames per second, it takes less than 2 seconds to go to frame 20.)

Flash Tools and Panels

The Flash GUI contains the Library panel, ActionScript panel, Drawing tools panel, and the Color Mixer. Each of these panels is a floating panel and can be dragged to any location around the Flash window.

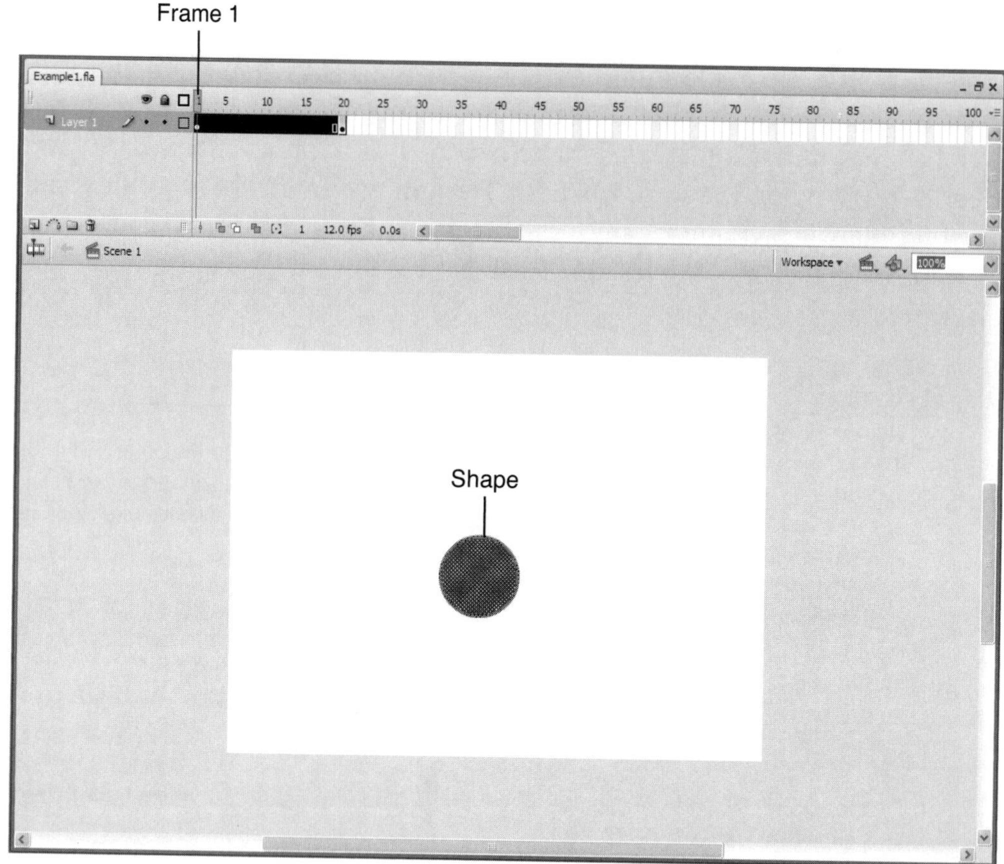

Figure 1.3
Initial movie clip.

The **Library** panel is where you can store the game assets required for the Flash movie. These include all the symbols, which includes graphics, movie clips and buttons (explained later in the chapter), and sound files, except for the vector objects, which are created on the stage and are not converted to symbols.

The **ActionScript** panel is the main area with which the developer interacts. It is in this panel that you insert the code to control the game assets (graphics and sound files) dynamically and execute the game loop. The game loop, in simple terms, checks for interactivity between the player and the game assets and renders the content to the screen. The scripting language used to write this code in Flash is ActionScript. This book uses ActionScript 3.0.

The **Drawing tools** panel can be categorized into three sections: selection tools, creation tools, and modification tools (see Figure 1.5).

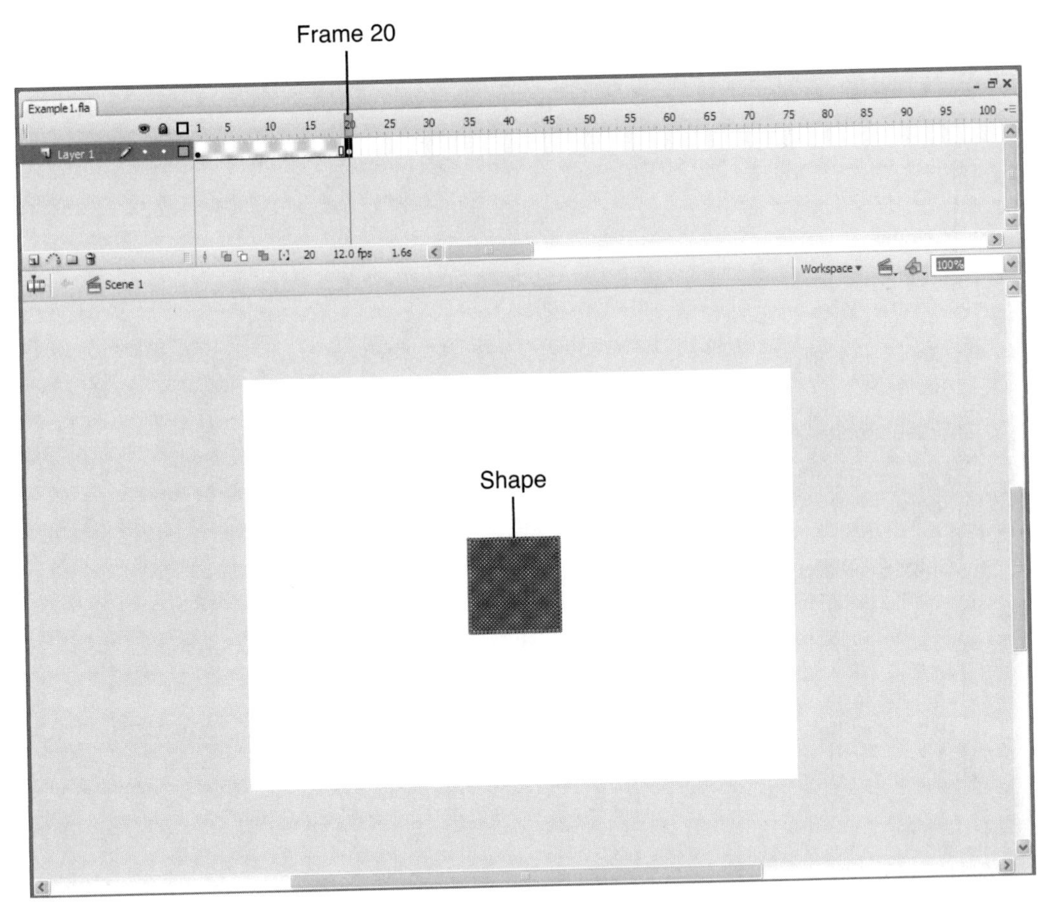

Figure 1.4
New movie clip.

Selection tools include the Arrow tool (black arrow), Sub Selection tool (white arrow), Free Transform tool, Gradient Transform tool, and the Lasso tool. These tools are used to select the already created or placed objects on the stage.

Creation tools include the Line tool, Text tool, Oval tool, Rectangle tool (which has additional tools that can be accessed by clicking on the small downward-pointing triangle), the Pencil, and the Brush tool.

Modification tools include the Ink Bottle, Paint Bucket, and Eraser. They are used for changing the attributes of the already created objects, such as the stroke color and the fill color, or for erasing a particular section of the drawing. To identify the different tools, move your cursor over each tool and wait for the pop-up tooltip description. It is a good idea to familiarize yourself with the different tools so you can quickly use them in later exercises.

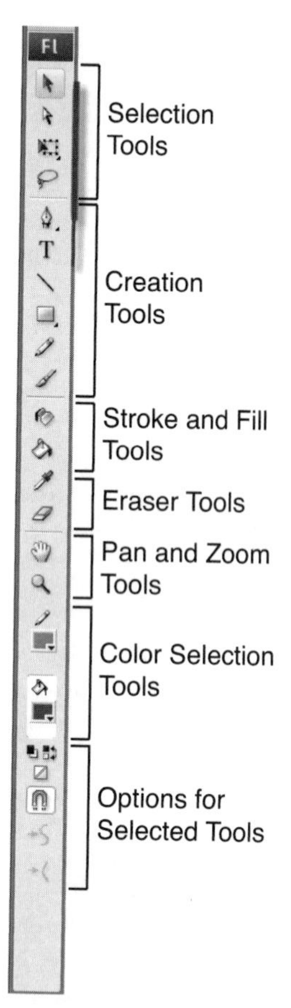

Figure 1.5
Drawing tools.

The Color Mixer palette is located on the right top corner of the Flash document. If you don't see it, select Color from the Window menu (see Figure 1.6). This palette provides options for choosing the foreground and background colors as well as for changing their alpha values. You can choose the type of fill from the available options—Solid, Linear, Radial, and Bitmap. Once you set the fill type to Linear, you can click on a particular shade in the color box and click on the little rectangular bar in the Color Mixer area. You should see a small icon (an envelope) on the rectangle. Double-click this icon and, from the Color pop-up window, click on any color to add that color to the Color Mixer. You can choose a few colors and add them to the Color Mixer area to get a range of colors. You can then use this color to fill your objects on the stage. The Color Mixer palette can also be moved around or collapsed, depending on your choice.

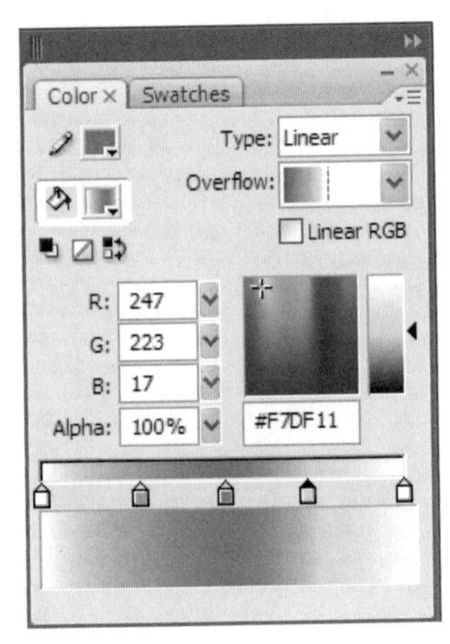

Figure 1.6
The Color Mixer.

Flash Symbols

Symbols are reusable objects created in the Flash authoring environment. Once a symbol is created, it is added to the library and can be reused in the current Flash movie or exported to other Flash movies. To use the symbol in the current Flash movie, drag the symbol from the library to the stage. The symbol on the stage is an instance of the main symbol in the library. You can consider the instance as a copy of the symbol. However, this instance can be modified by resizing or by changing the alpha value to meet the developer's requirements. The changes you make to the instance on the stage will not affect the symbol.

One of the main advantages of using a symbol in Flash is that the use of symbols reduces the size of the Flash file at run time because the file size is determined by the number of unique symbols in the Flash movie and not the number of times each symbol is used. Thus, it is a good idea to create and reuse symbols in a Flash movie to create efficient Flash files. There are three kinds of symbols you can build within Flash: *movie clips, buttons,* and *graphics.*

Movie clips and buttons are symbols that add interactivity. Code can be associated with these symbols to allow for this interactivity. These methods and properties are discussed in detail in Chapter 2.

Graphic symbols are useful when you have static graphics or bitmaps in the library and want to use them throughout your Flash document as backgrounds

Figure 1.7
A pirate.

Figure 1.8
A duck.

or just to lend some color to your Flash movie. Instances of graphic symbols can be dragged onto the stage and modified, but unlike movie clips and buttons, instances of graphics symbols cannot be programmed to provide interactivity.

Now it's time to have some fun. Open a new Flash document and use the Drawing tools to create some graphics. Also, play with the Color Mixer to get used to the different things you can do with the Flash authoring tool. See Figures 1.7 and 1.8 for examples of graphics that you can try, or use your imagination and create your own graphics.

This chapter provided an introduction to Flash. You learned the four main components in the Flash environment, including the stage, the Timeline, the tools and panels, and symbols. We further noted the difference between a keyframe and a blank keyframe on the Timeline and the purpose for each of these. You also learned about the different tools and panels, including the library, the

ActionScript panel, the Drawing tools, and the Color Mixer palette. Finally, you were introduced to the different kinds of Flash symbols. The next chapter will elaborate on ActionScript and symbols to prepare you for the rest of the games that you will develop.

Review Questions

1. What is Flash?
2. What is the difference between a keyframe and a blank keyframe?
3. Looking at the Color Mixer palette, what are the different types of fill options available in Flash?
4. What is the purpose of the ActionScript panel?
5. What are the three different types of symbols that you can create in Flash?
6. Assume that you want to create a Flash document that has an introduction to your game in frame 1. In frame 20, you would like to create a new scene with new symbols, backgrounds, text, and so forth. What type of frame would you use in frame 20: a keyframe or a blank keyframe?

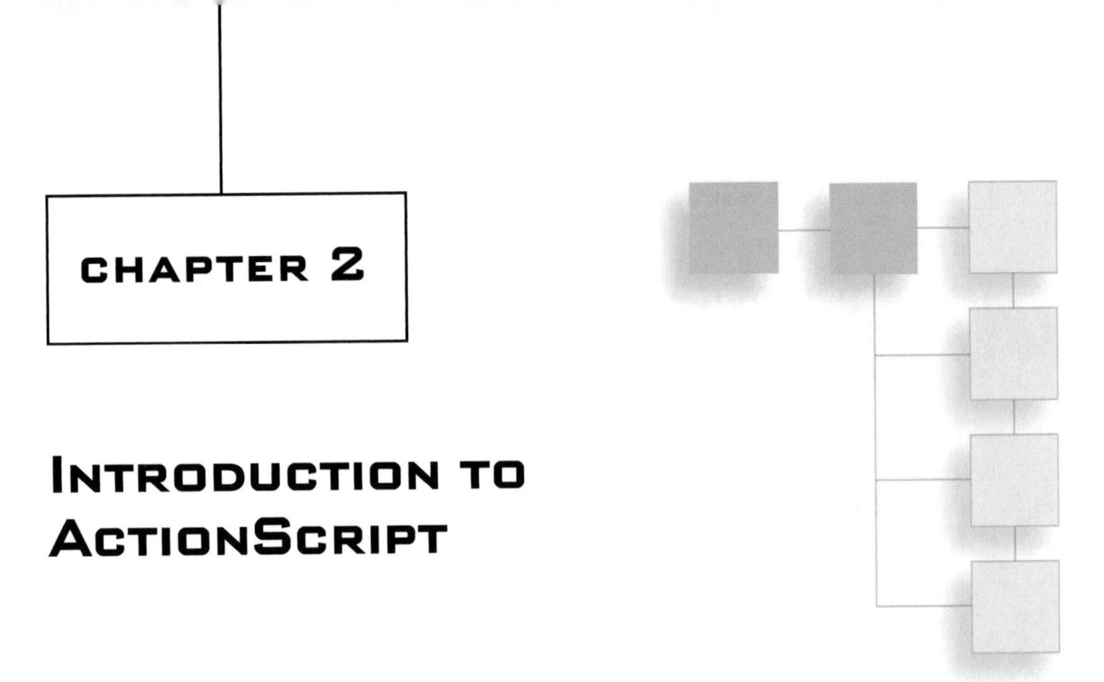

Introduction to ActionScript

- Create and use variables, data types, assignments, and expressions
- Use the trace function
- Comment code
- Understand the difference between keyframe code and object code
- Create movie clips and button symbols
- Learn the core properties of visual built-in classes: movie clip, button, and text field
- Understand static, dynamic, and input type text
- Add objects, instances, and properties

What Is ActionScript?

ActionScript is the scripting language used to control your Flash movie. ActionScript allows interactivity between the user and the Flash movie, which is essential in game programming. This chapter will introduce components—such as variables, data types, expressions, keyframe code, and object code—that are essential for creating such an interaction. We will also discuss the visual built-in classes (movie clips, buttons, and text fields) supported by ActionScript, because they are the building blocks for any Flash game that you create. This chapter includes two Flash document examples that will incorporate all the concepts discussed in the chapter.

Variables, Data Types, and Assignments

Variables are containers that can store data values. *Data type* specifies the type of data value stored in a variable and the type of operations that can be performed on that data value. ActionScript allows you to store the following basic data types: Number, String, Boolean, Null, Int, Unit, and Void. Number allows you to store decimal values and integer values; String stores values as text; Boolean stores two values, true and false; Null stores a null value default for a String variable; Int stores integer values; Unit stores a 32-bit unsigned integer; and Void stores an undefined value. *Assignment* is the process of assigning a value to a variable.

Following are some examples of creating variables:

```
var myName:String;
myName = "John";
var myScore1 : int = 90;
var myScore2 : Number = 100.20;
var result: Boolean = false
```

Keyframe Code

ActionScript 3.0 requires that all code be written in keyframes on the main Timeline. This is a major change from earlier versions of ActionScript, in which the code for the objects used in the game was written in many places, including in movie clips and buttons. ActionScript 3.0 supports code only in the main Timeline and in individual frames. This prevents writing code directly in instances of a button object since buttons don't have a Timeline. This method requires that a frame be converted to a keyframe before some code can be written in that frame—hence it can be referred to as *keyframe code.* It is also important to note that anytime you need to insert code in a frame (other than frame 1) on the main Timeline, you must insert a keyframe in that frame. To do that, you simply right-click on the frame and choose Insert Keyframe. A keyframe can also be inserted by clicking on the frame where a keyframe must be inserted and pressing F6. In addition, if you want the code in a particular frame on the main Timeline to make an object do something, you must refer to the instance of the object from the keyframe code. In this example, we are going to place the code in keyframe 1 of the main Timeline. Because the code is in frame 1, you do not need to insert a keyframe. Let's open Flash and open a new Flash document.

Exercise 2.1

Click on frame 1, layer 1 and open the Actions window, as shown in Figure 2.1. Type the following code:

```
stop();
//variable declarations;
var myName : String;
myName = "John";
var myScore1 : int = 100;
var myScore2:Number = 95.50;
var flag : Boolean = true;
//use trace to print the value of variables
trace(myName);
trace(myScore1);
trace(myScore2);
trace(flag);
```

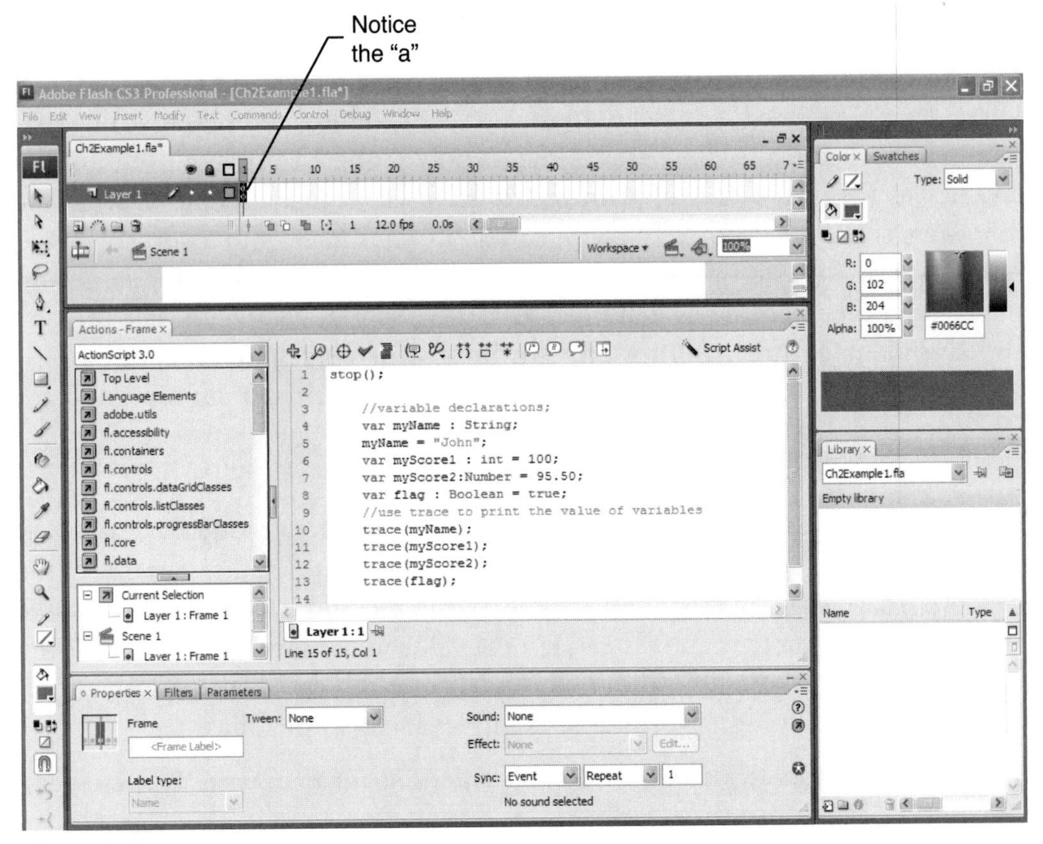

Figure 2.1
Keyframe code.

Figure 2.2
Example output.

Note

Notice the little "a" in frame 1. This denotes that there is some ActionScript code in frame 1. Anytime we place code in a frame, we see this little symbol.

Run the program now. You should see an output similar to Figure 2.2.

Explanation

There are several important aspects to take note of from Exercise 2.1 that pertain to good coding practices. First, look at the first line which has two // (parallel lines). These lines are used to comment your code. In other words, anything that you write on a line after the parallel lines is only visible to you as a programmer and not to the user or player. Comments are used to make a note of what the following code block does. It is important to comment your code so that it becomes easy for you or someone else at a later time to look at the code and understand the intention of that block of code. Second, you will notice that the code is indented. Indentation is only for improving readability; it is not a programmatic requirement. However, proper indentation practices are good for efficiency and debugging your code.

If you look at the Exercise 2.1 example code, you will notice that we have used two different ways to create variables. The first method is to create a variable and specify the data type on the first line and provide the value for that variable in the next line or even later in the program. The second method is to create the variable and specify the data type and also assign the value in the same line. Which is the right way? In fact, both are valid methods for creating variables in Flash. However, some points to note from these examples include the following:

The first method creates a `myName` variable with a String data type. This creates a container (a slot in memory), but it has no value assigned to it. This variable can only hold alpha numeric values because the data type of the variable is String. It is not necessary to give a value to a variable when you create it; the value can be passed on at a later point in time in the program, or you can assign a value when required. In this case, we assigned the value "John" to the variable `myName` in the very next line.

The second method creates the variable, specifies the data type, and then assigns the value to the variable, all in one line. This method was used to create the variables `myScore1`, `myScore2`, and `flag`. The data types used were Int (which stores integer values ranging from –2,147,483,648 [-2^{31}] to 2,147,483,647 [$2^{31}-1$], inclusive), Number (which stores both integers and floating points), and Boolean (which stores a value of true or false). Other data types supported by ActionScript 3.0 are Unit, Object, Null, and Void.

The most important thing to recognize about this code is that you must provide a data type for the variable when it is created. Avoiding this specification will result in compilation errors. Compilation errors are usually syntax errors caught by the language compiler before the computer program can be run.

Explicit data typing is important in programming as it will prevent any side effects in your program. For instance, if you have two variables with the same name and a data type was not stated, Flash could assign a string value to a numeric data type, which will cause problems in your code.

The Trace Function

Exercise 2.1 also included a `trace` statement. ActionScript uses the `trace()` function to display output to the user at run time. So, to print the value of `myName` from Exercise 2.1, you would type:

```
trace(myName);
```

The trace function is a built-in function that takes an *argument,* which is an expression or an object. In Exercise 2.1, we have used the `trace()` function to output the values of the four variables. More detailed coverage on functions will be provided in Chapter 3.

Expressions

An *expression* is a single statement or a set of statements that have to be evaluated and return a value. Typically, expressions are statements created by using variables, operators, and literal values. We have already discussed the concept of variables. Operators are symbols that perform specific actions. Examples are the symbols +, −, * , /, and so on. Operands are elements that are manipulated. Examples are 3, "Harry," and such. Here are some examples of expressions:

1. `num1`
2. `num1 + 3`
3. `num1 * (num2 – 4)`
4. `myName + "Smith"`

Example 1 is an expression that includes only a single variable. Example 2 is an expression of a variable to which a literal value is added with the + operator. Example 3 is an expression that has two variables and some operators. Example 4 is an expression, but the + operator here is not used in the arithmetic sense. It is instead used to join or combine the value of the variable `myName` (in this case, let us assume the value is `"John"`) and `Smith`, resulting in `John Smith`. This combining of two strings with the + operator, called a *concatenation*, is available in most programming languages. However, some programming languages use the `&` symbol instead of the + symbol.

Visual Built-In Classes

ActionScript has three visual built-in classes. These include movie clips, buttons and text fields. A discussion on each of these classes follows.

Movie Clips

A movie clip is a built-in object provided by Flash. An object is something that is created once and used many times. You reuse an object by creating an instance of this object. An object has properties that can be set and retrieved and methods or events that can be used to access it. Movie clips are essentially graphics that provide interactivity and hence are extremely valuable assets in a Flash movie. They have their own Timeline; you can insert code in the Timeline of the movie clip, which will execute at run time. Additionally, movie clips have properties that can be used to access and control the movie clip at run time from the Flash movie. Here is a list of common properties of a Movie Clip object.

`x`	Determines the x position of the movie clip on the stage
`y`	Determines the y position of the movie clip on the stage

`xscale`	Specifies the x scale (percentage from 0 to 1) for the movie clip
`yscale`	Specifies the y scale (percentage from 0 to 1) for the movie clip
`width`	Specifies the width of the movie clip
`height`	Specifies the height of the movie clip
`rotation`	Specifies the degree of rotation (0 to 360) for the movie clip
`alpha`	Specifies the transparency (0 transparent to 100 opaque) for the movie clip
`visible`	Sets the visible properties (true for visible and false for invisible) of the movie clip

Buttons

The Button object is a second type of visual built-in object provided by Flash. Buttons offer a great means to allow the player to interact with the game. Buttons have states and events.

Button States

The Button object has four states. These are the four states:

Up

Over

Down

Hit

You can access these button states at design time to provide interactivity to the user. For instance, when you create a button, you can change the color of the button for each state and observe the results at run time.

Mouse Events

Mouse events, which are accessible at run time, are also used to respond to the user's interaction with the button. Events are actions that can trigger something to happen in your program. For example, a mouse click on your Web browser is an event that can trigger the code to take you to another page. Some of the common mouse events are listed here:

```
CLICK

DOUBLE_CLICK

MOUSE_OUT

ROLL_OUT

ROLL_OVER

MOUSE_DOWN

MOUSE_OVER

MOUSE_UP

MOUSE_WHEEL

MOUSE_MOVE
```

Example program `ch2Example2.fla`, presented a little later in the chapter, will demonstrate the use of these concepts.

Text Field

The Text tool also has an important role in creating games. It is used to display instructions to the player, gather input from the player, or display scores or other run time textual elements to the player. To accommodate these tasks, Flash supports three types of text boxes:

- **Static text box.** This text box remains unchanged at run time (good to use for captions and headings).
- **Dynamic text box.** This text box can change at run time (good for displaying values from variables).
- **Input text box.** This text box accepts user input at run time (good for collecting user input and passing the input to variables).

Exercise 2.2

The main objective of this program is to illustrate the properties of movie clips and buttons discussed so far in this chapter. The idea in this example is that if the player clicks the Movie Clip Properties button, the movie proceeds to a scene that shows the different properties of the movie clip, and if the player clicks the Mouse Events button, the movie proceeds to the scene that shows the different events available for a button. This program has all the code in layer 1 and frames 1, 2, 3, and 4.

1. Open a new Flash document. Click on Insert, New Symbol and choose Movie Clip. You can also use `Ctrl+F8` to open the Create New Symbol dialog box.

2. Type `mc_ball1` for the symbol name. Your screen should now be similar to Figure 2.3.

3. Use the Oval tool and draw a circle on the stage. Fill the circle with any color you like. Your screen should now be similar to Figure 2.4.

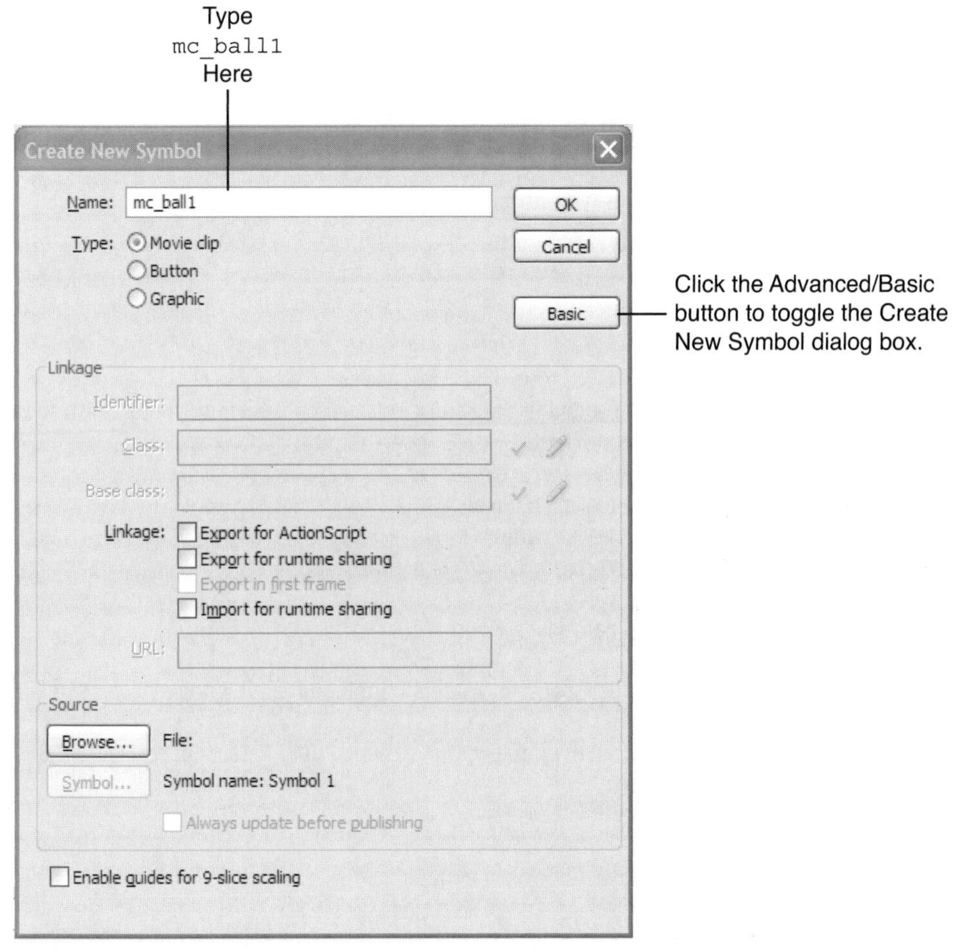

Figure 2.3
Type `mc_ball1` here.

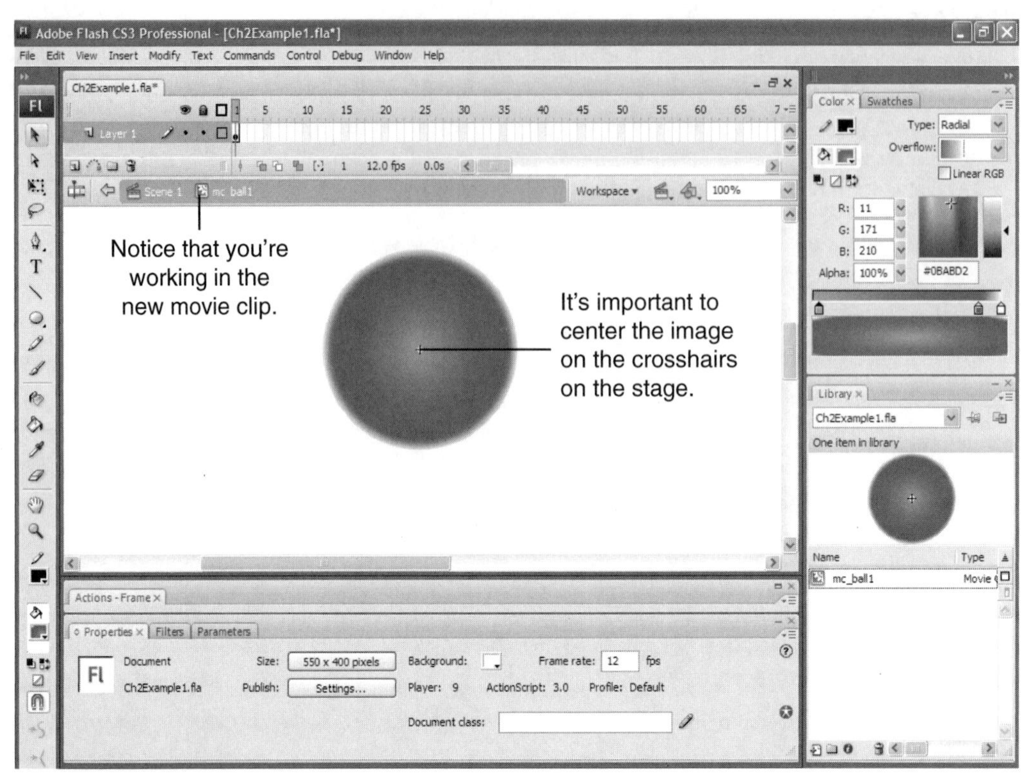

Figure 2.4
Fill the circle.

4. Check that this new movie clip is added to the library. This will be used in the program to show the different properties of a movie clip.
5. Click on Scene 1 to go back to the main Timeline.
6. To create a button, click on Insert, New Symbol and choose Button.
7. Type `btn_mybtn` for the button name (see Figure 2.5).
8. Use the Rectangle tool or any other shape to create a button, and fill it with any color you like.
9. Check that the button is added to the library. Your screen should be similar to Figure 2.6.
10. Click on Scene 1 to get back to the stage.
11. Let's add some color to the stage. Click on the stage.
12. If your Properties window is not open, click on Window and Properties or press Ctrl+F3.
13. You should see the Properties window, as in Figure 2.7.

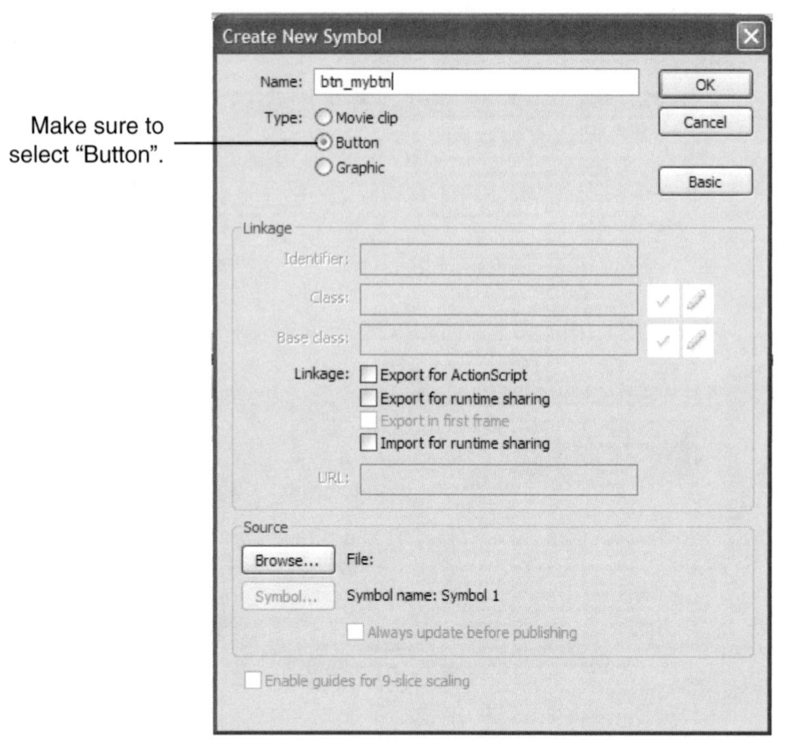

Figure 2.5
Create a button.

14. Click on the arrow next to the Background box and choose any color you like. This color will now be the background color of your stage.

15. Click on the Text tool and drag it onto the stage, and then type the text `Enter your name and press one of the buttons.`

16. Make sure that the Text tool is selected and drag and drop it onto the stage. While the text box is selected, click on the Properties window and choose Input Text for the type of text box, as shown in Figure 2.8.

17. Below the text type box, type `txtName`, as in Figure 2.8.

18. Make sure you are on Scene 1 and drag two instances of the button onto the stage.

19. Use the Text tool and type `Movie Clip Properties` on one of the buttons.

20. If your Properties window is not open, Click on Window and choose Properties to open it. In the Properties window, type `btn_mc` as the instance name for this button.

21. Use the Text tool and type `Button Properties` on the second button.

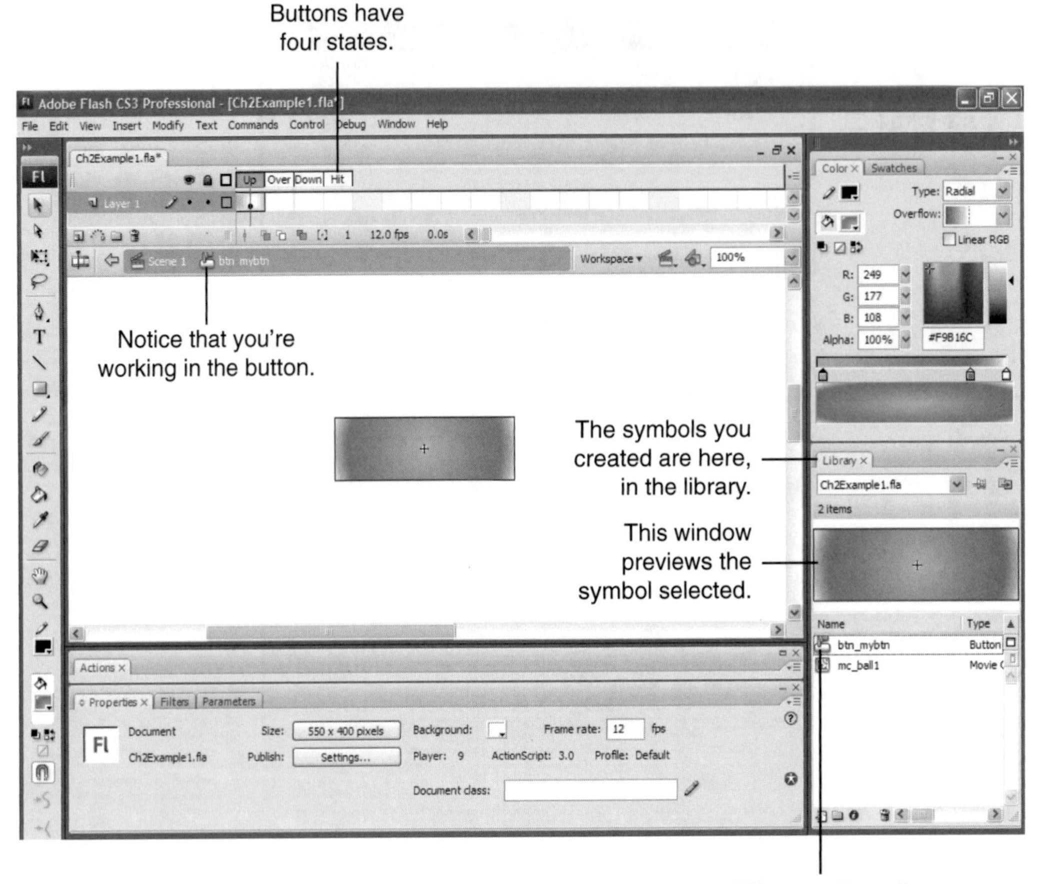

Figure 2.6
Add the button to the library.

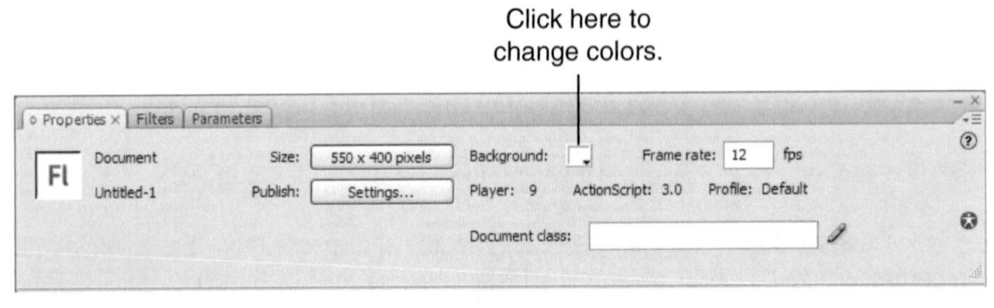

Figure 2.7
Properties window.

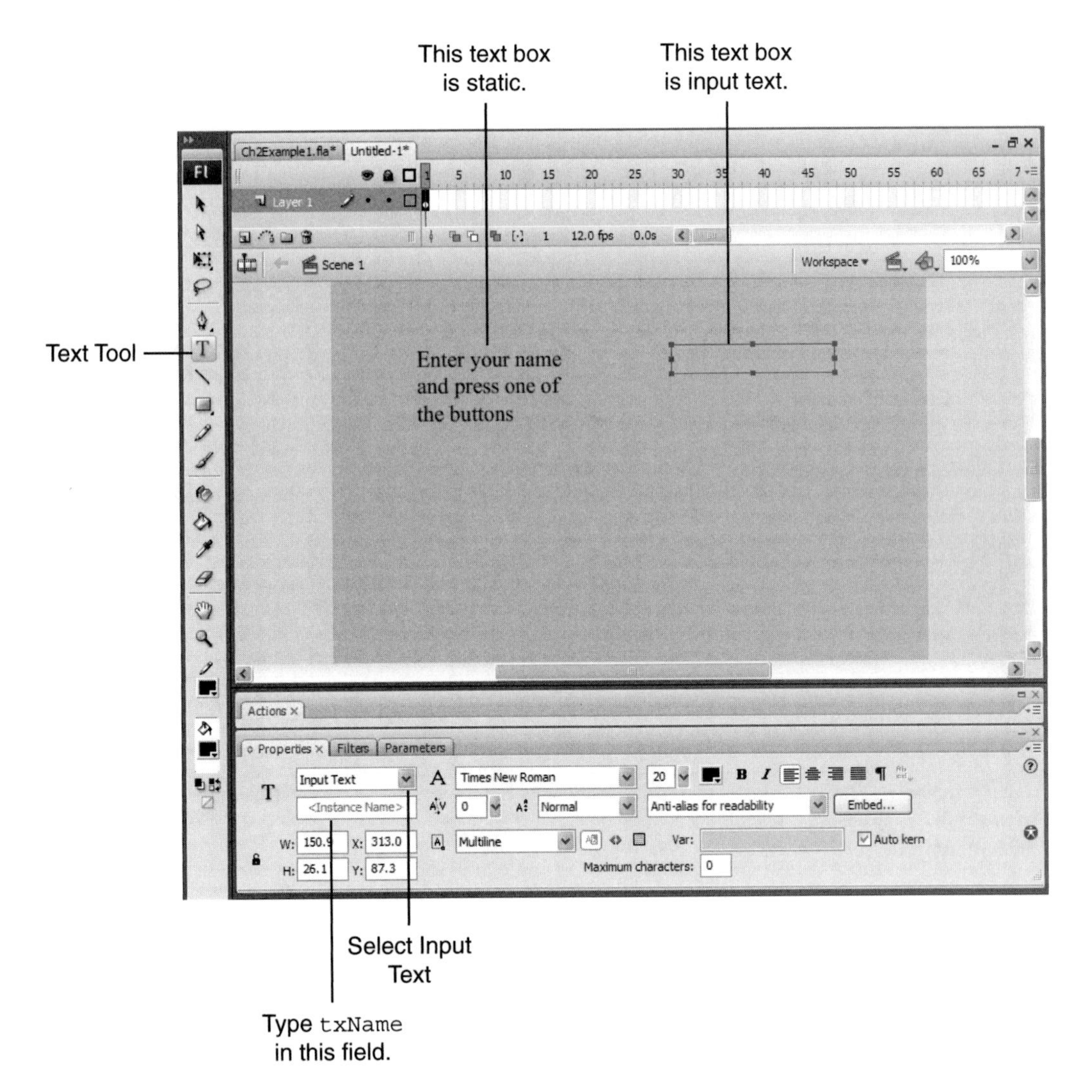
This text box is static.
This text box is input text.
Text Tool
Enter your name and press one of the buttons
Select Input Text
Type txName in this field.

Figure 2.8
Create an input box.

22. In the Properties window, type `btn_btn` as the instance name for this button.

23. Your screen should now look similar to Figure 2.9.

24. Click on frame 1 and open the Actions window.

25. Type the following text in the Actions panel:

```
stop();
var myName:String;
```

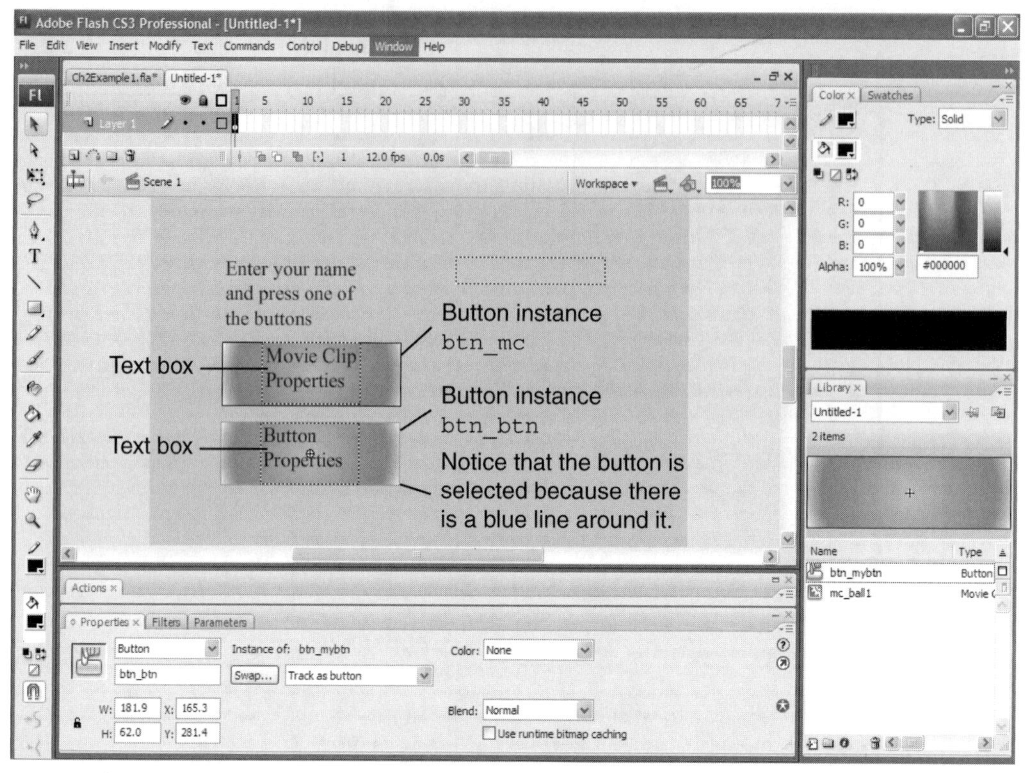

Figure 2.9
Add buttons.

```
function btn1_Click(myevent:MouseEvent): void {
      myName = txtName.text;
      gotoAndStop(2);
}

btn_mc.addEventListener(MouseEvent.CLICK,btn1_Click);

function btn2_Click(myevent:MouseEvent): void {
      myName = txtName.text;
      gotoAndStop(3);
}

btn_btn.addEventListener(MouseEvent.CLICK,btn2_Click);
```

Your screen should now be similar to Figure 2.10.

Explanation

The `stop()` command stops the movie from proceeding to the next frame. The name of the input text box that collects the player's name is `myName`. It is initialized to an empty string value.

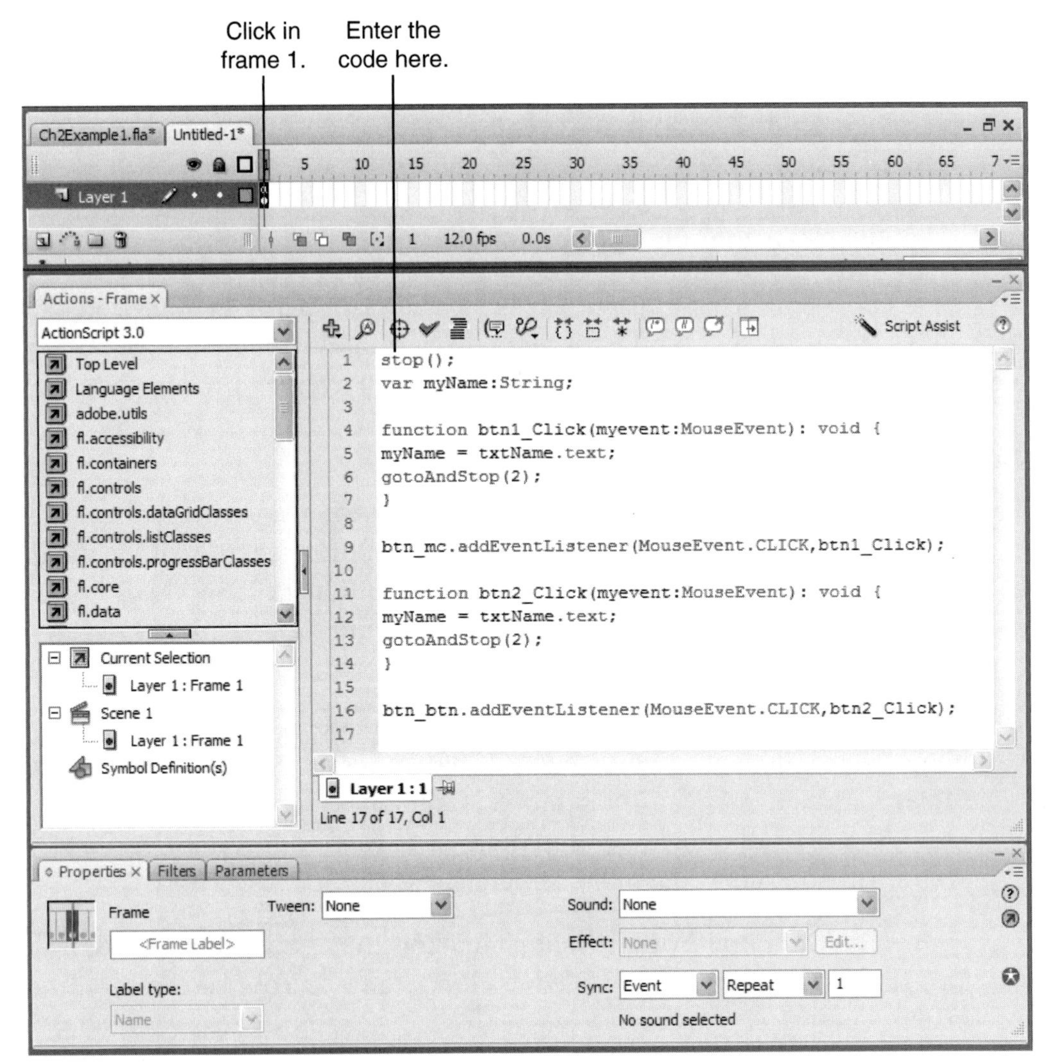

Figure 2.10
Actions-Frame.

The next block of code is important. We mentioned that Flash is an event-driven programming language. This means that the elements on the stage can respond to events that happen at run time. An example is where the player clicks a button or a collision occurs between two objects. In this example, the player clicks the `btn1_Click` button, which should then take him to the next scene, which has the code for the movie clip properties. The code that makes this happen must be written in a function that is triggered when the button is clicked. We add an event listener (`MouseEvent.CLICK`) to the `btn_mc`, which can recognize (listen to) when the mouse is clicked and triggers the function `btn1_Click`. The function has a code segment that:

- Takes the text typed into the `txtName` text box and assigns it to the variable `myName`
- Takes the player to frame 2 with the code `gotoAndStop(2)`

The same code is repeated for the `btn_btn`, which takes the player to frame 3 to look at the different events that can be triggered by clicking the mouse on the button. Examples of mouse events are click, double-click, roll over, and roll outside.

Activities for Frame 2

This frame contains several buttons. The idea is that when a particular button is clicked, the code associated with it will change one of the properties of the movie clip. For instance, clicking on the button with the caption `y button` changes the `y` property of the movie clip. So let's get started and build the activities for frame 2 to get a feel for the movie clip properties.

1. Before we move on, create a movie clip that can be manipulated in this frame. Make sure you are on scene 1. Click on Insert, New Symbol. Choose Movie Clip as the type of the symbol. Name this symbol `mc_ball1`. Use the Oval tool or Rectangle tool and draw a small circle or rectangle. Click on Scene 1 to go back to the main Timeline.
2. Right-click on frame 2 on the main Timeline and choose Insert Keyframe. You should see a small black filled circle in frame 2. Your screen should match Figure 2.11.

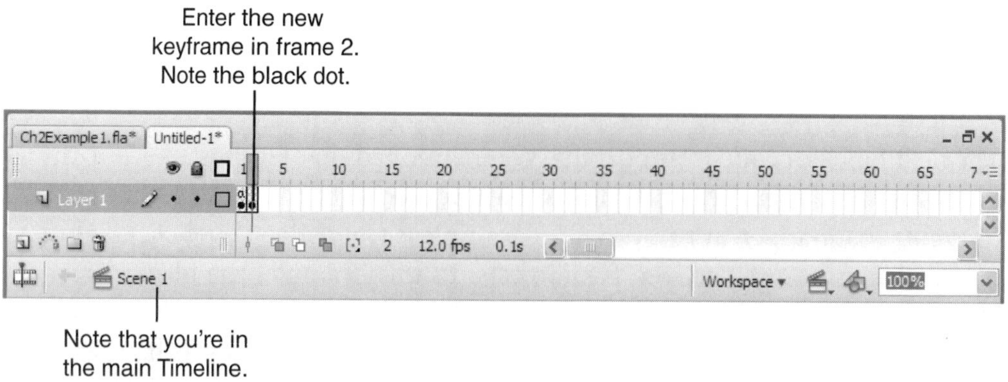

Enter the new keyframe in frame 2. Note the black dot.

Note that you're in the main Timeline.

Figure 2.11
Keyframe on frame 2.

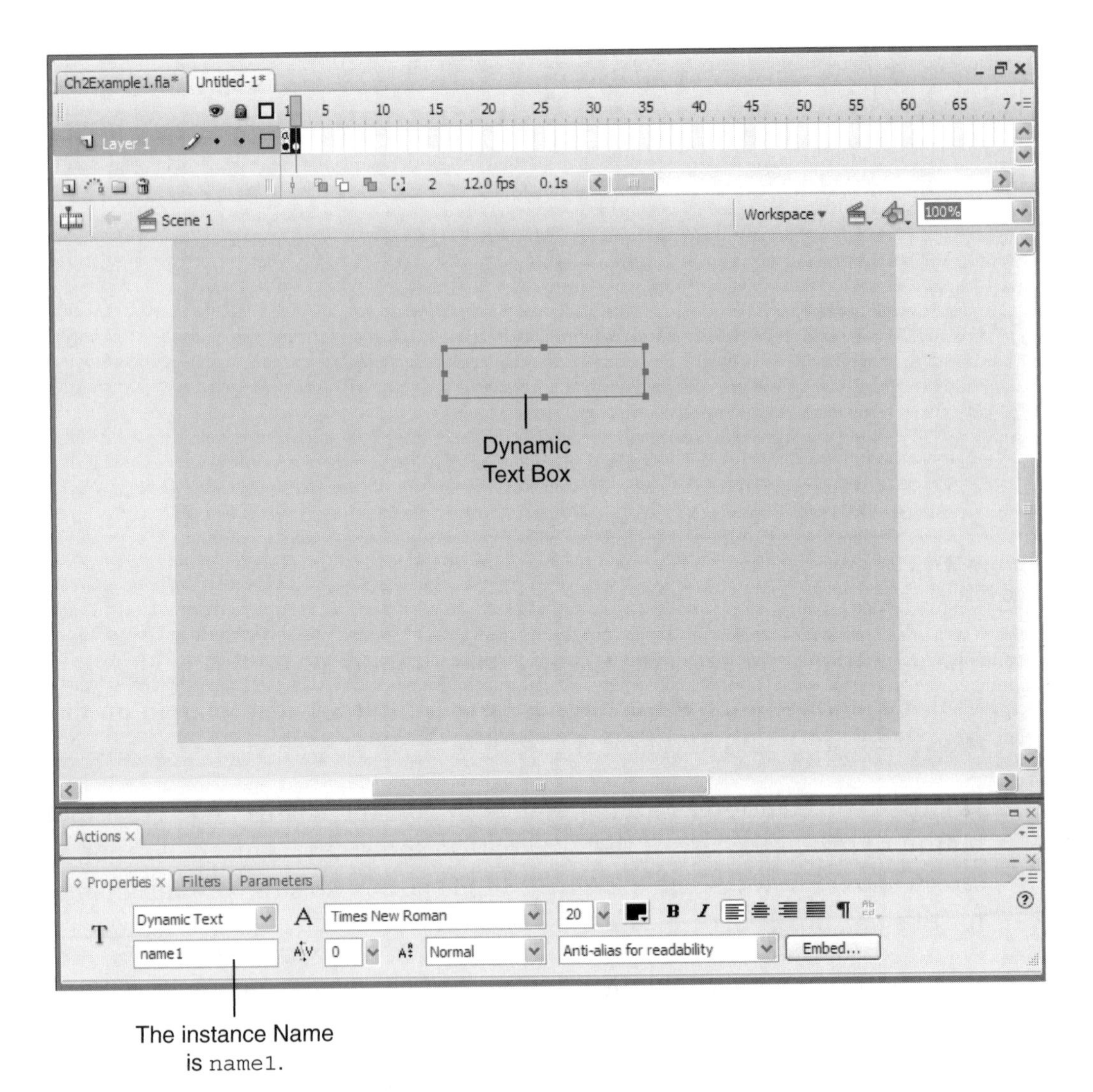

Figure 2.12
Change to dynamic text.

3. Delete all the text boxes and buttons on the stage. There should be nothing on the stage.

4. Use the Text tool and draw a text box on the stage and center it across the stage. Right-click on the text box and choose Properties. Change the text type associated with this text box to Dynamic Text, as shown in Figure 2.12. Type `name1` as the instance name for this text box.

5. Use the Text tool again and draw a text box on the stage. Type in `x`. Your screen should now be similar to Figure 2.13.

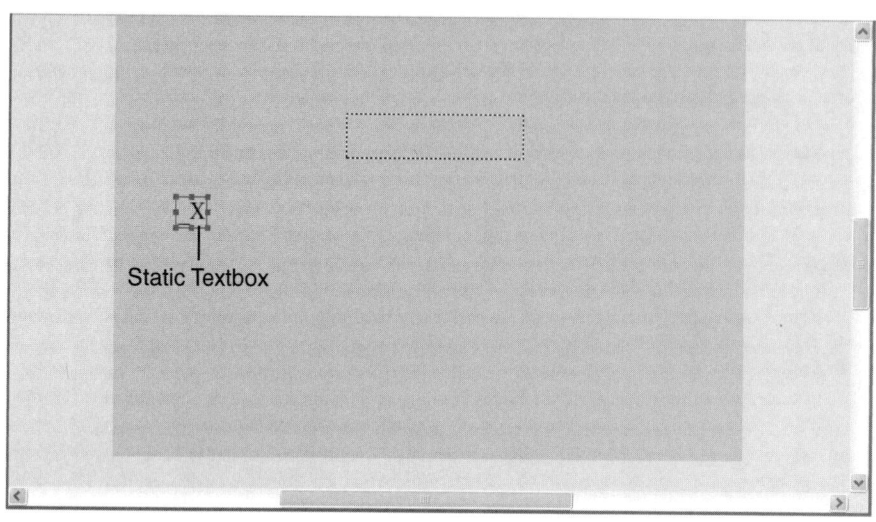

Figure 2.13
Add a label.

6. The next step is to create the buttons. Drag an instance of the `btn_mybtn` from the library to the stage and position it toward the left margin on the stage.
7. Use the Free Transform tool (▫) in the toolbox and change the size of the button to match the size of the little button shown in Figure 2.14. Your screen should now resemble Figure 2.14. Type `btn_x` as the instance name for this text box.
8. Drag the Text tool onto this little button and type the + symbol on it. Your screen should now be similar to Figure 2.15.
9. In a similar manner, drag seven more instances of the `btn_myBtn` from the library and place them on the stage, as shown in Figure 2.16. Include seven instances of the text boxes, too, to correspond to the text beside each button. Your screen should be similar to Figure 2.16. The names for the buttons are given in Table 2.1. The left column corresponds to the text caption, and the right column corresponds to the name of the button.
10. The last step is to drag the movie clip that is going to be manipulated onto the stage. Drag an instance of `mc_ball1` to the stage and place it on the center of the stage, below the buttons. Type `mc_ball1` as the instance name for this instance. Your screen should be similar to Figure 2.17. This completes the design of the interface for frame 2.

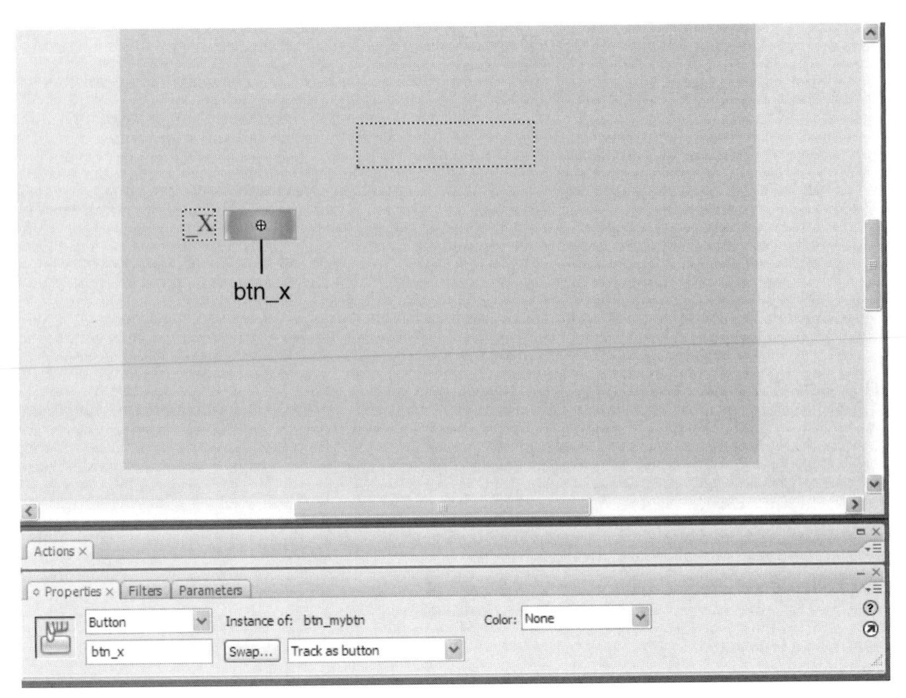

Figure 2.14
Add a button.

Figure 2.15
Button with +.

11. Click on frame 2, open the Actions window, and type the following code:

```
stop();

name1.text = myName + " Experiment with the Movie Clip Properties";


function buttonx(myevent:MouseEvent): void {
      mc_ball.x +=5;
}

btn_x.addEventListener(MouseEvent.CLICK,buttonx);

function buttony(myevent:MouseEvent): void {
      mc_ball.y +=5;
}
```

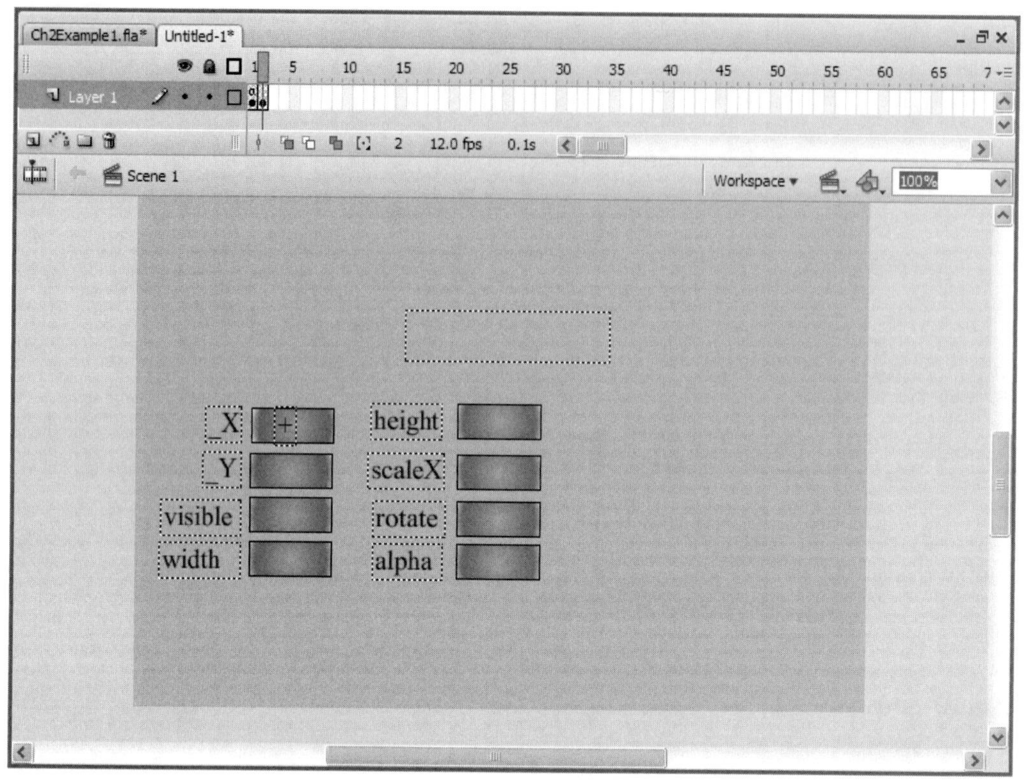

Figure 2.16
Completed screen with buttons and text boxes.

Table 2.1

Caption	Instance Name for the Button
x	btn_x
y	btn_y
visible	btn_visible
width	btn_width
height	btn_height
scaleX	btn_scaleX
rotate	btn_rotate

```
btn_y.addEventListener(MouseEvent.CLICK,buttony);

function buttonV(myevent:MouseEvent): void {
      mc_ball.visible = false;
}
```

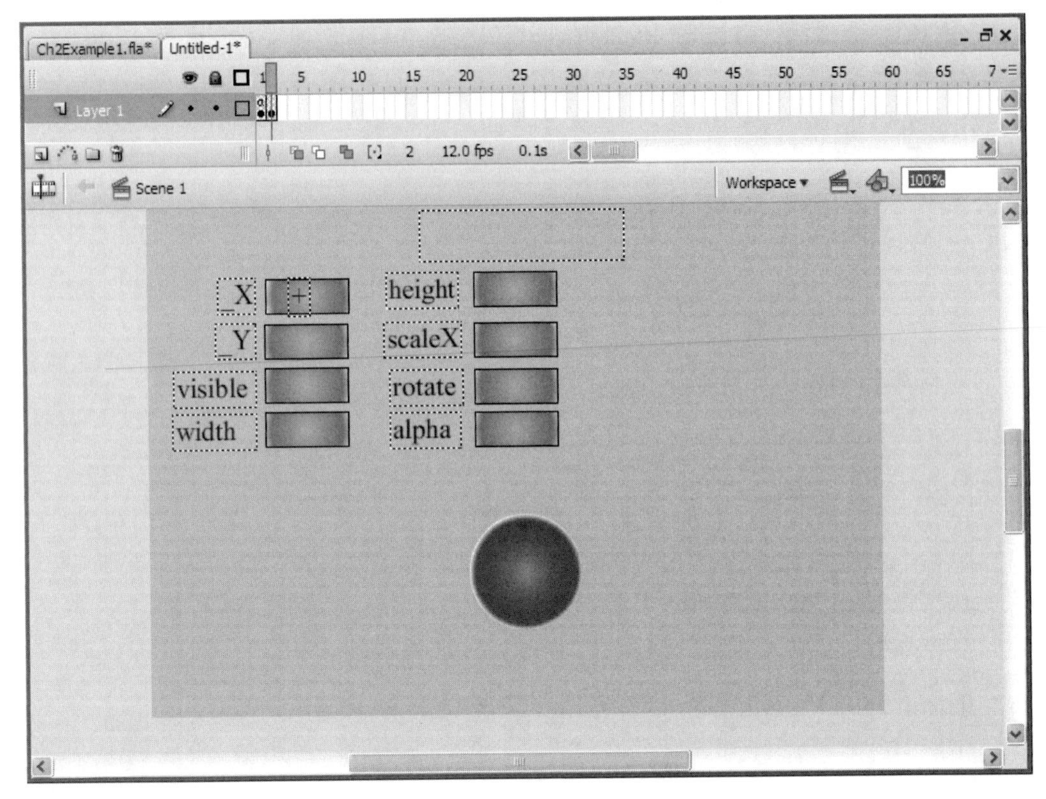

Figure 2.17
Completed stage.

```
btn_visible.addEventListener(MouseEvent.CLICK,buttonV);

function buttonW(myevent:MouseEvent): void {
      mc_ball.width += 5;
}

btn_width.addEventListener(MouseEvent.CLICK,buttonW);


function buttonH(myevent:MouseEvent): void {
      mc_ball.height += 5;
}

btn_height.addEventListener(MouseEvent.CLICK,buttonH);

function buttonS(myevent:MouseEvent): void {
      mc_ball.scaleX = .30;
}
```

```
btn_scaleX.addEventListener(MouseEvent.CLICK,buttonS);

function buttonR(myevent:MouseEvent): void {
      mc_ball.rotation += .30;
}

btn_rotate.addEventListener(MouseEvent.CLICK,buttonR);


function buttonA(myevent:MouseEvent): void {
      mc_ball.alpha = .50;
}

btn_alpha.addEventListener(MouseEvent.CLICK,buttonA);
```

12. Your screen should match Figure 2.18. Make sure you see Layer 1 : 2 at the bottom, as in Figure 2.18. This ensures that you are on layer 1, frame 2.

13. The `stop()` function, as seen earlier, stops the movie from proceeding to the next frame.

14. `name1` is the name of the dynamic text box that gets the string value `myName + "Experiment with the Movie Clip Properties"`. `myName` is the name of the variable that has the user-typed name from the previous scene, and the rest of the string (`"Experiment[...]"`) is concatenated with it. Notice that the + sign, when used in the context of strings, is the concatenation operator, which is used to join one or more strings and/or variable values.

The rest of the code is to demonstrate the properties of a movie clip. Each time the player clicks on one of the buttons, a specific property of the movie clip is executed. The button's click event triggers the execution of that specific code. The explanation for the button's click event remains the same as in the code for frame 1. Table 2.2 presents the explanation for this section of the code.

Try and experiment with this code by changing the values for `width`, `height`, `x`, `y`, `rotate`, `scale`, `rotation`, and `alpha` and observe the changes in the movie clip. Make sure to try negative values for `x`, `y`, `width`, and `height` properties.

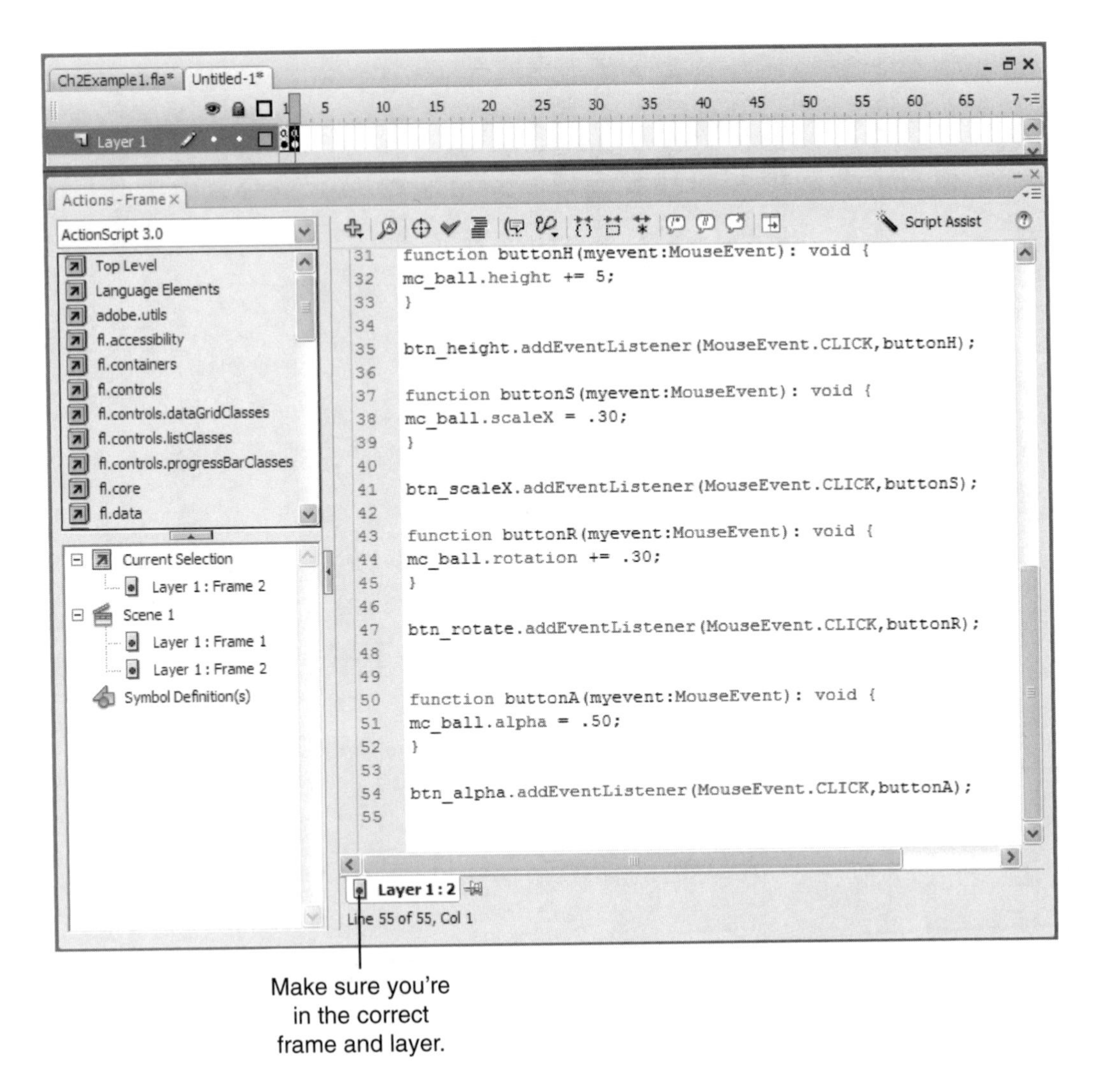

Figure 2.18
Check layer and frame.

Activities for Frame 3

This frame contains the code to illustrate the events available for a mouse that can be listened to by a button as discussed earlier in the chapter.

1. Right-click on frame 3 and choose Insert Keyframe.
2. Delete everything from the stage.
3. Use the Text tool and draw a text box on the stage and center it across the stage. Right-click on the text box and choose Properties. Change the text

Table 2.2 Movie Clip and Button Controls in Frame 2

Name of the Button	Code to Change the Property of the Movie Clip	Function Name	Explanation

btn_x	function buttonx(myevent:MouseEvent): void {
	mc_ball.x +=5;
	}
	
	btn_x.addEventListener(MouseEvent.CLICK,buttonx);
		buttonx	Moves the movie clip by 50 pixels to the right.
			
			The click event is added to btn_x so it can be triggered when the user clicks the button. Once the click event is triggered, it calls the function buttonx, which will move the movie clip by 50 pixels to the right.
			
			The explanation for the click event applies to all the rest of the buttons where the click event triggers a function that modifies a specific property of the movie clip, so it will not be repeated.

btn_y	function buttony(myevent:MouseEvent): void {
	mc_ball.x +=5;
	}
	
	btn_y.addEventListener(MouseEvent.CLICK,buttonx);
		buttony	Moves the movie clip lower by 50 pixels.

btn_visible	function buttonV(myevent:MouseEvent): void {
	mc_ball.visible = false;
	}
	
	btn_visible.addEventListener(MouseEvent.CLICK,buttonV);
		buttonV	Sets the visible property of the movie clip to true or false. In this case, it is set to false.

btn_width	`function buttonW(myevent:MouseEvent): void {`
	`mc_ball.width += 5;`
	`}`
	
	`btn_width.addEventListener(MouseEvent.CLICK,buttonW);`
		buttonW	Increases the width of the movie clip by 5 pixels.

btn_height	`function buttonH(myevent:MouseEvent): void {`
	`mc_ball.height += 5;`
	`}`
	
	`btn_height.addEventListener(MouseEvent.CLICK,buttonH);`
		buttonH	Increases the height of the movie clip by 5 pixels.

btn_scale	`function buttonS(myevent:MouseEvent): void {`
	`mc_ball.scaleX = .30;`
	`}`
	
	`btn_scaleX.addEventListener(MouseEvent.CLICK,buttonS);`
		buttonS	Scales down the movie clip to 30% of its original size.

btn_rotate	`function buttonR(myevent:MouseEvent): void {`
	`mc_ball.rotation += 200;`
	`}`
	
	`btn_rotate.addEventListener(MouseEvent.CLICK,buttonR);`
		buttonR	Rotates the movie clip by 200 degrees.

btn_alpha	`function buttonA(myevent:MouseEvent): void {`
	`mc_ball.alpha = .50;`
	`}`
	
	`btn_alpha.addEventListener(MouseEvent.CLICK,buttonA);`
		buttonA	Sets the transparency of the movie clip to 50% of its original alpha value.

type associated with this text box to Dynamic Text, as shown in Figure 2.12. Type `name2` as the instance name for this text box.

4. Drag an instance of the `btn_mybtn` from the library to the stage and provide it with the instance name `mybtn`.

5. Open the Actions window and make sure it says Layer 1, Frame 3. Type the following code:

```
stop();

name2.text = myName + "Experiment with the Movie Clip Properties";

function btnpress(myevent:MouseEvent): void {
trace("you clicked me");
}

myBtn.addEventListener(MouseEvent.CLICK,btnpress);


function btnrollover(myevent:MouseEvent): void {
trace("you rolled over me");
}

myBtn.addEventListener(MouseEvent.ROLL_OVER,btnrollover);

function btnreleaseoutside(myevent:MouseEvent): void {
trace("your mouse is outside of me");
}

myBtn.addEventListener(MouseEvent.MOUSE_OUT,btnreleaseoutside);
```

As in frame 2, the `stop()` function prevents the Flash movie from proceeding to the next frame. It also displays the name typed by the player in a dynamic text box `name2`. The rest of the code illustrates some of the available mouse events, and the explanation is provided in Table 2.3.

Note

ActionScript 3.0 is case sensitive. So if you type `mybtn` instead of `myBtn` your code will not work!

Now is a good time to extend the code and try other events listed earlier in the chapter, such as `DOUBLE_CLICK`, `MOUSE_UP`.

Table 2.3 Mouse Events

Event	Code	Explanation

CLICK	`function btnpress(myevent:MouseEvent): void {`
	`trace("you clicked me");`
	`}`
	`myBtn.addEventListener(MouseEvent.CLICK,btnpress);`
		Happens when the mouse is clicked—prints "you clicked me."

ROLL_OVER	`function btnrollover(myevent:MouseEvent): void {`
	`trace("you rolled over me");`
	`}`
	`myBtn.addEventListener(MouseEvent.`
	`ROLL_OVER,btnrollover);`
		Happens when the mouse rolls over the button—prints "you rolled over me."

MOUSE_OUT	`function btnreleaseoutside(myevent:MouseEvent):`
	`void {`
	`trace("your mouse is outside of me");`
	`}`
	`myBtn.addEventListener(MouseEvent.MOUSE_OUT,`
	`btnreleaseoutside);`
		Happens when the mouse moves outside the button—prints "your mouse is outside of me."

Interacting with the Button States

In this section we will look at providing interactivity with button states. The button's fill color will be changed for different states, so you have different colors for different states of the button.

Before you start, make sure you are on the main Timeline (which is Scene 1) so that we can create a button and then change its behavior.

1. Click on Insert, New Symbol, and choose Button as the type of symbol. Type `btn_mybtn2` as the name of the symbol.

2. Click on the Oval tool and draw a button on the stage. Fill it with any color you like. Your screen should now match Figure 2.19. This is the color of the button when the mouse is up, meaning that the mouse has not been clicked. This is the default state for the button.

3. The next step is to provide some action when the mouse is over the button. Click on the square below the Over box.

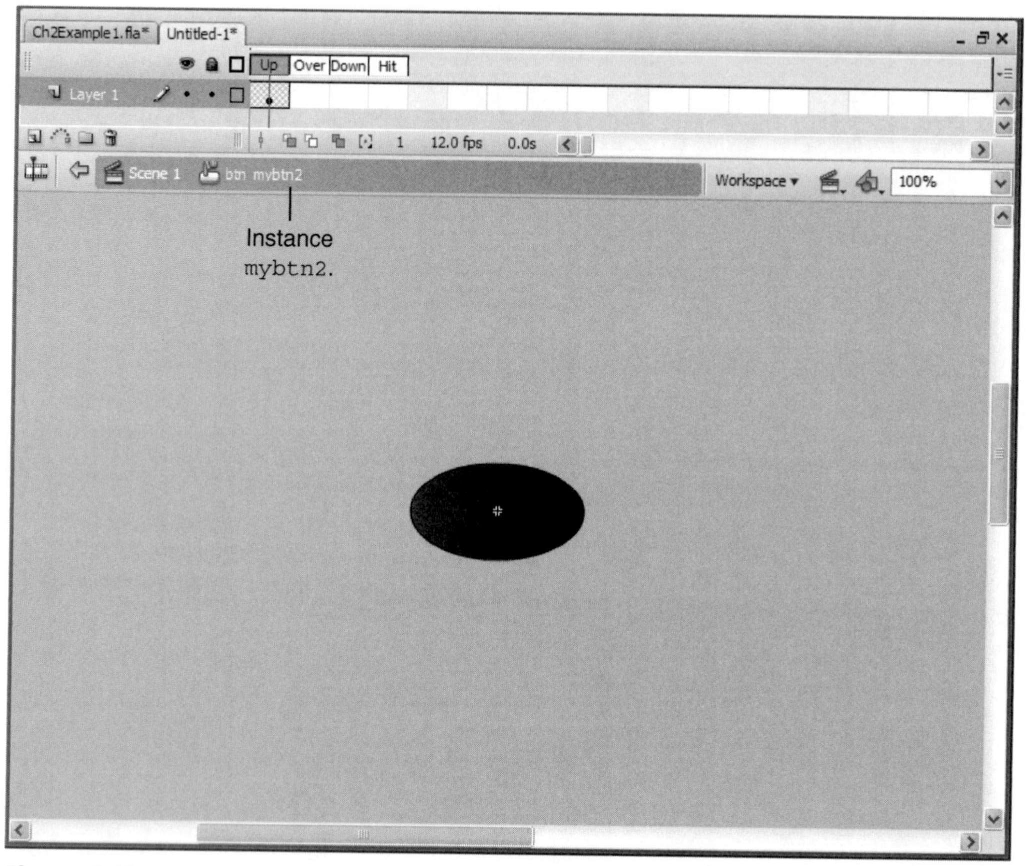

Figure 2.19
Create a button.

4. Right-click on this square and choose Insert Keyframe. You should see a little dot in the square. Your screen should match Figure 2.20.

5. Double-click the button and change the fill color to any color of your choice. This is the color of the button when the mouse is over the button.

6. Click on the square below the Down box. Right-click on this square and choose Insert Keyframe. Double-click the button instance and change the fill color to any color of your choice. This is the color of the button when the mouse is down, or clicked on the button.

7. The last state is the hit state. This state defines the clickable area of the button. Unlike the other states, it is not visible at run time. Therefore, in most cases the interactivity you have for the Up state can be copied to the Hit state.

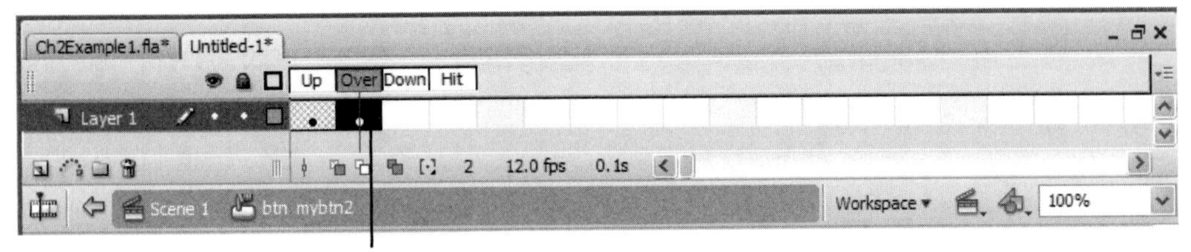

Figure 2.20
Button, Over state.

8. To test this button, go back to Scene 1, click on frame 3, and drag an instance of the new button to the stage. Run the Flash movie and try experimenting with the different states of the button by placing your mouse over the button, pressing the mouse down on the button, and observing the changes in color.

Summary

In this chapter, we looked at the building blocks required to create a Flash document. We looked at ActionScript (the scripting language used in Flash movies), the different properties of the movie clip, and buttons. We also looked at the events supported by the button object such as mouse `CLICK`, mouse `ROLL_OVER`, and so forth, etc. and the different states of the button. All of these concepts will provide you with a good foundation to start developing Flash games from Chapter 3 onward.

Review Questions

1. What is the possible side effect of not declaring a data type for a variable when creating it?
2. What is the difference between object code and keyframe code?
3. What is an expression? Give an example of an expression to take a number and calculate 20 percent of that number.
4. What properties must you use if you want to (a) change the movie clip's opacity, (b) set the movie clip to a certain percentage of its original size, and (c) make a movie clip invisible?
5. What are the two ways to interact with a button? In which of these two methods can you include code for a button?

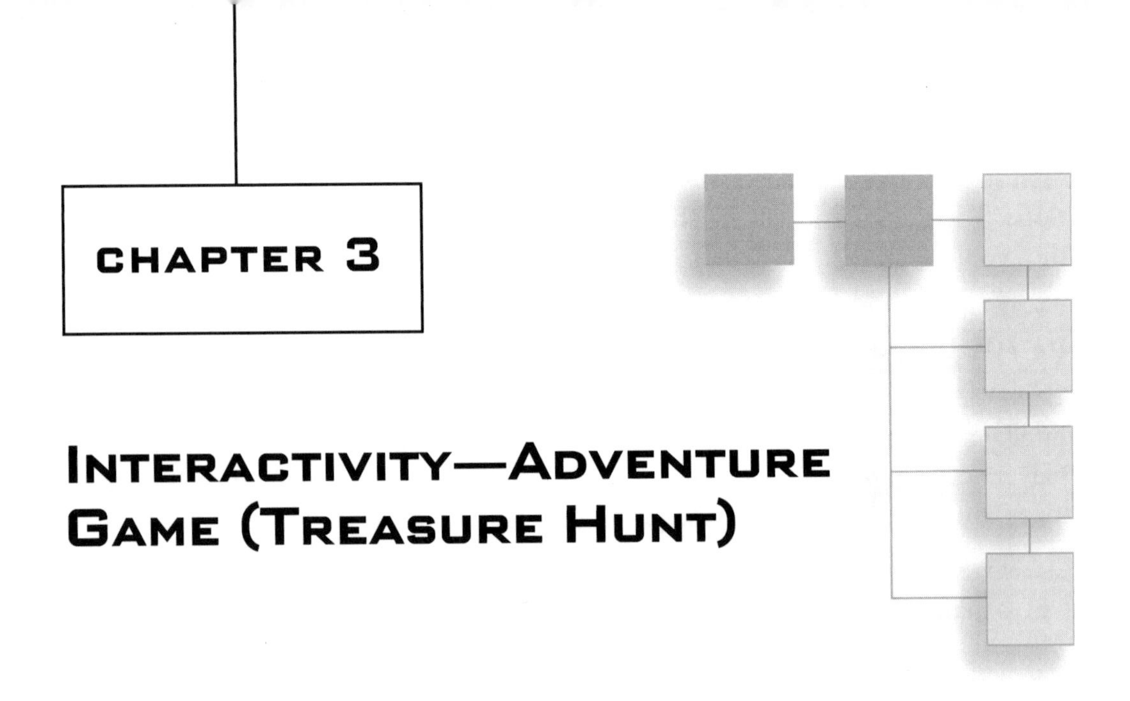

Interactivity—Adventure Game (Treasure Hunt)

Basic Software-Engineering Principles

The software-engineering process involves analysis, design, implementation, and testing.

Developing complex software systems requires good analysis and problem-solving skills. Good software begins with good design. Programming languages are just tools used to implement that design. Here are the features of a good design:

- **Correctness.** The software should closely match the requirements.
- **Robustness.** The software should operate as expected over a period of time under different circumstances.
- **Ease of use and validation.** It should be easy to test the software and easy for end users to use the product.
- **Maintainability.** The software should be easy to maintain and should operate efficiently.
- **Reusability.** Modules should be designed so that they can be reused.
- **Scalability.** The software should be able to grow along with growing future requirements without major changes to the code or design.
- **Portability.** The end product should be able to execute in a new environment with minimal changes.

Object-oriented design (OOD) is based on objects or entities and their operations. The designer identifies the objects in the problem and the operations that these objects need to perform.

Introduction to Game Design

Game-design process can help you structure your ideas and build your game intelligently and efficiently and help you turn your finished product into one that players can enjoy. *Design* refers to everything about your plan, including your idea, your code, audio, and the graphical elements of your game.

- Every game should have rules and objectives and criteria for success or failure.
- The game designer should provide an environment or terrain with objects or assets, such as robots, spaceships, animals, characters, balls, etc.
- The game should have a story line that involves character development.
- The player should be able to achieve a goal (e.g., solve a puzzle, shoot spaceships, or win money).
- The game should have some challenge associated with it.
- Periodically, rewards (like collection of points or money) should be given to the player.
- A game should provide variety with incentives for the player so that it is fun to play.
- The game should be easy to learn but tough to master.
- Rules should be simple, and quick feedback should be available through the game.
- Sound effects should be used to increase fun and excitement.

Importance of a Storyboard

The first thing you should do is determine the basic idea behind your game. Is it a shooting game, a maze or puzzle, an adventure game, or some mixed combination? What is the objective of the game? Does the main character rescue others? Does he kill bad characters or just explore a strange environment? What time frame is your game set in, or does it even have a time frame? Keep your audience in mind and target your idea to fit. Then decide on the look and feel of your game.

A *storyboard* tells the story, scene by scene, through the use of rough sketches of each scene. A storyboard basically enables you to create a visual layout of the entire game, based on the story. Having a storyboard to reference helps ensure that you don't lose sight of the story when you get into heavy development.

Even if your game is a simple action game, developing a story line helps you to establish the landscape and think up creatures to populate your game world. Putting your game in the context of a story also brings the game player closer to your world. For games in which the story is a more integral part, it is often useful to develop a storyboard along with the story line.

A storyboard also makes experimentation possible. You can try out new things and easily change your story line when it is in the storyboard stage.

In a storyboard, you should put screen shots of scenes of your Flash program in an order that clearly tells your story. Plan your story so that the visual images and the script can be clearly understood by reading your storyboard. Make sure there is a smooth, clear, logical flow from shot to shot and scene to scene.

Functions

A function in Flash is a block of ActionScript code that can be reused.

A function can be simply defined as a block of code that does a specific task and returns a specific value. A function can take as input values called arguments or parameters that it uses to complete its task. For example, you could have a function to calculate area of a circle given the radius. This calculation requires the circle's radius, which can be passed as a parameter or argument to the function. The function uses this value to calculate the area and returns the area to the main program.

If you pass more parameters than the function requires, the extra values are ignored. If you don't pass a required parameter, the empty parameters are assigned the `undefined` data type, which can cause errors during run time.

To call a function, simply use the function name and pass any required parameters. Parameters appear within parentheses after the function name and are separated by commas. A function with no parameters must be called with an empty pair of parentheses. For example:

```
isNaN(someVar);
getTimer();
```

A function should have a return type identifying the type of data it returns. Example: `Number` if it returns a number and `String` if it returns text. If the function does not return anything, `void` is used as the return type.

The following example is a function named `areaOfCircle` with the parameter `radius`. The return type is `Number` because the value returned by this function is a number.

```
function areaOfCircle(radius:Number):Number {
   return Math.PI * radius * radius;
}
```

A corresponding function call for the above function would be as follows:

```
var area:Number = areaOfCircle(5);
```

In the above code, 5 is the radius. The variable `area` accepts the value returned by the function `areaOfCircle()`. Note that the data type of area `Number` should be the same as the return type of the function.

Built-In Functions in Flash

Flash has built-in functions that let you access certain information and perform certain tasks, such as getting the version number of the Flash Player that is hosting the .swf file (`getVersion()`). Functions that belong to an object are called *methods.* Functions that don't belong to an object are called *top-level functions.* Some common built in functions are described below:

stop() Function

```
stop() : Void
```

This function stops the .swf file that is currently playing. The most common use of this action is to control movie clips with buttons.

gotoAndStop Function

```
gotoAndStop([scene:String], frame:Object) : Void
```

This function sends the playhead to the specified frame in a scene and stops it in that frame. If no scene is specified, the playhead is sent to the frame in the current scene. You can use the scene parameter only on the main Timeline, not within Timelines for movie clips or other objects in the document.

In the following example, a document has two scenes: sceneOne and sceneTwo. sceneOne contains a frame label on frame 10, called newFrame, and also two buttons, myBtn_btn and myOtherBtn_btn. The following ActionScript is placed on frame 1, scene 1 of the main Timeline:

```
stop();
myBtn_btn.addEventListener(MouseEvent.CLICK, btnClickHandler1);
function btnClickHandler1(event:MouseEvent):void
{
gotoAndStop("newFrame");
}

myOtherBtn_btn.addEventListener(MouseEvent.CLICK, btnClickHandler2);
function btnClickHandler2(event:MouseEvent):void
{
gotoAndStop("sceneTwo",1);
}
```

When the user clicks myBtn_btn, the playhead moves to frame 10 in sceneOne and stops. When the user clicks on myOtherBtn_btn, the playhead moves to frame 1 in sceneTwo and stops.

gotoAndPlay Function

```
gotoAndPlay([scene:String], frame:Object) : Void
```

This function sends the playhead to the specified frame in a scene and plays from that frame. If no scene is specified, the playhead goes to the specified frame in the current scene. You can use the scene parameter only on the main Timeline, not within Timelines for movie clips or other objects in the document.

```
gotoAndPlay("newFrame");
      gotoAndPlay("sceneTwo",1);
```

When the user clicks myBtn_btn, the playhead moves to frame 10 in sceneOne and plays from that frame. When the user clicks on myOtherBtn_btn, the playhead moves to frame 1 in sceneTwo and plays from that frame.

Note the difference between `gotoAndPlay()` and `gotoAndStop()`. The former plays from the scene and/or frame specified, and the latter just stops at the scene and/or frame specified.

Events and Event Handlers

An *event* is something that happens (e.g., a mouse click on a button, an image loading). Events usually occur as a result of human interaction with the browser (e.g., selecting a document to load, entering form information). `CLICK` is an event that occurs when you click with the mouse on the object. `RELEASE` is an event that occurs after you click and release the mouse on the object. There are many other events that were discussed in Chapter 2.

Event handlers are methods that handle events in the movie. They are basically functions that are invoked when certain events occur. They allow programmers to control what happens when specific events occur.

Every component broadcasts events when the user interacts with it. For example, a `MouseEvent.CLICK` event occurs when a button is clicked. ActionScript code is written to handle an event. This code executes when the event occurs.

ActionScript 3.0 introduces a single event handling model. To create an event handler in ActionScript 3.0, we need to add an event listener using `addEventListener()`, which is a method that can be called on any object in the event flow. We cannot attach ActionScript code to a movie clip; it needs to be attached to an event listener.

The following example registers a `MouseEvent.CLICK` event on a button with instance name `myBtn`.

```
myBtn.addEventListener(MouseEvent.CLICK, btnClickHandler);
function btnClickHandler(event:MouseEvent):void
{
gotoAndStop(1);
}
```

`myBtn` is the instance name of the object, and `clickHandler()` is the event handler, which is a function that holds ActionScript that is executed when the mouse click event occurs on `myBtn`. In the preceding code, the function `gotoAndStop(1)` is invoked when the event occurs, taking the user to frame 1.

In this chapter, we will build a simple adventure game using event handlers. The game is built with the `MouseEvent.CLICK` event. We will create movie clips, buttons, event listeners, and event handlers, and we will use one built-in function: `gotoAndStop()`.

Sample Adventure Game

Figure 3.1 shows a flowchart, which is the simplest form of a storyboard, for the game we are going to create in this chapter. The rectangular boxes can be replaced by your actual screen shots to make it a storyboard.

Creating the Movie Clip for the Program

1. Open the Flash application. When prompted to choose what type of Flash document to create, you should select ActionScript 3.0.

2. From the main menu bar, click on Insert, New Symbol and choose Movie Clip.

3. Type `pirate` for the symbol name.

4. Use the Drawing tools to create an image of a pirate, similar to the one shown in Figure 3.2.

5. Click on scene 1 to go back to the main Timeline. The new movie clip will be added to the library.

Creating the Button for the Program

1. From the main menu bar, click on Insert, New Symbol, and choose Button.

2. Type `btn_mybtn` for the button name.

3. Use the Rectangle tool or any other shape to create a button, and fill it with any color you like.

4. Use the Text tool and add a label by typing `Start` and position it on top of the button.

5. Click on scene 1 to go back to the main Timeline. At this point the button will also be added to the library.

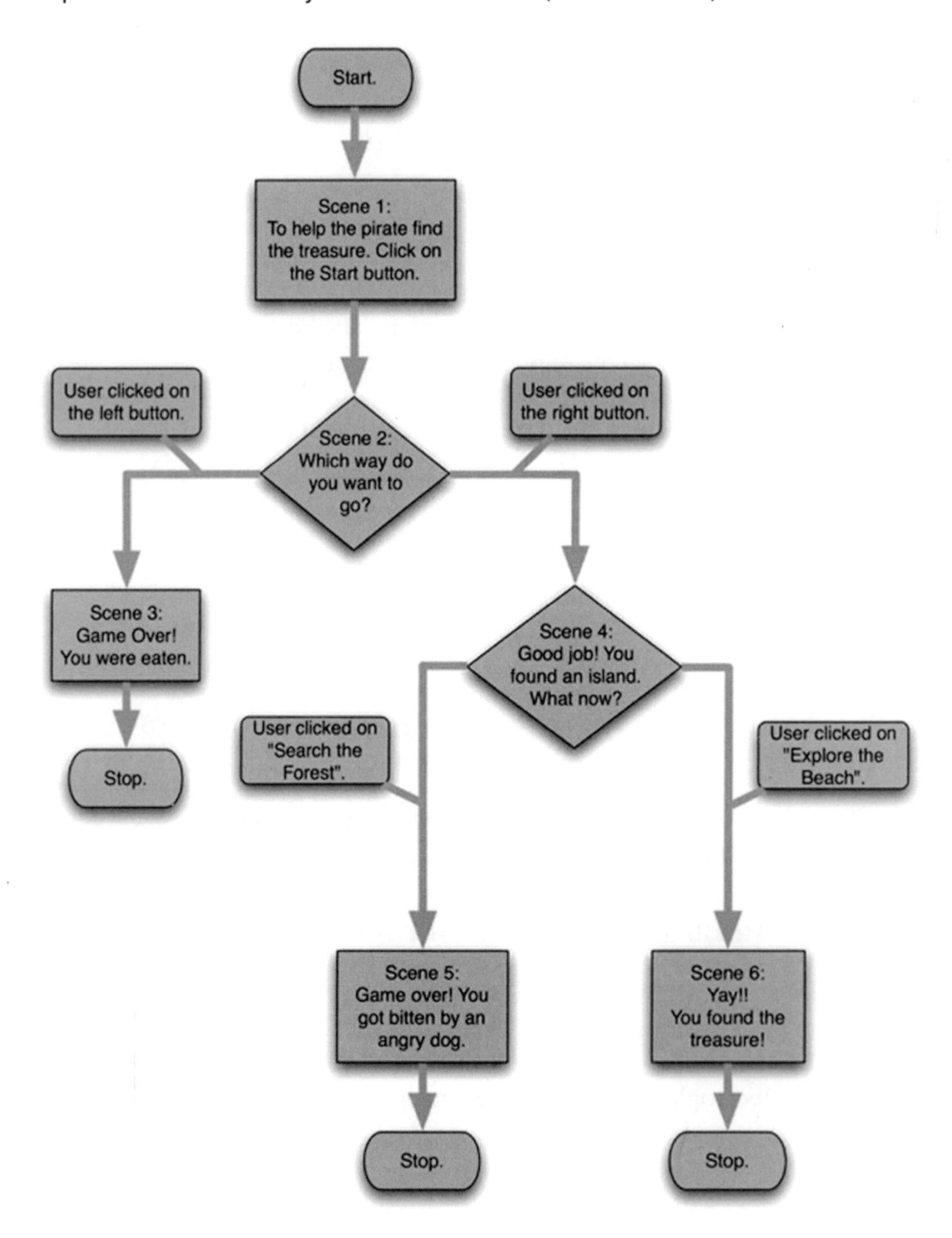

Figure 3.1
Storyboard flowchart for the adventure game.

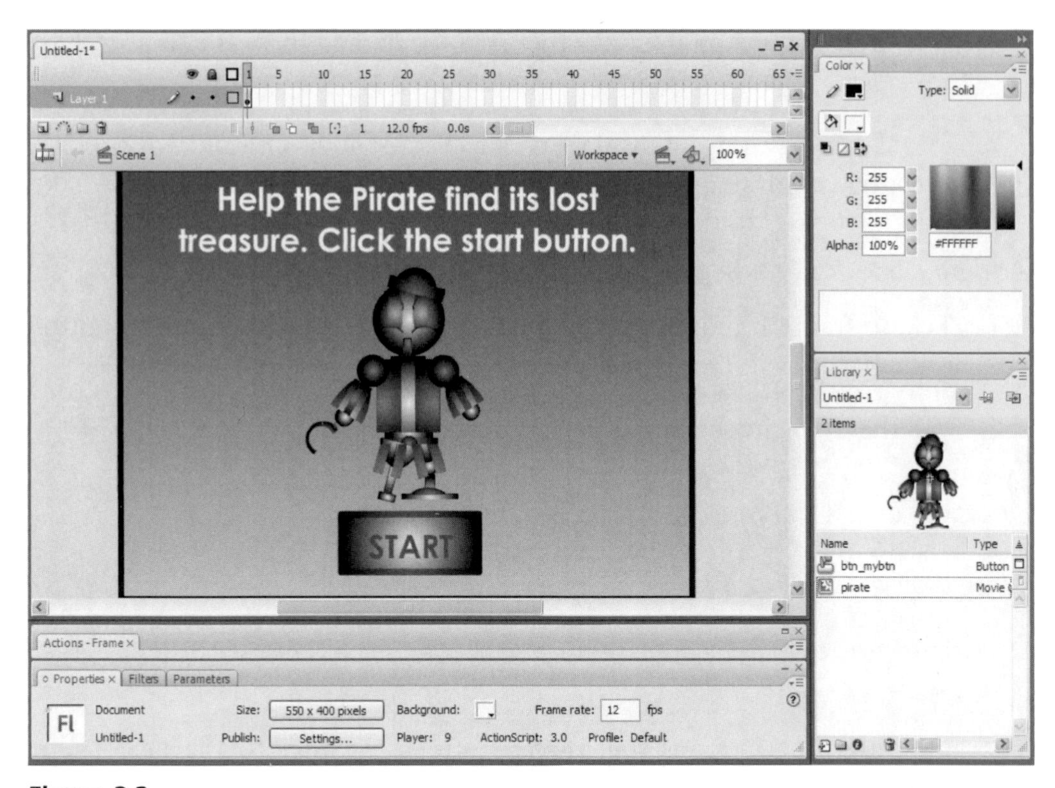

Figure 3.2
Layer 1, frame 1 activities.

Activities for Layer 1, Frame 1

1. Click on layer 1, frame 1.
2. Create a background. From the Tools panel click on the Rectangle tool, draw a rectangle that covers the entire stage, and fill it with gradient colors.
3. Click on the Text tool and click on the stage to create a text box. While the text box is selected, click on the Properties window and choose Static Text for the type of text box.
4. Enter the following text into it: `Help the Pirate find its lost treasure. Click the start button.`
5. From the library, drag an instance of the previously created button onto the stage.

6. Click the Start button and give the instance name `btn_start` to it in the Properties panel.
7. From the library drag an instance of the `Pirate` movie clip and position it to the center of the stage. Your screen should look like Figure 3.2.

Adding Code for Frame 1

1. Click on frame 1 and open the Actions window by pressing the F9 button on the keyboard.
2. Type the following code in the Actions panel for frame 1:

```
stop();
function buttonClick(myevent:MouseEvent): void
{
      gotoAndStop(2);
}
btn_start.addEventListener(MouseEvent.CLICK,buttonClick);
```

The `stop()` command stops the movie from proceeding to the next frame. `btn_start` is the instance name of the Start button. We defined the event handler using a function called `buttonClick`. The function takes the user to frame 2 using `gotoAndStop(2)`. `MouseEvent.CLICK` is an event that occurs when the user clicks on the Start button. This event invokes the `buttonClick` function.

This completes the activities for layer 1, frame 1. See Figure 3.3 for details.

Figure 3.3
Code for layer 1, frame 1.

Activities for Layer 1, Frame 2

1. Press F6 to create a keyframe. It copies the contents of the first frame to the new frame.
2. Delete the Start button and the static text.
3. Create a circle and delete half of it to create the hull of the ship. Then draw a flag post and attach a flag to construct a ship. You can drag the pirate onto the ship.
4. Add a static text box and input the following: `Which way do you want to go?`
5. Create two more buttons shaped as arrows, one pointing right and one pointing left.
6. Drag the buttons and place one toward the left and the other toward the right on the rectangle you drew earlier.
7. Select the buttons and give the instance name `btn_left` to the button pointing to the left and `btn_right` to the button pointing to the right. Your screen should now match Figure 3.4.

This completes the design of the interface for frame 2.

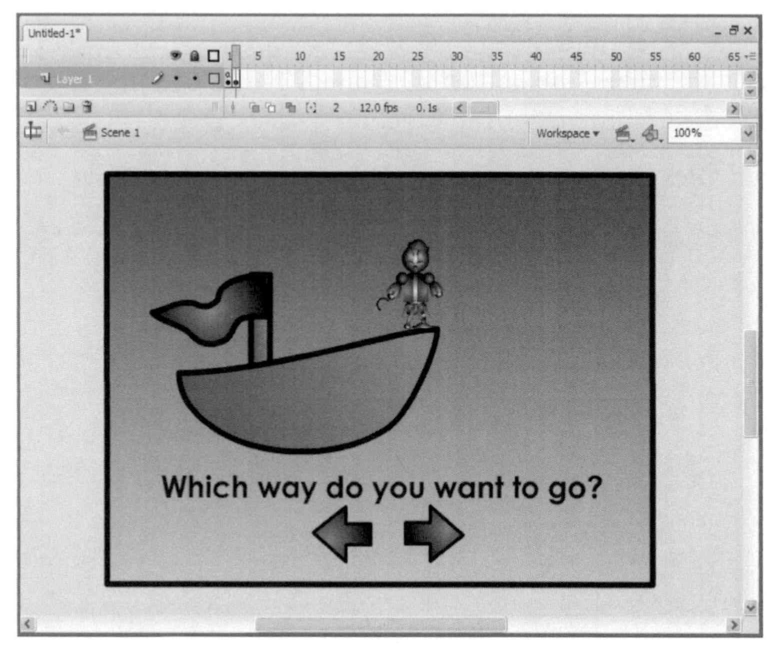

Figure 3.4
Activities for layer 1, frame 2.

Adding Code for Frame 2

1. Click on frame 2 and open the Actions window by pressing the F9 key on your keyboard.

2. Type the following text in the Actions panel:

```
stop();
function buttonClickleft(myevent:MouseEvent): void {
      gotoAndStop(3);
}
btn_left.addEventListener(MouseEvent.CLICK,buttonClickleft);

function buttonClickright(myevent:MouseEvent): void {
      gotoAndStop(4);
}
btn_right.addEventListener(MouseEvent.CLICK,buttonClickright);
```

The code in this frame mimics a decision-making mechanism. The `stop()` command stops the movie from proceeding to the next frame. An event listener is associated with the button `btn_left`, which invokes the event handler `buttonClickleft()`, which executes the built-in function `gotoAndStop(3)` when the button is released. This moves the movie to frame 3, specified as the argument for the function `gotoAndStop()`. Similarly, an event listener is associated with `btn_right`, which invokes the event handler `buttonClickRight()`, which executes the function `gotoAndStop(4)` when the button is released. This moves the movie to frame 4, specified as the argument for the function `gotoAndStop()`.

This completes the activities for layer 1, frame 2. See Figure 3.5 for details.

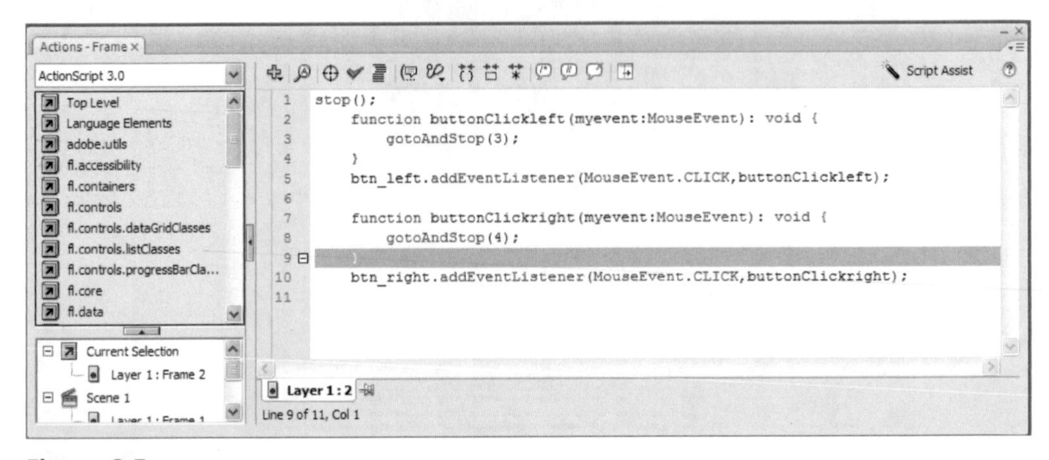

Figure 3.5
Code for layer 1, frame 2.

Activities for Layer 1, Frame 3

1. Press F6 to create a keyframe.
2. Delete everything from this frame.
3. Draw a scary creature. (See Figure 3.6.)
4. Add the following text to a static field: `Game Over. You got eaten!!!`
5. Create a button that allows the user to play again (Start Over, in Figure 3.6) and give it the instance name `btn_playagain`.

Adding Code for Frame 3

1. Click on frame 3 and open the Actions window by pressing the F9 key on your keyboard.
2. Type the following text in the Actions panel:

```
stop();
function buttonPlayagain(myevent:MouseEvent): void {
```

Figure 3.6
Activities for layer 1, frame 3.

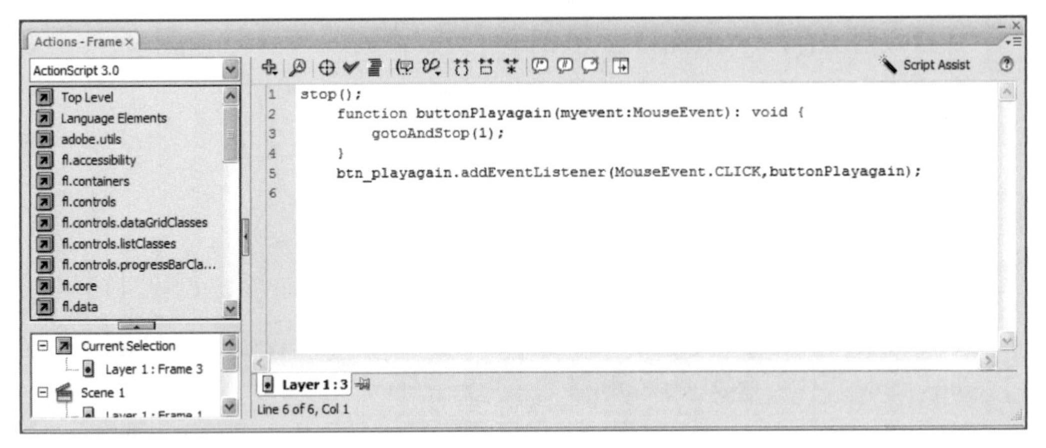

Figure 3.7
Code for layer 1, frame 3.

```
    gotoAndStop(1);
}
btn_playagain.addEventListener(MouseEvent.CLICK,buttonPlayagain);
```

An event listener is associated with `btn_playagain`, which invokes the event handler `buttonPlayagain()`, which executes the function `gotoAndStop(1)` when the button is released. This moves the movie to frame 1, specified as the argument for the function `gotoAndStop()`.

This completes the activities for layer 1, frame 3. See Figure 3.7 for details.

Activities for Layer 1, Frame 4

1. Press `F6` to create a Keyframe.
2. Change the gradient of the background and add a small hemisphere at the bottom using the Circle tool to create the background for the fourth frame.
3. Delete the text `Game Over` and the scary character image.
4. Drag the pirate movie clip onto the center of the stage.
5. Using the Text tool, add the text `Good Job!!! You found an island. What now?`
6. Drag two instances of arrow buttons onto the stage and position them so one points toward the left and the other points toward the right. Use the

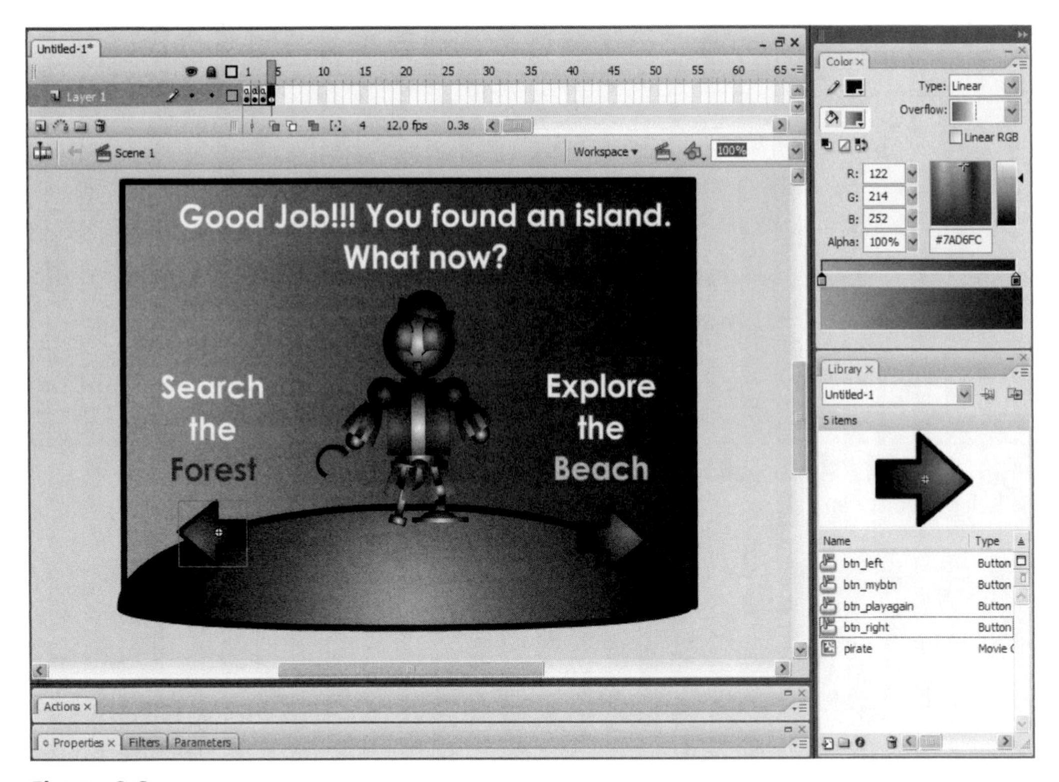

Figure 3.8
Activities for layer 1, frame 4.

Text tool to add the label `Search the Forest` under the left-pointing arrow and `Explore the Beach` under the right-pointing arrow. See Figure 3.8.

7. Select the respective buttons and give them the instance names `btn_search` and `btn_explore`.

Adding Code for Frame 4

1. Click on frame 4 and open the Actions panel by pressing the F9 key on your keyboard.
2. Type the following text in the Actions panel:

```
stop();
function buttonClicksearch(myevent:MouseEvent): void {
      gotoAndStop(5);
}
```

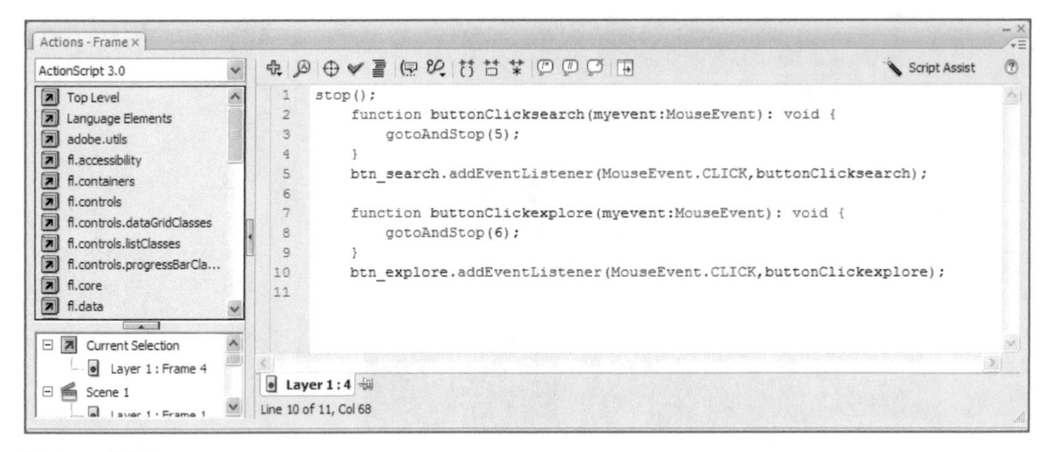

Figure 3.9
Code for layer 1, frame 4.

```
btn_search.addEventListener(MouseEvent.CLICK,buttonClicksearch);

function buttonClickexplore(myevent:MouseEvent): void {
      gotoAndStop(6);
}
btn_explore.addEventListener(MouseEvent.CLICK,buttonClickexplore);
```

An event listener is associated with the button `btn_search`, which invokes the event handler `buttonClicksearch()`, which executes the built-in function `gotoAndStop(5)` when the button is released. This moves the movie to frame 5, specified as the argument for the function `gotoAndStop()`. Similarly, an event listener is associated with `btn_explore`, which invokes the event handler `buttonClickexplore()`, which executes the function `gotoAndStop(6)` when the button is released. This moves the movie to frame 6, specified as the argument for the function `gotoAndStop()`.

This completes the activities for layer 1, frame 4. See Figure 3.9 for details.

Activities for Layer 1, Frame 5

1. Press F6 on the keyboard to create a keyframe.
2. Remove the buttons and their labels and the pirate.
3. Draw an angry dog or drag an appropriate graphic from the library to the stage. See Figure 3.10.

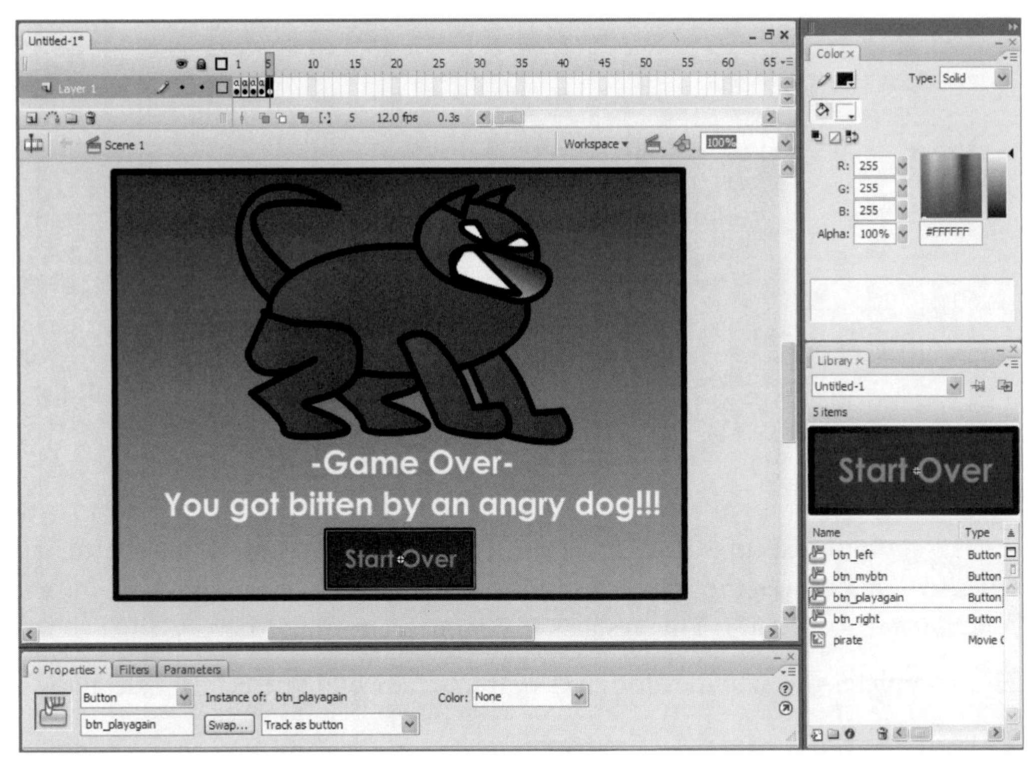

Figure 3.10
Activities for layer 1, frame 5.

4. Add the following text as a label: `-Game Over- You got bitten by an angry dog!!!`

5. Drag an instance of the button to play again and give it the instance name `btn_playagain`.

Adding Code for Frame 5

1. Click on frame 5 and open the Actions panel by pressing the F9 key on your keyboard.

2. Type the following text in the Actions panel:

```
stop();
btn_playagain.addEventListener(MouseEvent.CLICK,buttonPlayagain);
```

An event listener is associated with `btn_playagain`, which invokes the event handler `buttonPlayagain()`. (Note: We do not rewrite the function `buttonPlayagain()` because it has already been written for frame 3.)

Figure 3.11
Code for layer 1, frame 5.

`btnPlayagain()` executes the function `gotoAndStop(1)` when the button is released. This moves the movie to frame 1, specified as the argument for the function `gotoAndStop()`. This restarts the game from frame 1.

This completes the activities for layer 1, frame 5. See Figure 3.11 for details.

Activities for Layer 1, Frame 6

1. Press F6 on the keyboard to create a keyframe.
2. Change the background to show something related to treasure. You can use images of money bags or gold coins. See Figure 3.12.
3. Change the caption to `Yay!!! You've found the Treasure.`
4. Drag an instance of the Play Again button and give it the instance name `btn_playagain`.

Adding Code for Frame 6

1. Click on frame 6 and open the Actions panel by pressing the F9 key on your keyboard.
2. Type the following text in the Actions panel:

```
stop();
btn_playagain.addEventListener(MouseEvent.CLICK,buttonPlayagain);
```

An event listener is associated with `btn_playagain`, which invokes the event handler `buttonPlayagain()`. Again, as in frame 5, we do not rewrite the function `button-Playagain()` because it has already been written for frame 3. `btnPlayagain()`

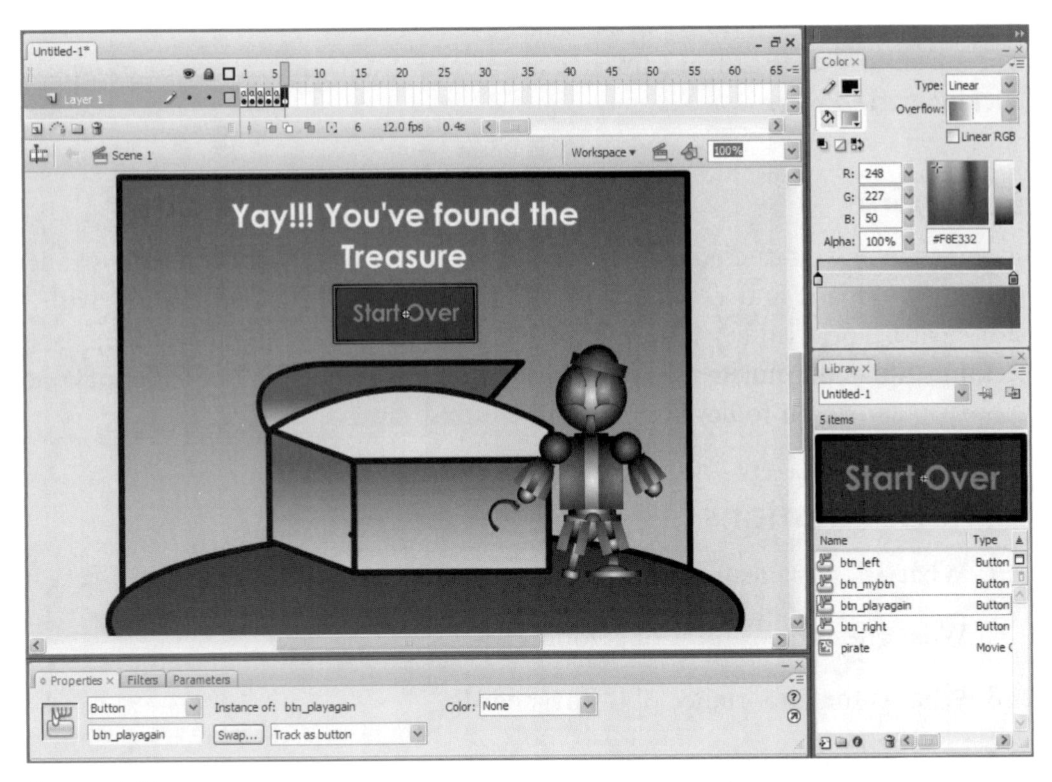

Figure 3.12
Activities for layer 1, frame 6.

Figure 3.13
Code for layer 1, frame 6.

executes the function `gotoAndStop(1)` when the button is released. This moves the movie to frame 1, specified as the argument for the function `gotoAndStop()`. This restarts the game from frame 1.

This completes the activities for layer 1, frame 6. See Figure 3.13 for details.

The adventure game code is complete now. Save your code and test the movie by clicking Ctrl+Enter.

Summary

In this chapter, you studied software and game design. You learned the importance of the storyboard and created a very simple adventure game starting with a storyboard. You used key frames, movie clips, buttons, and event handlers using ActionScript and simulated simple decision making using basic ActionScript code. Now you can go on to develop more interesting games.

Review Questions

1. What are some features of good software design?
2. What are some features of a good game?
3. What is the importance of a storyboard?
4. What is a movie clip and what is a button?
5. What is a function? Mention some built-in functions in Flash.
6. What is a function parameter?
7. What is an event? Name some event handlers.
8. What does the `goToAndStop(3)` function do?

Project

Create another adventure game. This time make it an educational game.

1. Create four question frames. Each frame should ask one question.
2. Create a fifth frame, telling the user that he won the game.
3. Create a sixth frame, telling the user that he lost the game.
4. Have two buttons on each question frame: one for the right answer and the other for the wrong answer.

5. When the user clicks on the right answer, take him to the next question frame.

6. Finally, when all questions are answered correctly, take him to the fifth frame. Allow the user to replay the game (starting from the first frame).

7. When the user clicks on the wrong answer, take him to the sixth frame. Allow the user to start over from the first frame and try again.

8. Keep the questions very simple. For example:

   Question: 100 + 12=?
   Answer Button: 112 (correct answer)
   Answer Button: 102 (wrong answer)

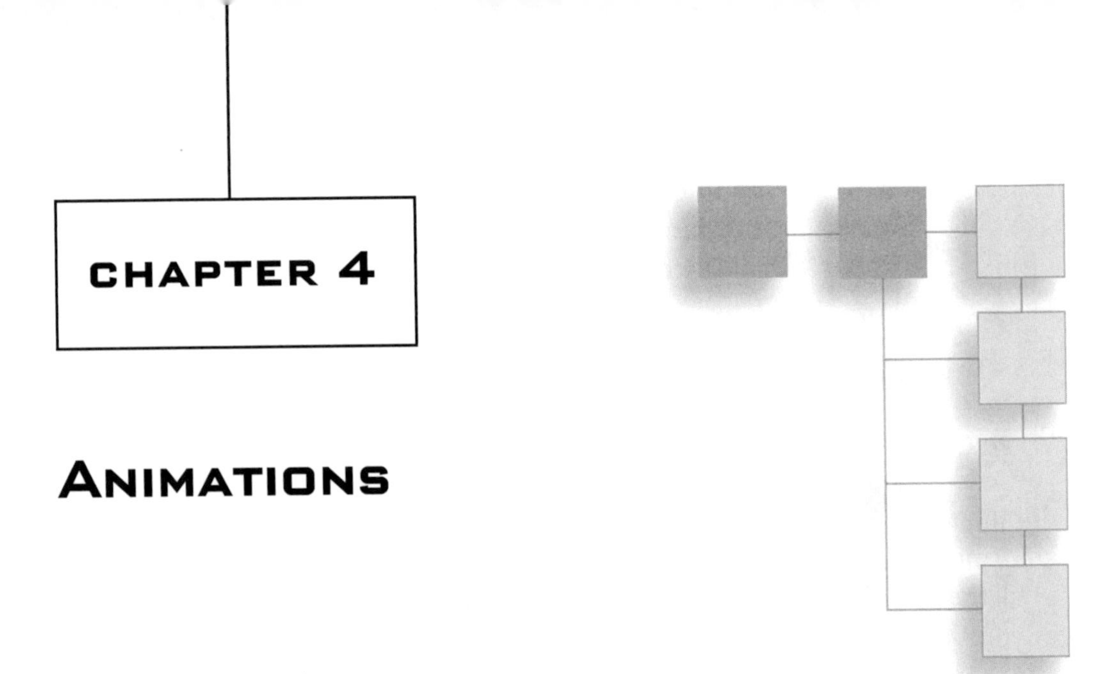

Animations

- Understand the meaning of animation
- Understand the different types of animation
- Develop Flash animations using tweening
- Develop Flash animations using cel animation and ActionScript animation
- Use Onion Skin to animate Flash objects
- Understand Masking
- Create a custom cursor
- Create a rollover effect

Introduction to Animation and Visual Effects

Animation can be simply defined as a series of pictures containing objects that when displayed consecutively at a particular speed, the differences between pictures give the perception of object movement, rotation, or transformation.

The *frame rate*, the speed at which an animation is played, is measured in number of frames per second. A frame rate that's too slow causes the animation to appear jerky; a frame rate that's too fast will cause a flickering effect instead of smooth movement.

You need to think about frame rate when working with animations because it can affect the performance of your .swf file and the computer that plays it. You also need to consider the frame rate setting because it affects how smoothly your animation plays.

For example, an animation set to 12 frames per second (fps) in the Property Inspector plays 12 frames each second. If the document's frame rate is set to 24 fps, the animation appears to animate more smoothly than if it ran at 12 fps. However, your animation at 24 fps also plays much faster than it does at 12 fps, so the total duration (in seconds) is shorter. Therefore, if you need to make a five-second animation using a higher frame rate, it means you need to insert additional frames to fill those five seconds than at a lower frame rate—which raises the total file size of your animation. A five-second animation at 24 fps typically has a higher file size than a five-second animation at 12 fps, depending on your assets and how you are animating the content. Five seconds at 12 fps means ($5 \times 12 =$) 60 frames, and 5 seconds at 24 fps means ($5 \times 24 =$) 120 frames. This means that an increase in fps increases the number of frames needed for the effect, which then may require more storage for the additional frames.

Types of Animation

There are many techniques used for 2D animation, and you will learn a few of them in this chapter. The artist draws the scene using a mouse and tools available in Flash such as brushes, pencils, spraying tools, erasers, and so on. A series of similar images are linked together to simulate movement, as you will see below.

Tweened Animation

Tweened animation is an effective way to create movement and changes over time while minimizing file size and development time. In tweened animation, Flash stores only the values for the changes between frames. In tweened animation, we create the objects in key positions by inserting keyframes and modifying the properties such as color, position, and size, and transitional shapes are created by Flash.

Flash can create two types of tweened animation:

- motion tweening
- shape tweening

Motion Tweening

In motion tweening, you define properties such as position, size, and rotation for an instance, a group, or a text block at one point in time and then change those properties at another point in time. After you do so, you can apply the motion tween between those two frames, and Flash will automatically create the frames between the first and last frames. You can also apply a motion tween and assign a path for it to follow.

Exercise 4.1

1. Open a new Flash document.
2. Draw a rectangle on the stage. Add a keyframe to frame 10. Move the rectangle to another part of the stage.
3. Create a motion tween. You can create a motion tween using one of the following methods:
   - Click anywhere between the two frames in the layer. Select Motion in the Tween option in the Property Inspector. See Figure 4.1.
   - Right-click on any frame and select Create Motion Tween. See Figure 4.2.

Another way to create a motion tween is as follows.

1. Create the first keyframe for the animation.
2. Insert a rectangle.
3. Insert the number of frames you want in the Timeline.
4. Select Insert, Timeline, Create Motion Tween.
5. Move the rectangle to the new location on the stage. Flash automatically creates the ending keyframe. See Figure 4.3.

Tweening Motion Along a Path

Motion guide layers let you draw paths along which tweened instances, groups, or text blocks can be animated. You can link multiple layers to a Motion Guide layer to have multiple objects follow the same path. A normal layer that is linked to a Motion Guide layer becomes a guided layer. To create a motion path for a tweened animation, do the following:

1. Create a motion-tweened animation sequence. If you check the checkbox for Orient to Path in the Properties panel, the baseline of the tweened

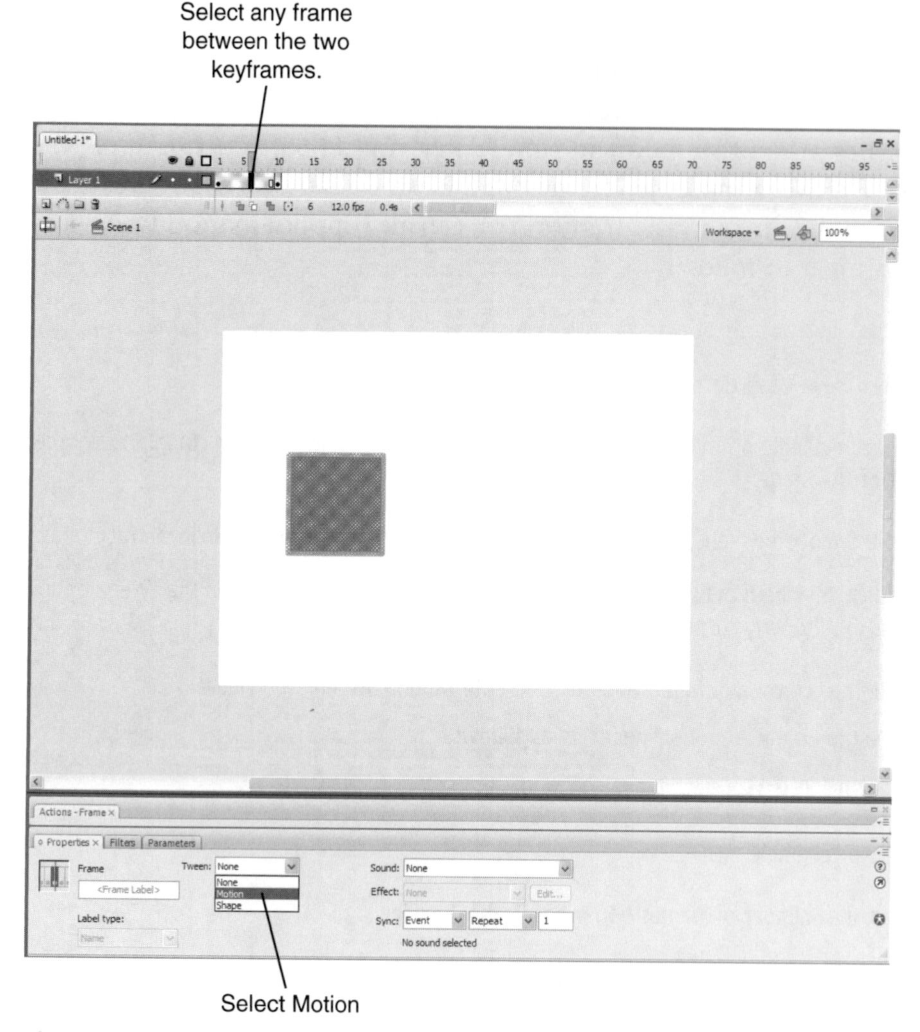

Select any frame between the two keyframes.
Select Motion

Figure 4.1
Creating a motion tween by selecting a frame.

element orients to the motion path. If you check the Snap checkbox, the registration point of the tweened element snaps to the motion path.

2. Select the layer containing the animation and select Insert, Timeline, Motion Guide. Alternatively, you can right-click the layer containing the animation and select Add Motion Guide from the context menu. Flash creates a new layer above the selected layer with a motion guide icon to the left of the layer name. See Figure 4.4.

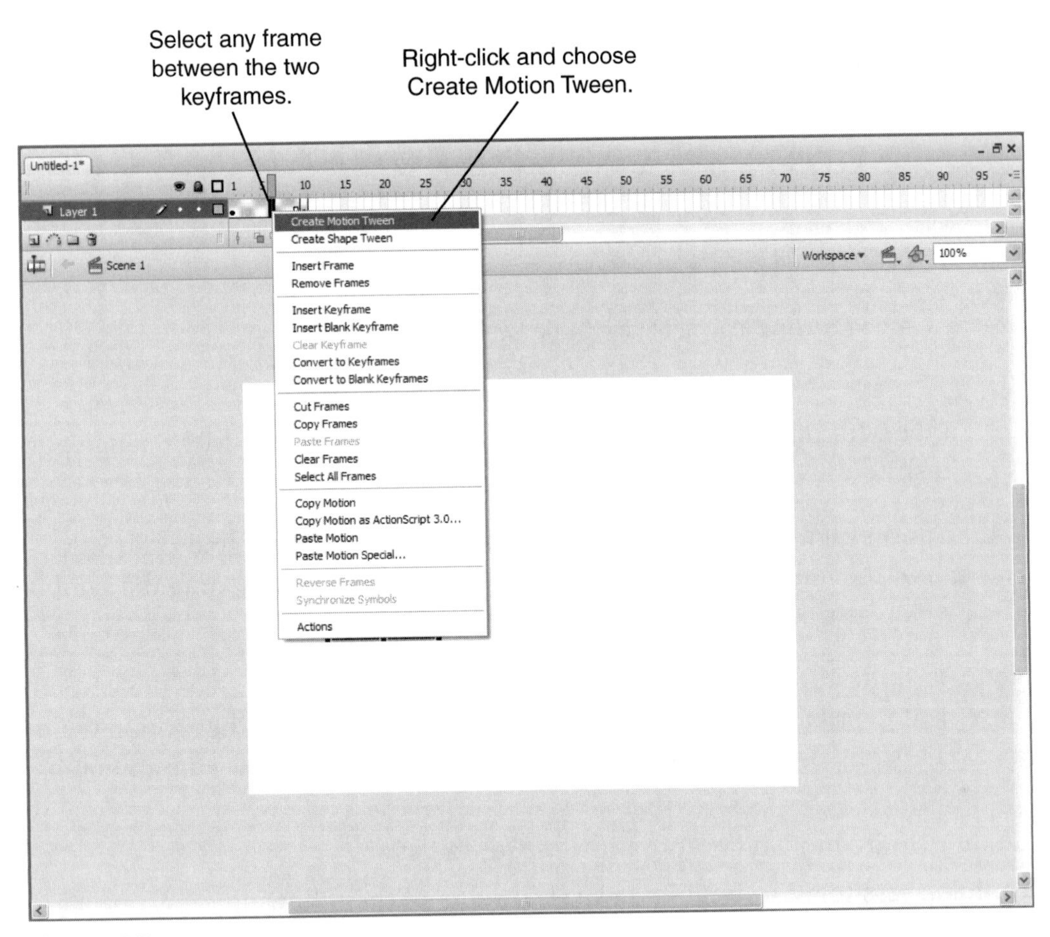

Figure 4.2
Creating a motion tween by right clicking on a frame.

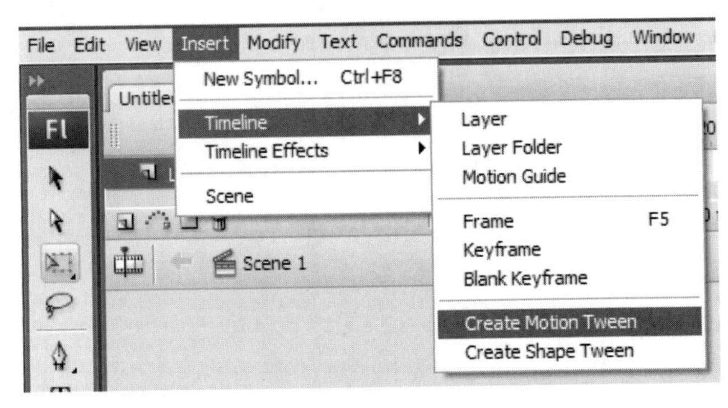

Figure 4.3
Creating a motion tween using the menu.

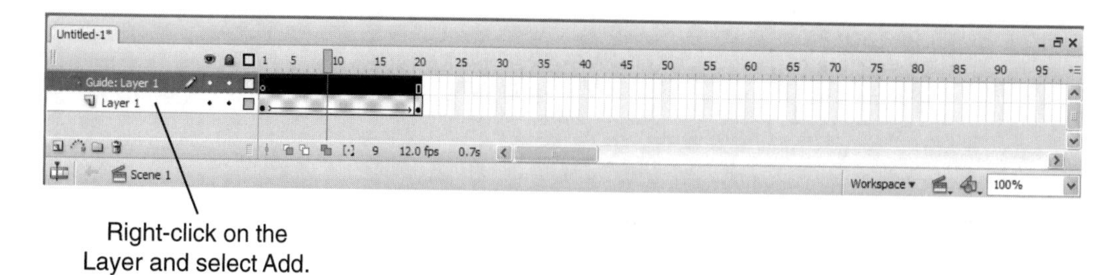

Figure 4.4
Creating a motion tween using the Motion Guide layer.

3. In the Motion Guide layer, use the Pen, Pencil, Line, Circle, Rectangle, or Brush tool to draw the desired path.
4. Snap the center to the beginning of the line in the first frame and to the end of the line in the last frame. For best snapping results, drag the symbol by its registration point.

Note: To hide the Motion Guide layer and the line so that only the object's movement is visible while you work, click in the Eye column on the Motion Guide layer. The group or symbol follows the motion path when you play the animation.

Linking/Unlinking Layers to a Motion Guide Layer

To link layers to a Motion Guide layer, do one of the following:

- Drag an existing layer below the Motion Guide layer. The layer is indented under the Motion Guide layer. All objects on this layer automatically snap to the motion path.
- Create a new layer under the Motion Guide layer. Objects you tween on this layer are automatically tweened along the motion path.
- Select a layer below the Motion Guide layer. Select Modify, Timeline, Layer Properties and select Guided in the Layer Properties dialog box.

To unlink layers from a Motion Guide layer, select the layer you want to unlink and do one of the following:

- Drag the layer above the Motion Guide layer.
- Select Modify, Timeline, Layer Properties and select Normal as the layer type in the Layer Properties dialog box.

Shape Tweening

In shape tweening, you draw a shape at one point in time and then change that shape or draw another shape at another point in time. In the first frame's properties, select Shape from the Tween drop-down menu. Flash interpolates the values or shapes for the frames in between, thus creating the animation. The shape changes from the first shape into the second shape.

By tweening shapes, you can create an effect similar to morphing, making one shape appear to change into another shape over time. Flash can also tween the location, size, color, and opacity of shapes.

Exercise 4.2

1. Open a new Flash document.
2. First add three layers for a total of four layers. Name layer 1 Background, layer 2 Objects, layer 3 Flower, and layer 4 Branch.
3. Let's start with the Background layer. In frame 1 create a night sky by placing a blue rectangle around the screen.
4. Right-click on the 30th frame and click on the Insert Keyframe option.
5. Now change the color of the rectangle to orange or any other warm color to create a morning sky.
6. Click on any frame between 1 and 30, and in the Properties toolbar, select Shape from the Tween drop-down menu. There should be an arrow pointing from the first to the 30th frame, and the frames should be colored in light green. If you test your animation now (Ctrl+Enter), then you will have a rectangle changing color from blue to orange.
7. Lock the Background layer. Now move to the Objects layer. In frame 1, create two objects: a gray half circle for the moon and a yellow circle for the sun.
8. Place the half circle (moon) in the upper left-hand corner of the screen. Place the sun in the upper right-hand side but off of the screen.
9. Click on the 30th frame. Just like with the Background layer, create a keyframe. Now move the moon off of the screen to the left and move the sun onto the screen on the top right.
10. Create a motion tween for the Objects layer by right-clicking on any frame between 1 and 30 and selecting Create Motion Tween. Lock the layer so that changes can't be made on the Objects layer.
11. In the Flower layer, in frame 1 create a circle of any color combination for a flower bud. Place the flower bud near the bottom-center of the stage.

12. Click on the 30th frame and insert a keyframe.
13. In the 30th frame, replace the flower with one that has petals. Make sure that the flower is in the same place.
14. Right-click between the two keyframes and select Create Shape Tween. If you play the animation now, you should have a background changing color along with the moon moving and the sun coming up. The flower should also be blooming. Now lock the Flower layer.
15. Now go to the Branch layer. In the first keyframe, use your Brush tool to make a thin green stem from the bottom of the screen diagonally with a branch off of it that connects to the flower bud.
16. Create a keyframe on the 30th frame.
17. Go over the bud using the Brush tool, but this time use a thicker brush so that the branch is thicker. You can also create more branches sprouting out.
18. Click on a frame between 1 and 30 and select Shape from the Tween drop-down menu in the Properties toolbar.
19. Now lock the Branch layer. Drag the Branch layer below the Flower layer. This will make the flower appear on top of the stem. If you click on frame 1, you should see something like Figure 4.5. If you click on any frame between 1 and 30, your screen should look like the one in Figure 4.6. If you click on frame 30, your screen should look like Figure 4.7.
20. To make the animation play only once, open the Actions frame for the 30th frame and type `stop();`.

Your animation is complete. If you run it, the background should change, the sun and moon should move, the flower should grow, and the branch should sprout out.

Your output screen should resemble the one in Figure 4.8.

Cel Animation (Traditional Frame by Frame)

In cel animation, we follow the traditional principle of creating the objects in each frame. For example, if we want to simulate the animation of a person walking, then we have to draw the different positions of the leg while walking, right from lifting the leg to dropping it on the ground again.

A frame-by-frame animation changes the contents of the stage in every frame and is best suited to a complex animation in which an image changes in every frame instead of simply moving across the stage. This type of animation increases the

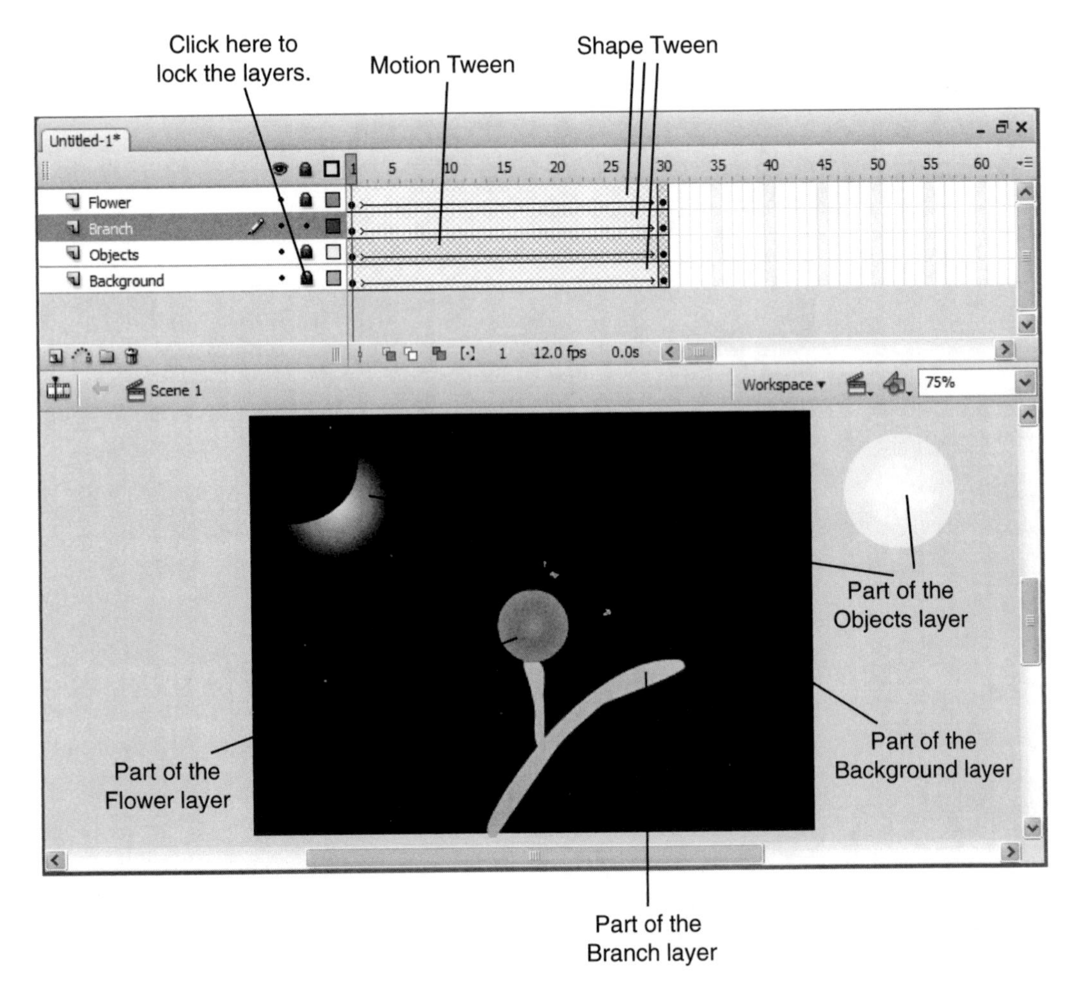

Figure 4.5
Shape tweening—frame 1.

file size more rapidly than tweened animation because Flash stores the values for each keyframe.

To create a frame-by-frame animation, you define each frame as a keyframe and create a different (typically modified) image for each frame. Each new keyframe on a layer typically contains the same contents as the keyframe preceding it because the contents of a frame are copied to the next keyframe when you select a frame and press F6. By selecting a frame and pressing F6, you can modify each new keyframe in the animation incrementally.

Often you use the Onion Skin feature to view incremental changes between each keyframe. This and other features are described in the following section of this chapter.

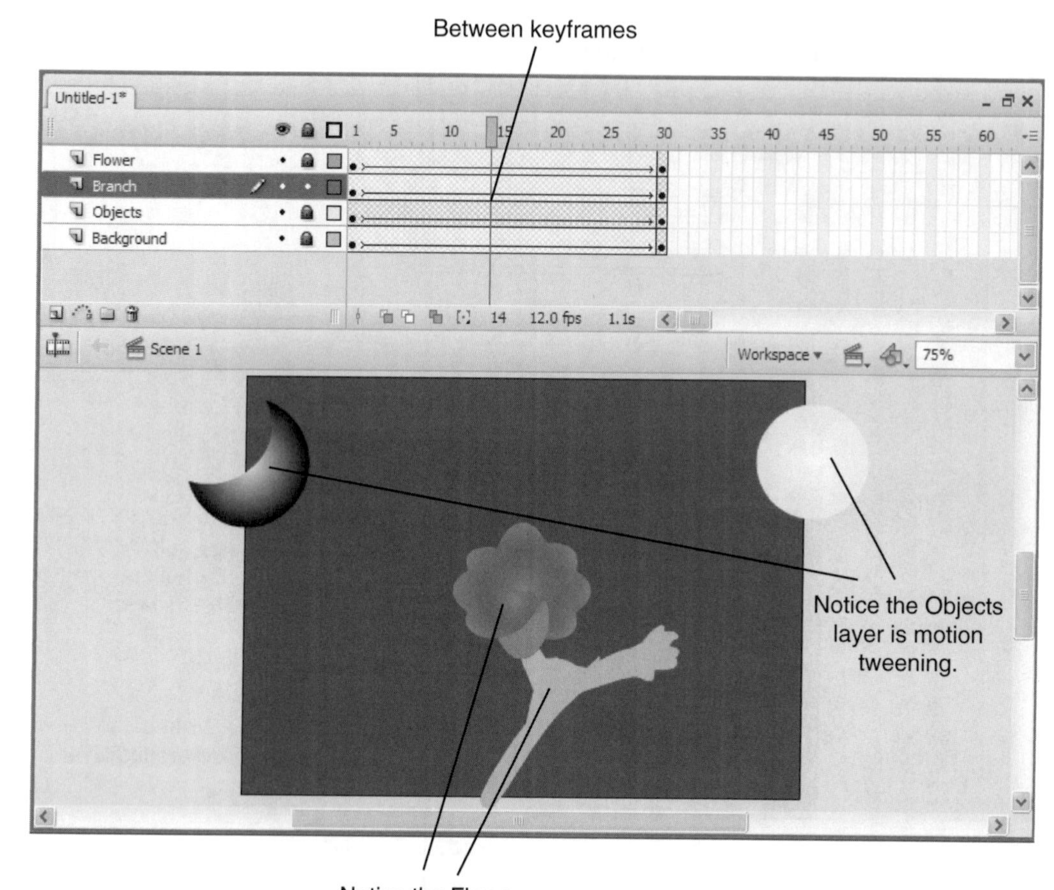

Figure 4.6
Shape tweening—frame 14.

Other Visual Effects

Flash provides other techniques that help make animation visually appealing. Some of these techniques are explained in this section.

Onion Skinning

Onion Skinning allows you to see a faint ghost image of the previous frame so you can see where you want to place the artwork for the next frame. First you need to add a new layer on your stage. In the next exercise, you will draw and animate a flower on this layer.

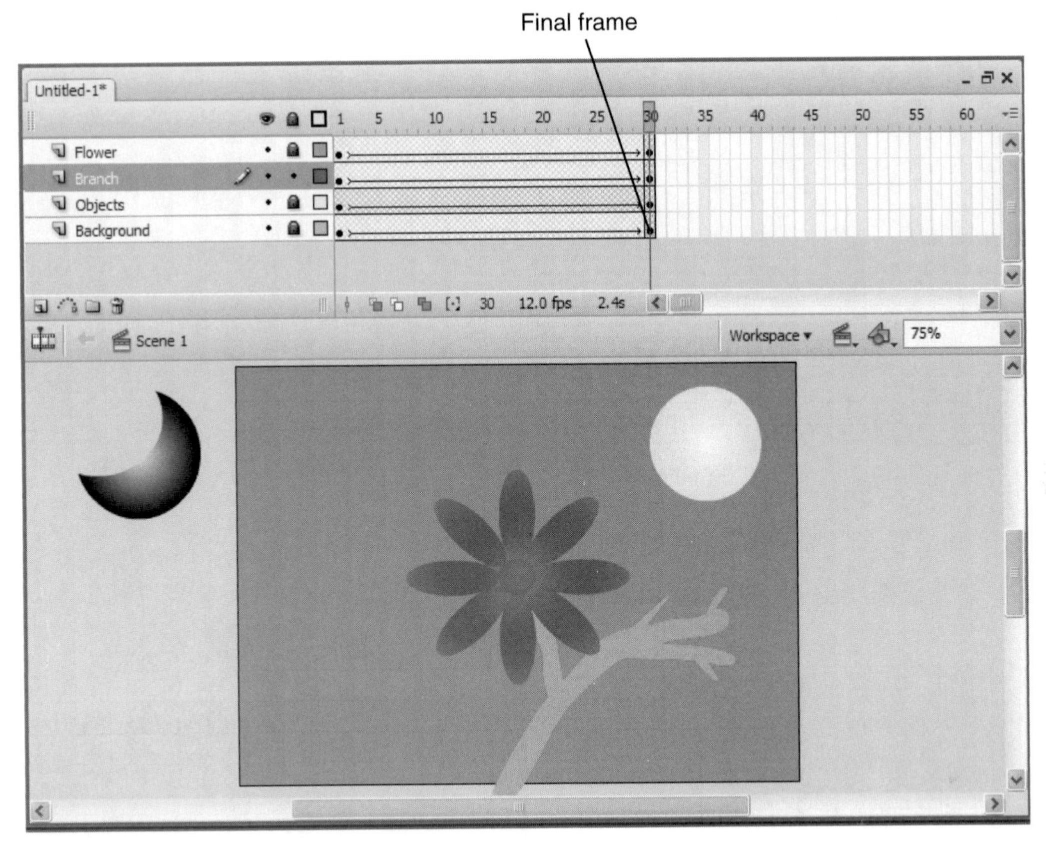

Figure 4.7
Shape tweening—frame 30.

Figure 4.8
Shape tweening—output.

Figure 4.9
Draw a flower.

Exercise 4.3

1. Open a new Flash document.
2. Rename the default layer Flower.
3. In the Flower layer, draw a flower on the stage. See Figure 4.9.
4. Select frame 2 and insert a keyframe.
5. In frame 2, drag your cursor around the flower to select it, and use the Free Transform tool to rotate it.
6. At the bottom of the Timeline there is a row of five buttons. When you mouse over the second button from the left you'll see the tip Onion Skin. Click on the second button to turn on Onion Skinning. You will see a faint ghost image where your first frame was. See Figure 4.10.
7. Add a new keyframe. With the Free Transform tool selected, rotate, scale, etc. your flower with its registration point placed at bottom center. Continue to add keyframes for each change that you make to the flower. Continue to make transformations. Stop after transforming on frame 5. Choose Control, Loop Playback to set your playback in a loop. Then select Control, Play to see your animation repeat. Select Control, Stop to stop playback.
8. Play with and modify your movie. Add as many keyframes as you wish and make the movie as long as you wish.

Masking

Masking is defining a particular region or area in the existing layer (changing it to a Mask layer) through which you want to view the contents of the layer below. Masking enables you to view the contents of a layer below through the region defined in the Mask layer.

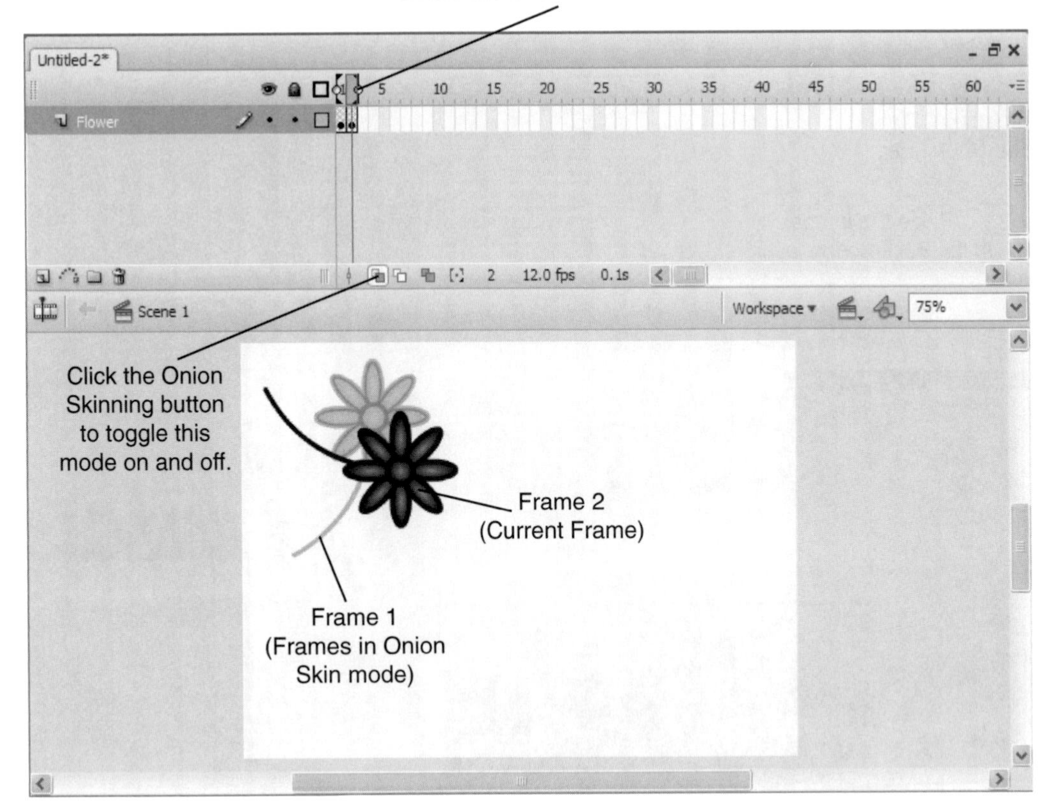

Figure 4.10
Onion Skinning.

Exercise 4.4

Inserting and Renaming Layers

1. Open a new Flash document.

2. Add a new layer. You need two layers to mask an object. Rename the top layer Mask and the layer below that Background. See Figure 4.11.

3. Import a picture to the stage on the Background layer, as you can see in Figure 4.12. Select the Background layer, and then choose File, Import, Import to Library. Select an image file and click Open. Drag an instance of this image to the stage.

4. Using the Oval tool from your toolbox, draw a circle in your Mask layer and delete its border. See Figure 4.13.

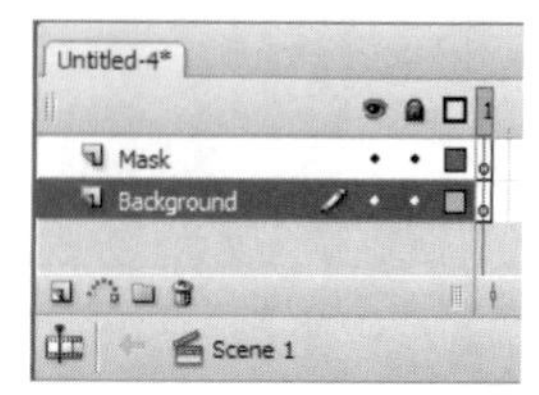

Figure 4.11
The Mask layer.

Place the image
in the Background layer.

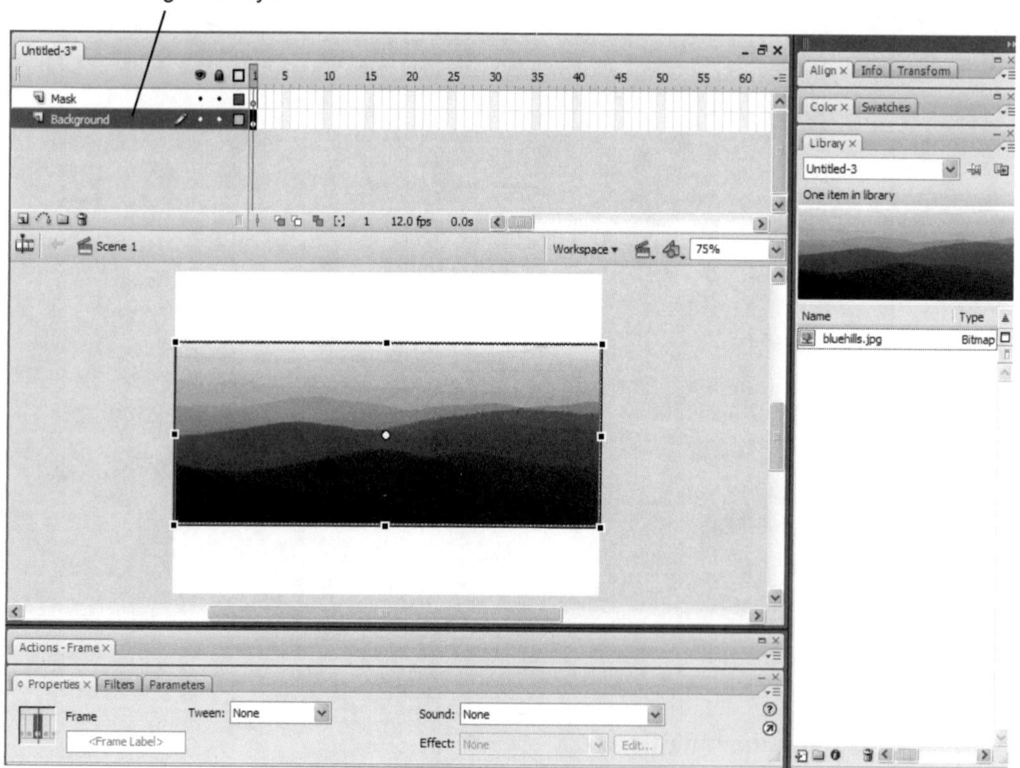

Figure 4.12
A background image in the Background layer.

5. Drag the circle to one end of your picture.

6. Now go to frame 40 of your Mask layer and press F6 to insert a new keyframe. See Figure 4.14.

7. Now go to frame 40 of your Background layer and press F5 to insert frames, so that the background image is available all through your mask. See Figure 4.15.

8. Select frame 40 of your Mask layer. Drag the circle to the other end of your picture. See Figure 4.16.

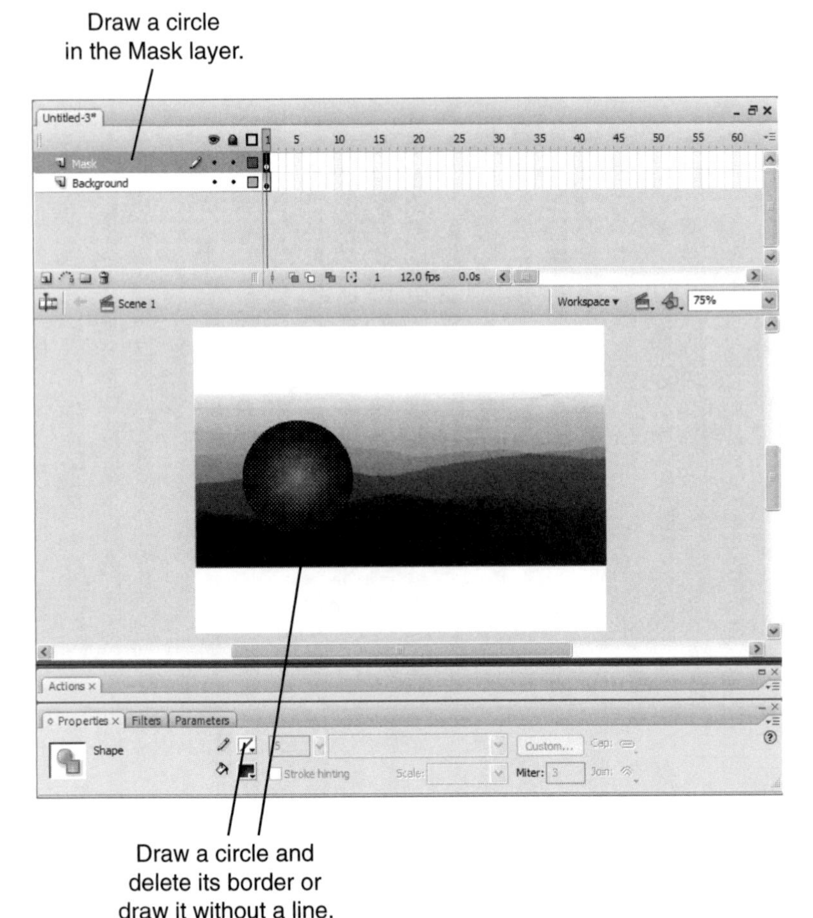

Figure 4.13
A ball in the Mask layer.

9. You can use shape tween (for filled-in objects) or motion tween (for graphic symbols). Go back to frame 1 of your Mask layer and select Shape from the Tween drop-down menu in the Properties tab. See Figure 4.17.

10. Right-click on the Mask layer (the area where you named the layer, not where the frames exist) and select Mask. See Figure 4.18. Your resulting screen should look like Figure 4.19.

A Custom Cursor

The system default cursor is the white cursor. If you want to have a custom cursor replace the default system cursor, you need to create a movie clip symbol, which would act as a custom cursor, and then apply a built-in function of Flash

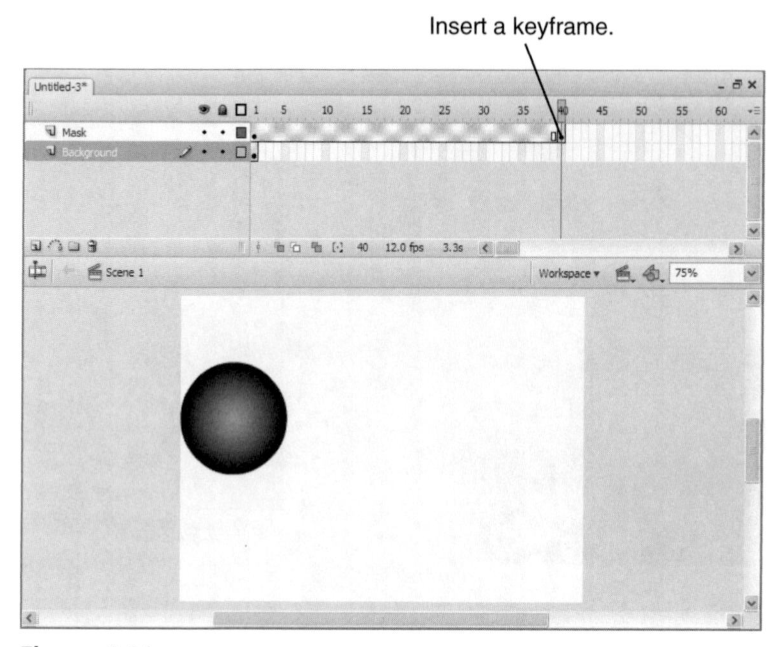

Figure 4.14
Insert a new keyframe in the Mask layer.

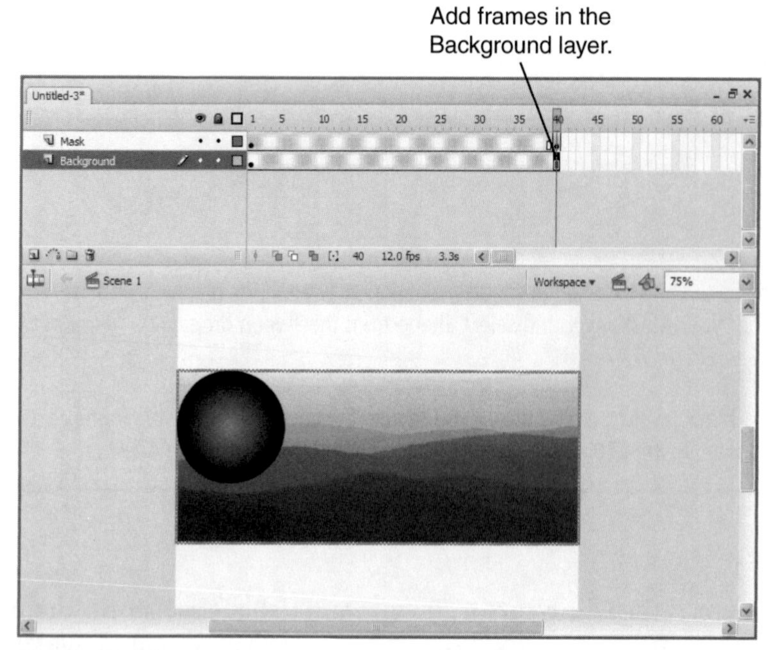

Figure 4.15
Insert keyframes in the Background layer.

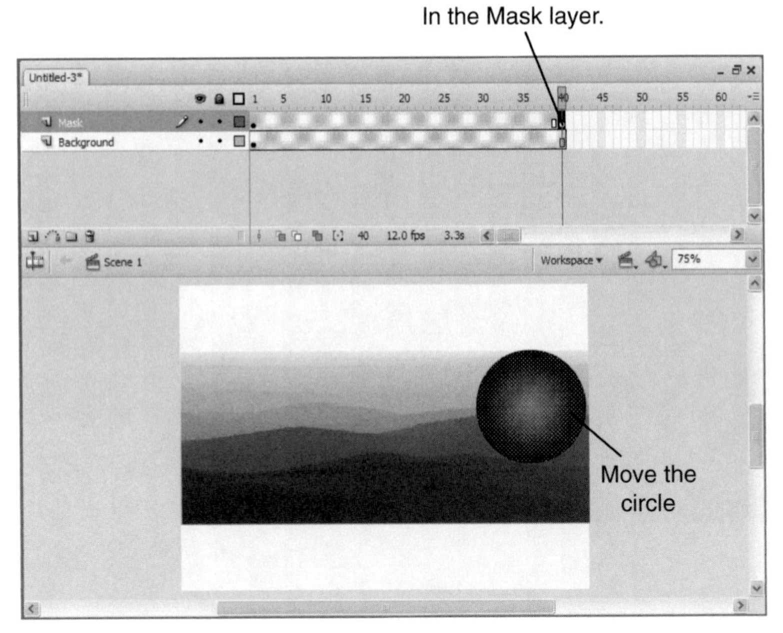

Figure 4.16
Drag the circle to the other end.

ActionScript, `startDrag()`, which enables you to drag the movie clip. Apart from this, you need to hide the default cursor, which you can access through built-in mouse methods of ActionScript.

Exercise 4.5

1. Begin by starting a new movie. Select Insert, New Symbol. Name it cursor and select behavior type Movie Clip. Inside this movie clip, make the cursor that you want. You can make it animated if you want to.

2. Next you want to get back to the main scene by clicking Scene 1 on the top left of the screen. If your Library window is not already open, open it by choosing Window, Library. Click and drag the cursor from the library onto any place in the white working space, the stage.

3. Go to the Instance tab and name the cursor movie clip instance `cursor_mc`. See Figure 4.20.

4. Lastly, right-click on the first keyframe on the top Timeline and select Actions. Paste the following code into the Actions window:

```
cursor_mc.startDrag(true);
Mouse.hide();
```

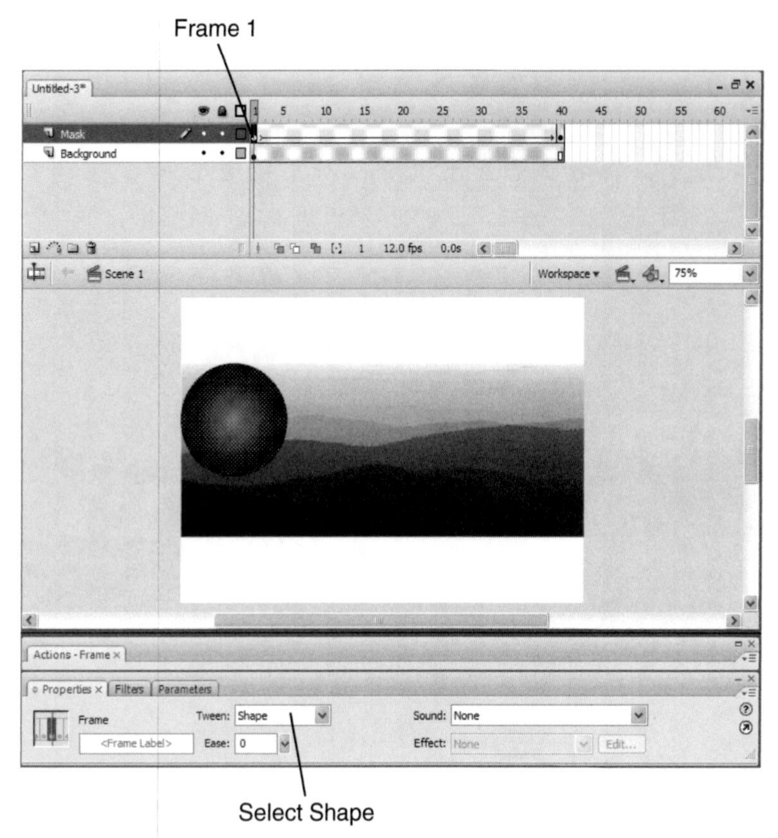

Figure 4.17
Shape tween.

Text Animation

You can add simple text animation from the menu bar options.

Exercise 4.6

1. Open a new Flash document.
2. Create text on the stage using the Text tool.
3. Keeping the text selected, from the menu bar, choose Insert, Timeline Effects, Transform/Transition, Transition. See Figure 4.22.
4. In the new window that opens, you can create custom text animation by changing the properties in the left pane. To view the changes, click on Update Preview. See Figure 4.23.
5. Once you are satisfied with the changes, click on the OK button, and Flash will generate the layers and frames required to create the animation. Now test your movie (Ctrl+Enter).

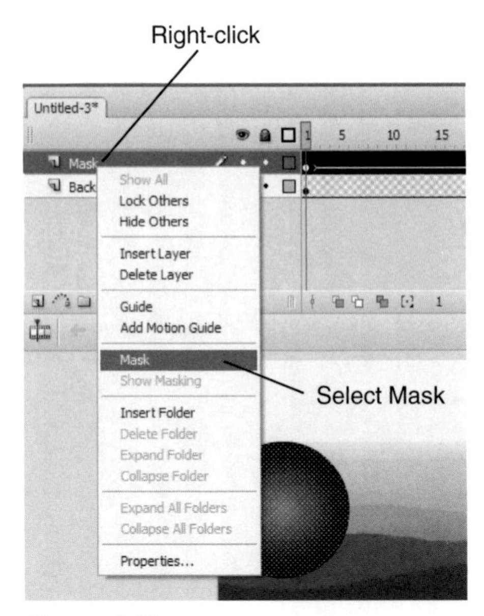

Figure 4.18
Before Masking.

Figure 4.19
After Masking.

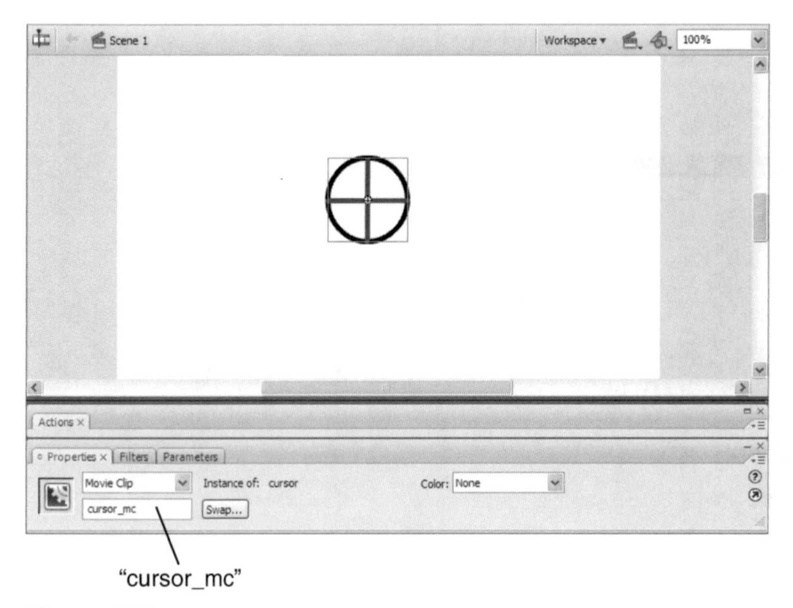

Figure 4.20
The cursor movie clip.

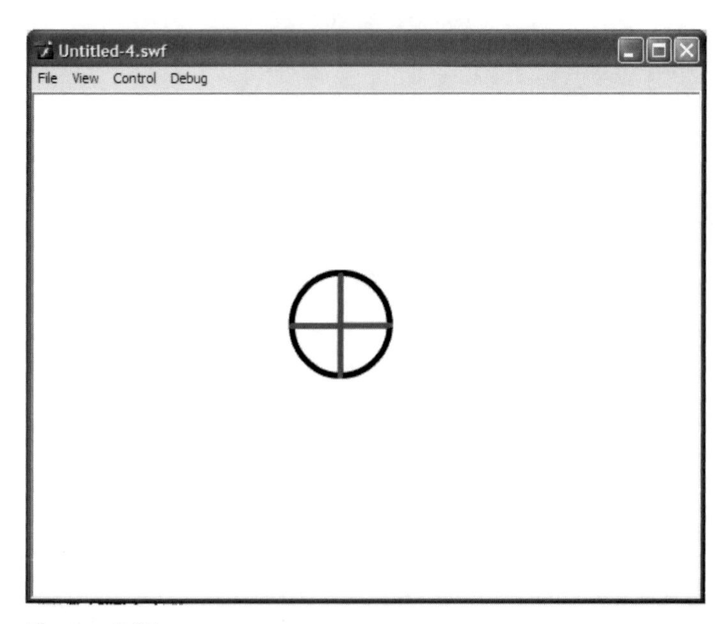

Figure 4.21
Movie Clip instance.

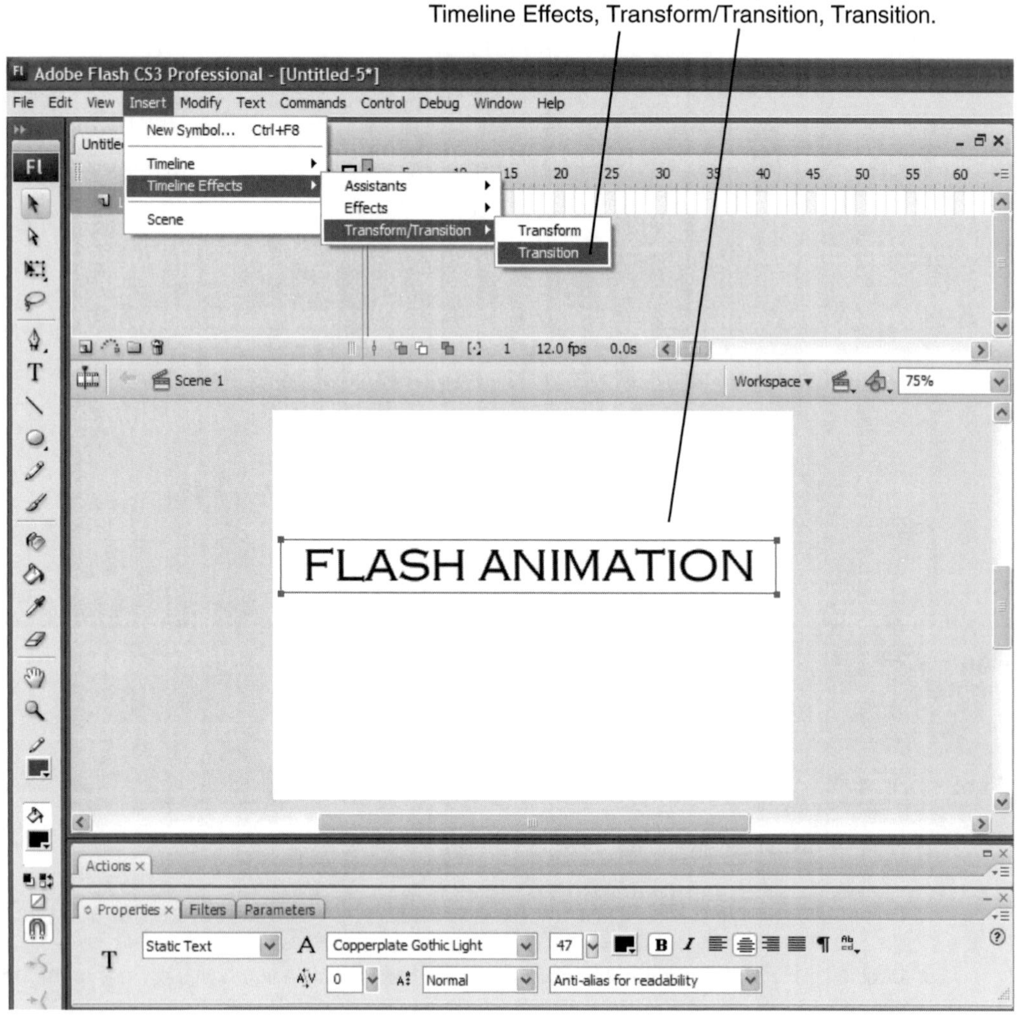

Figure 4.22
Text animation.

Rollover Effects

You've undoubtedly noticed that often when you roll your cursor over certain areas on a Web page, some sort of animation plays (such as leaves falling or flowers growing), even though you haven't clicked on anything. Flash buttons have four states: Up, Over, Down, and Hit. The Hit button state is used to create the region or area that should act as the hit area. This hit area is not visible during run time of the Flash movie and is visible only during the design time as a light blue transparent object. Buttons and their states were presented earlier in Chapter 2.

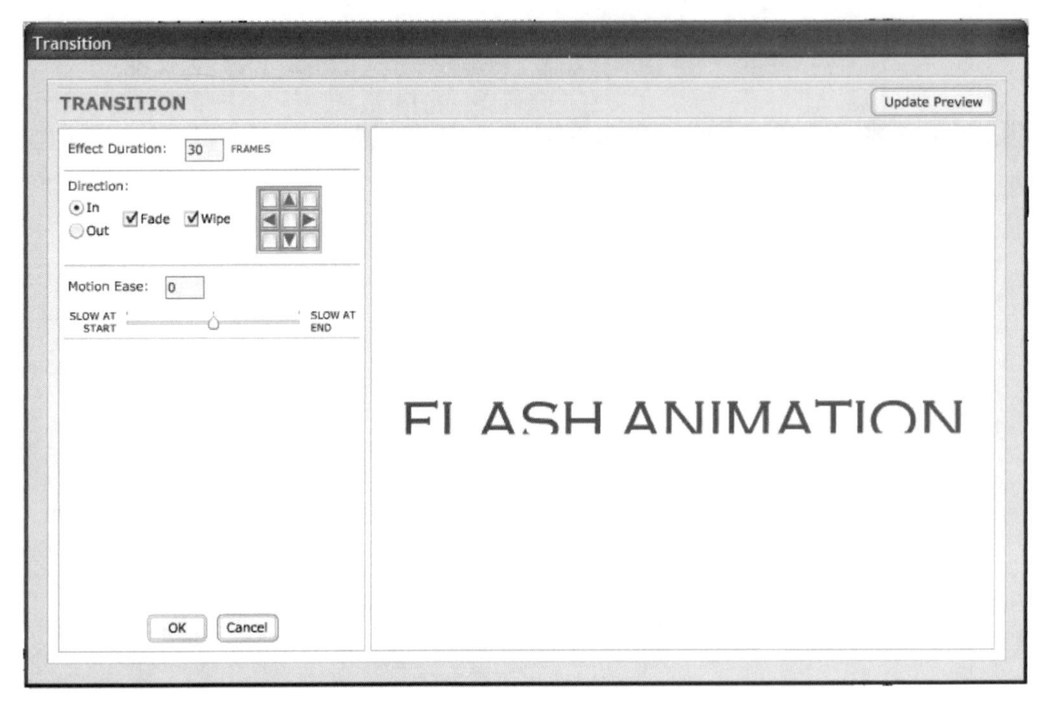

Figure 4.23
Transition.

Exercise 4.7

1. Open a new Flash document.
2. Draw a small circle and, keeping the circle selected, press F8 and convert it to a button.
3. Double-click on this button to edit it. You will see that the circle you have drawn is in the Up state.
4. In layer 1, simply drag the little rectangle by grabbing the circular keyframe icon (not the playhead but the black rectangle from the Up state) and drop it in the Hit state. So now you have empty fills in the Up, Over, and Down states and the filled button in the Hit area. See Figure 4.24.
5. Click on Scene 1 to return to the stage. Now you can see the light blue shade of the button.
6. Now select the button and press F8 again. This time convert it to a movie clip. This way you have created a movie clip with a button in its first frame.
7. Double-click the movie clip to enter its edit state.
8. Select the button and give it the instance name `play_btn` in the Properties tab.

9. From the second frame onward, create an animation of falling stars or something that fascinates you (the button is in the first frame). Use motion tweens for special effects. See Figure 4.25. To create a star animation, follow these steps:

   a. Press F7 to create a blank frame so that the button is not duplicated.
   b. Put an image of a star there and scale it small.
   c. Click on frame 12 and press F6.
   d. Put an image of a star there and scale it big. You can also change the star's location here.
   e. Select the second frame, and in the Properties tab, apply motion tween. In the Properties panel, choose CW for Rotate and enter `1` for Times. This will rotate the star when it is animating.
   f. Now drag the playhead over the Timeline to see a preview of your animation.

10. Create a new layer and call it Actions. Here in frame 1 you can write the following ActionScript.

```
stop();
function playClick (evt:MouseEvent):void {
play();
}
play_btn.addEventListener(MouseEvent.ROLL_OVER,playClick);
play_btn.removeEventListener(MouseEvent.ROLL_OUT,playClick);
```

11. The `stop()` action stops the movie clip from playing the animation. The first frame of the movie clip has an invisible button so nothing is visible on the stage except for the light blue Invisible button. See Figure 4.26. The code is just changing the event to the `ROLL_OVER` state when the mouse is on the button, and then when the mouse is out the event is removed.

12. Click on Scene 1 to return to the main Timeline and select the movie clip. Press Ctrl+D to duplicate the movie clip and place them all around the stage. See Figure 4.27.

13. Press Ctrl+Enter to test the movie and see the animation playing. Figure 4.28 presents sample output. It appears that there is nothing on the stage, but in fact we have movie clips that have animation that plays when you roll over the invisible buttons.

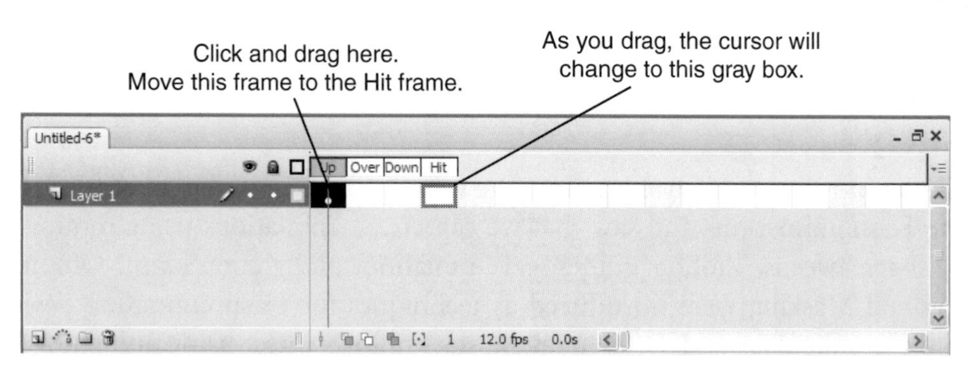
Click and drag here.
Move this frame to the Hit frame.
As you drag, the cursor will
change to this gray box.
Untitled-6*
Up
Over
Down
Hit
Layer 1
1
12.0 fps
0.0s

Figure 4.24
The button Hit area.

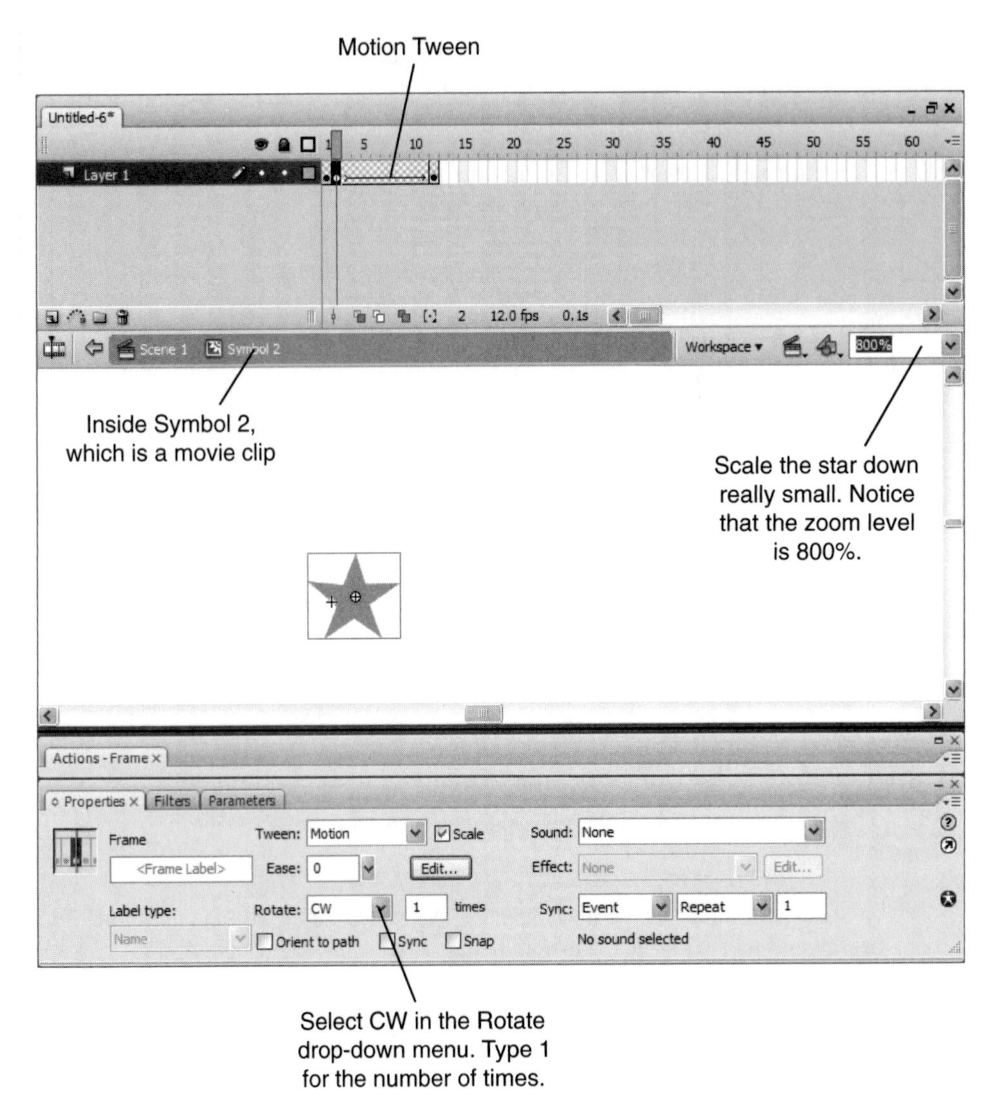

Figure 4.25
A star animation.

Summary

This chapter introduced Flash animation. We went through a number of examples to create Flash animations and saw that we can create animations using motion tweens, shape tweens, motion guides, cel animation, and ActionScript. Onion Skinning and Masking were introduced as techniques for Flash animation. We created a custom cursor and, lastly, a falling stars rollover effect using animation. These examples should enable you to start creating your own animations.

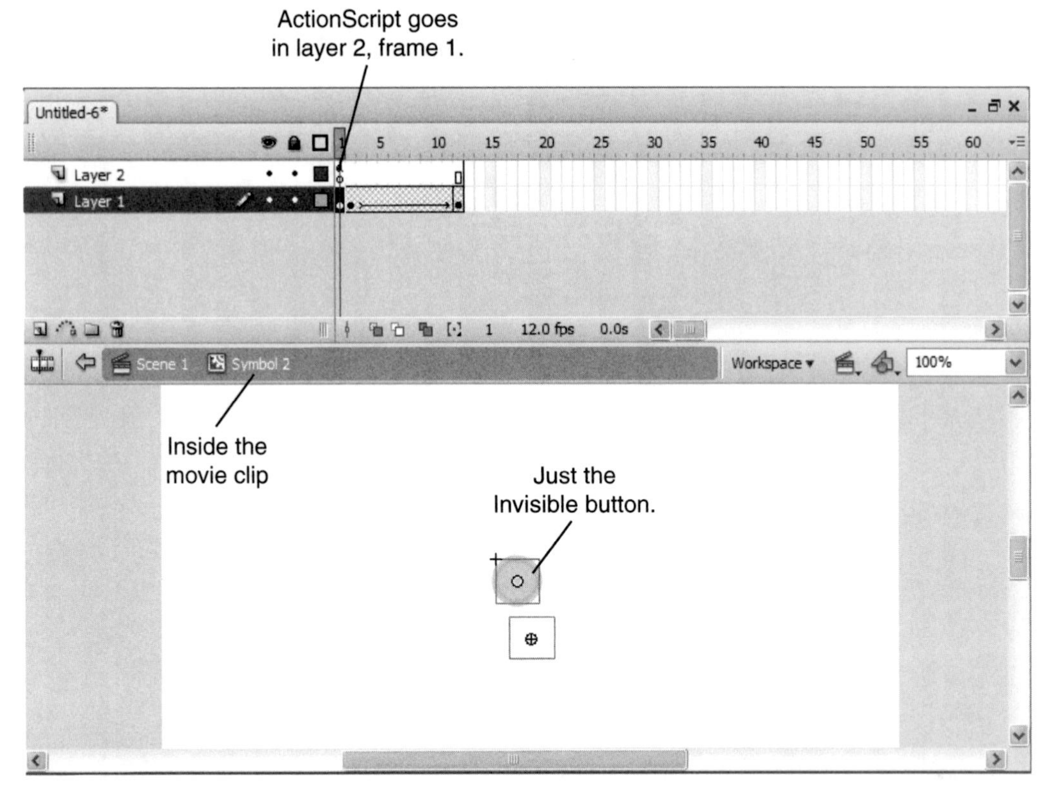

Figure 4.26
ActionScript for the first frame.

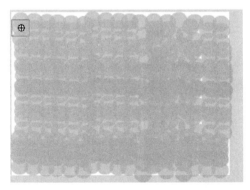

Figure 4.27
Copy instances of the movie clip on the screen.

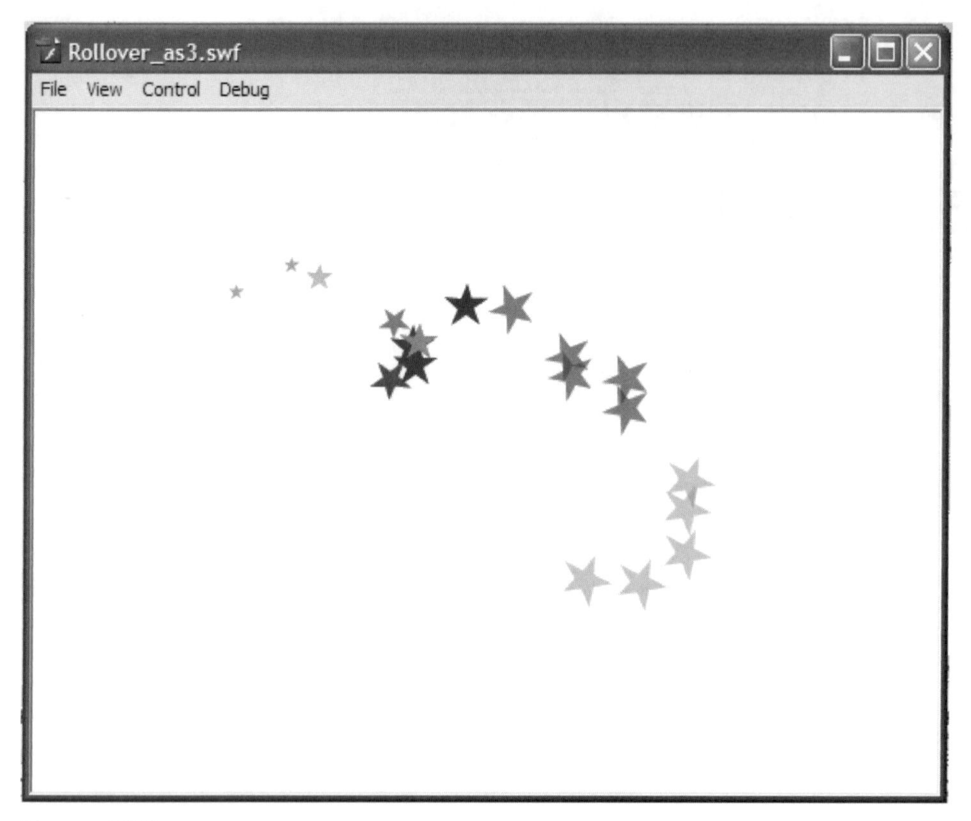

Figure 4.28
Completed star animation.

Review Questions

1. What is animation?
2. What are the two types of tweening?
3. What is cel animation?
4. How is the motion guide helpful in animation?

Projects

1. Use motion guide to create an animation of a flying kite.

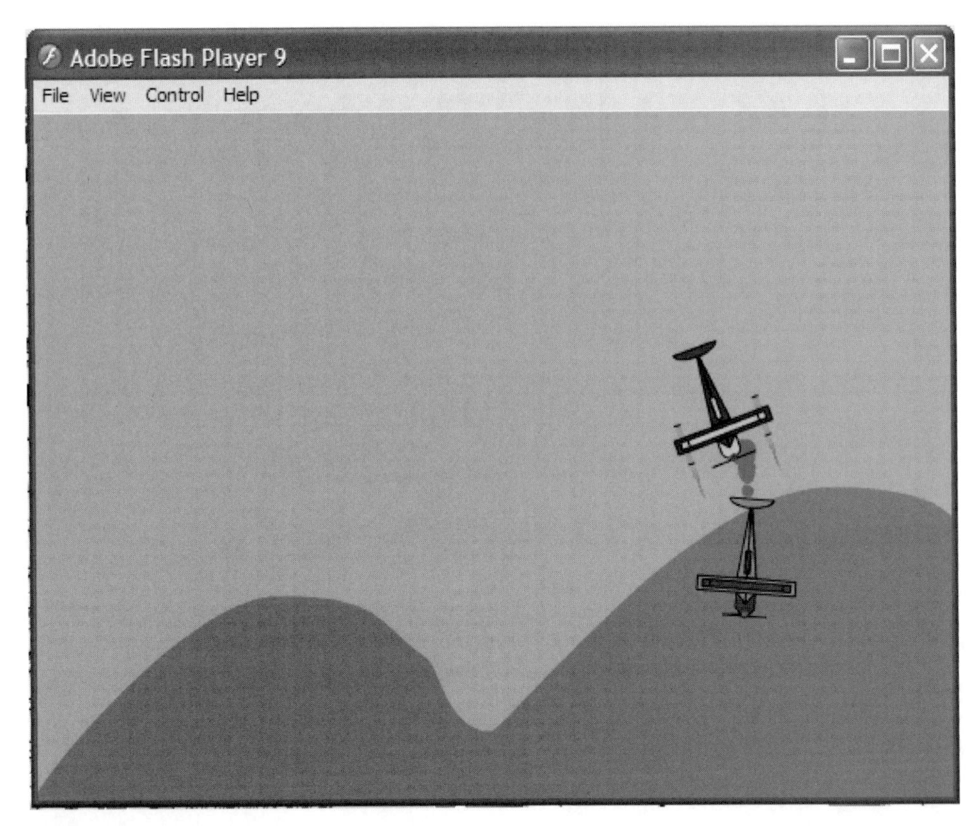

Figure 4.29
Motion tween: two airplanes.

2. Use motion tweening to create an animation of two airplanes. Make one airplane follow another airplane. Your output should look something like Figure 4.29.
3. Create a blue square and, using shape tweening, make that square grow into a blue car.

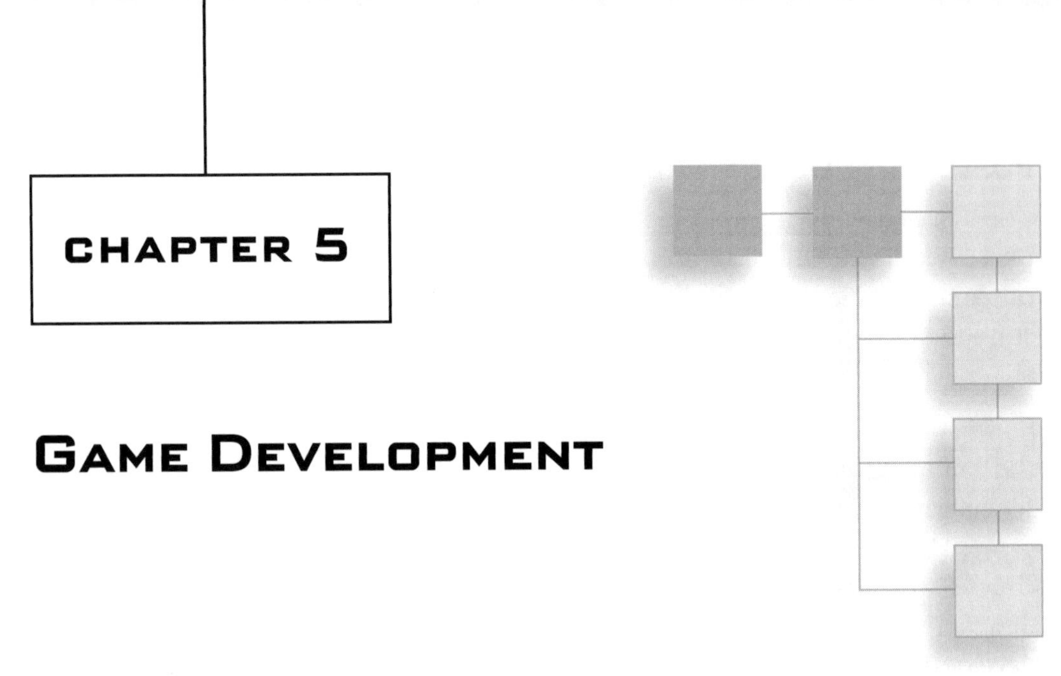

Chapter 5

Game Development

- Use the software-engineering model to design, develop, and test a Flash game
- Import and use movie clip symbols
- Create instances of movie clips and buttons
- Use the layers and frames on the Timeline
- Control an instance of the symbols with arrow keys
- Create and use a timer
- Use the Hit Test function
- Manage and use a scorecard
- Use built-in functions

The Game Plan

We will use the traditional software-engineering process to design (phase 1), develop (phase 2), and test (phase 3) a game in Flash. The design phase includes the story line, identifying the objects to be used in the game, determining their roles, etc. The development phase includes the coding of the objects used in the game. The testing phase includes running the movie clip and debugging the errors.

Phase One: Design Phase

The first phase in game development is the game design. This is a very important phase because it will serve as a blueprint for your game. In this phase, you plan out and document your audience for the game, develop the story line, sketch the storyboard, determine and create the characters for your game, and identify the characters' roles.

So what is *game design?* Game design includes aspects of the game that are vital to the game and cannot be changed. Changing these aspects would make it a different game. So the first step is to identify these unchangeable aspects of the game. They include (a) a story line, (b) a storyboard, (c) different game pieces (of course, the shapes, sizes, and colors of these pieces can change based on the designer's interests), and (d) the roles played by each game piece. Let's start developing the design of the game.

A. Story Line

The story line of this game is that there is evidence that the earth is going to be invaded by aliens in the year 2020. The aliens plan to invade by landing their deadly spaceships on the earth. These spaceships carry harmful chemicals that can pollute the atmosphere and create incurable viruses among the inhabitants of the earth, so scientists are building tanks to fire at these spaceships before they land to prevent entry of harmful chemicals. Scientists are encouraging entrepreneurs to bid for projects to build these tanks. They are testing the models by simulating the scenario of alien spaceships entering Earth and check the effectiveness of the tank's ability to knock down the alien spaceships. The minimum number of alien ships that must be destroyed by the tank is 10 in 30 seconds. The company that meets this goal will be asked to build some of the tanks for the year 2020. This game is going to test one such scenario with one tank. To add more activity on the screen, the game also uses some instances of hovercrafts that move horizontally on the screen.

The game essentially checks on how many alien ships can be fired by the player with his tank in 30 seconds. After 30 seconds, the game halts, and the player is given his score and a message (winner or loser) with a choice to play again or quit.

B. Storyboard

This phase is similar to the concept of a flowchart or UML (Unified Modeling Language) used in software development. Basically, we sketch the scenes to

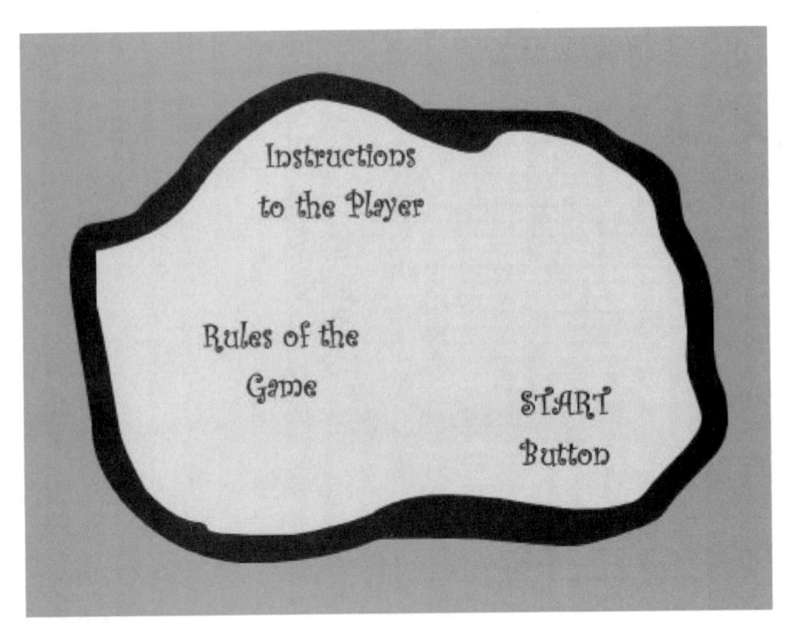

Figure 5.1
Introduction scene.

determine the flow of the game just as we would use flowcharts to describe the data flow in a program. Figures 5.1, 5.2, and 5.3 are the sketches for the storyboard. Notice that we just used some rough images or text to represent the game pieces and the flow of the story line. This is done intentionally to illustrate that at this stage the story line is more important than the actual graphics.

The elements required for the game are:

- an instructions scene
- some instances of alien spaceships
- a sound file to be played in case of collision
- hovercraft
- a tank
- a scoreboard
- a timer control
- display message
- option to play again or quit

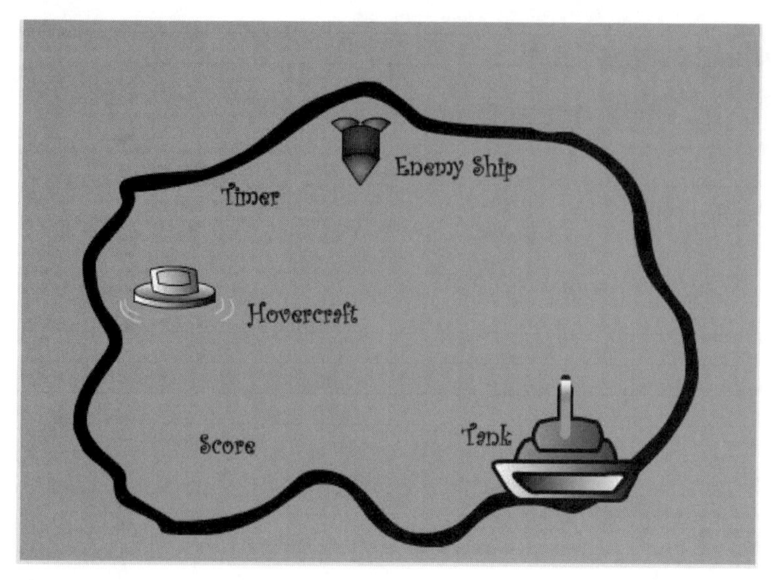

Figure 5.2
Game pieces.

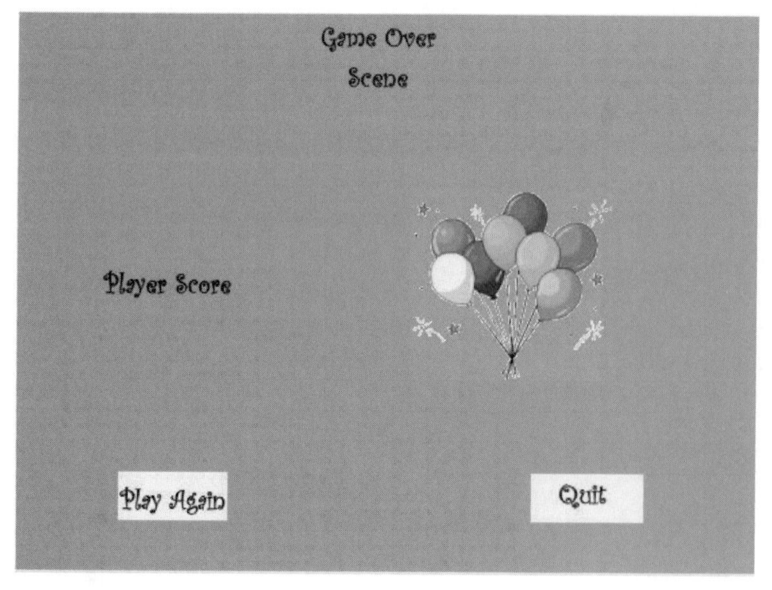

Figure 5.3
Game over scene.

C. Creating the Game Pieces

This section will discuss some concepts involved in creating the movie clips required for this game. Emphasis will be placed on presenting the techniques to create the movie clips, such as nested movie clips, rather than on the artistic aspect of the graphics. In fact, this is one place where we see that game design and development cover several aspects and is a highly collaborative effort. These aspects include story line, graphics, animations, coding, and proof of concept. It is not necessary for one individual to have all these talents, and that is what we are about to demonstrate here. As far as this tutorial is concerned, you can create the graphics simply with geometric shapes to see how they work. After that, you can use your imagination or your team members' help to create the required graphics movie clips or use the movie clips provided in the tutorial. You can also use the Internet to download some images for a tank object, a missile, and a hovercraft and convert them to movie clips. Of course, when using the Internet, pay attention to the copyright policy pertaining to those images.

Note

If you like to use the movie clips or sound files provided in this movie, you can open shootingtank.fla provided as part of this tutorial in Flash and copy the movie clips from the library (found on the right side of the window) and paste them into your new Flash document's library.

Exercise 5.1

Create the Alien Spaceship

1. Start Macromedia Flash and open a new Flash document. Make sure you choose ActionSript 3.0.

2. Click on Insert, New Symbol, and name the symbol `mc_enemyship`. Make sure that the symbol is of type movie clip.

3. Use the tools in the toolbox to draw a triangle or a shape similar to the shape in Figure 5.4 to create an enemy spaceship.

Figure 5.4
Enemy spaceship.

4. Click on Scene 1 to get back to the main Timeline.

5. Save the file as `spaceInvaders`.

Create the Hovercraft

1. Click on Insert, New Symbol, choose Movie Clip and name the symbol `mc_hovercraft`.

2. Draw a hovercraft similar to the image in Figure 5.5 or use any shape you like to create the hovercraft. Do not click on Scene 1 yet.

3. Next, we apply motion tweening to enable the hovercraft to move horizontally across the screen. To do this, while you are still in the Timeline of the hovercraft, simply right-click on frame 48 and insert a keyframe.

4. Drag the hovercraft to the right, to position it roughly below the 40th frame.

5. Leave the hovercraft in its new position, and right-click anywhere between the first and 48th frame. Select Create Motion Tween.

6. Click on Scene 1.

7. To test that your hovercraft is working, drag an instance of the hovercraft to the stage and press Ctrl+Enter. You should see the movie clip move horizontally across the scene. Once it correctly moves across the screen, remove the hovercraft from the stage.

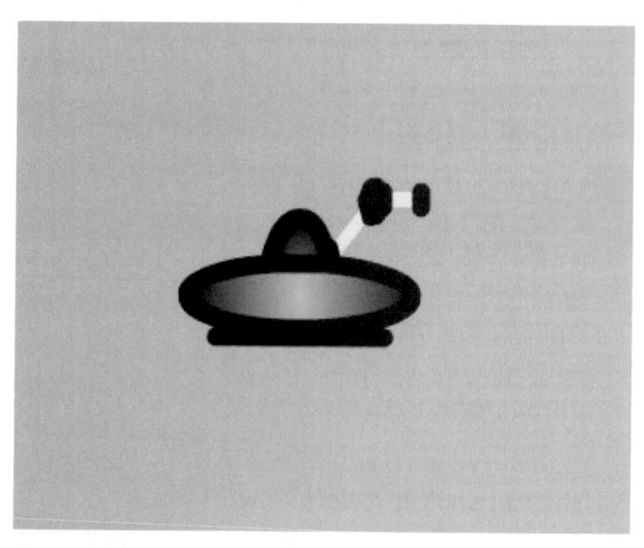

Figure 5.5
Hovercraft.

Note

By the way, this process of building a project and testing it in small modules is one type of software development model called the Incremental Model of Software Development, in which we test each module of the software being developed as soon as it is completed. For example, testing that the hovercraft you built actually works is one increment of your total game development process.

Create the Tank

The tank consists of two movie clips: the missile and the body of the tank, named `tank`. The missile is nested in the tank movie clip. So, let's start on the missile first.

The Missile

1. Click on Insert, New Symbol, choose Movie Clip, and name the symbol `missile`.
2. Open the Actions window for this missile, and in frame 1, type `stop();` This will prevent the missile from automatically playing the animation that we will apply to it in the next two steps. See Figure 5.6.
3. Draw a vertical beam; do not return to Scene 1 yet.
4. This time we want the missile to go upward, so we need to create a motion tween that moves the beam vertically upward.

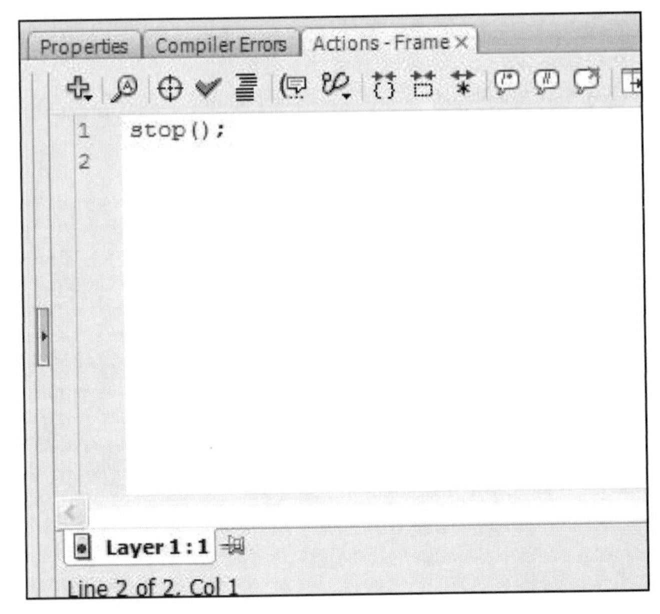

Figure 5.6
Missile code.

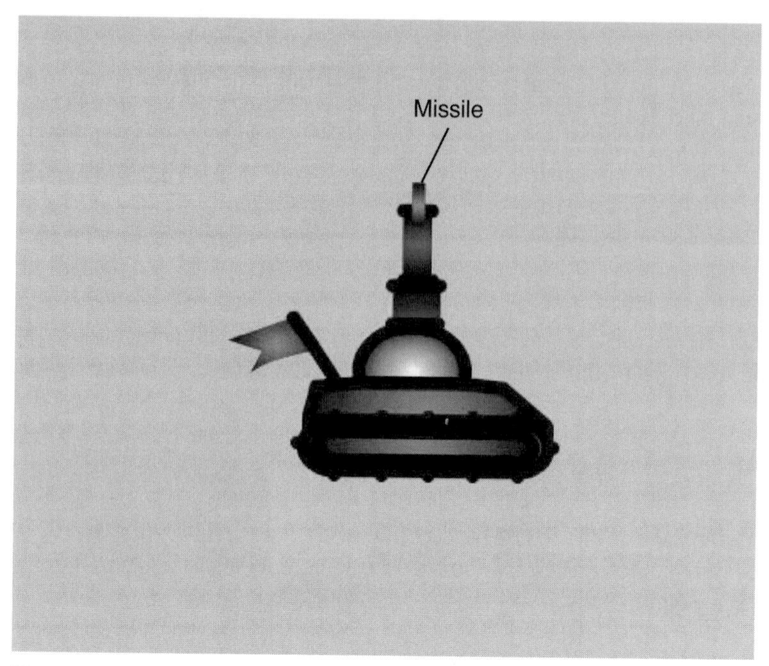

Figure 5.7
A tank.

5. Right-click on frame 20 and click Insert Keyframe.
6. Drag the missile upward roughly two to three inches from its current position.
7. Leave the missile in the new position. Right-click anywhere in between the first and 20th frames and select Create Motion Tween. Go back to Scene 1. Save your file.

The Tank

1. Click on Insert, New Symbol, choose Movie Clip, and name the symbol `tank`.
2. Use any shape that you like to create the body of the tank.
3. Drag an instance of the missile onto the stage, and place it just on the tip of the tank so it becomes a part of the tank.
4. In the Properties window, type `mc_missile` as the instance name for this missile. (See Figure 5.7.) Click on Scene 1 to return to the main Timeline.

Create the Stopwatch

1. Create a new symbol, choose the Graphic option for the type of symbol, and name it `stopwatch`. We choose a graphic type because this symbol does not have any code associated with it.

Figure 5.8
A stopwatch.

2. Use the Rectangle or Oval tool to draw and color the stopwatch image; look at Figure 5.8 if you need a reference image. Remember that this is just an image—it has no functionality at this stage, so it can be any image you fancy.

3. Go back to Scene 1 and save your file.

Add a Sound File

1. Browse the Internet and find a sound file that is suitable for a crash, or use the sound file from the .fla file on the CD provided with this book.

2. Click on File, Import and choose Import to the Library.

3. Browse to the folder that has the sound file and import it to the library.

4. Right-click on the sound file and choose Linkage.

5. In the pop-up window, check the Export for ActionScript box and Export in First Frame. These checks will enable the file to be available for use at run time. Type `crash` in the Class box. Type `flash.media.Sound` for the base class. This will ensure that you have used the sound file of your choice (crash) as the class from which you can create a specific instance in your code. This code also states that the crash class belongs to the base class, `flash.media.Sound`, which accommodates the sound files. See Figure 5.9.

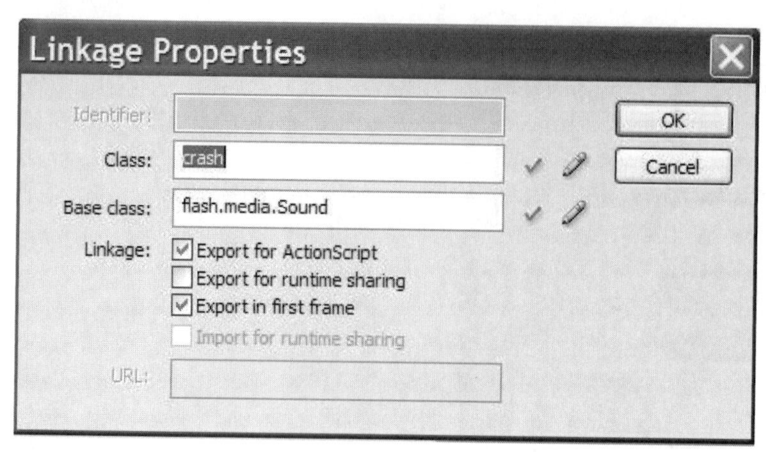

Figure 5.9
Sound file class.

This completes the steps involved in creating the pieces required for this game. The next section describes the role played by each of the pieces in the game.

D. Roles for the Pieces in the Game

- All instances of alien spaceships will randomly move toward the earth from the sky.
- Instances of the hovercraft will move horizontally across the stage. (This is used only for some activity on the stage at this point. You can later enhance your game by adding a `hitTest()` function to the game to detect collisions with the hovercraft and add or delete points, depending on how you want to use this hovercraft in the game.)
- An instance of the tank on the ground controlled by the player will try to attack the alien spaceship by firing missiles on it and to prevent the spaceship from falling down. Missiles are fired when an enemy ship is coming down to prevent the enemy from attacking the ground. At this time, the following actions take place:
  - If the enemy ship gets hit by a missile from the tank, the sound file is played and the enemy ship disappears.
  - The scoreboard is incremented, and the player gets a point.
  - These steps repeat until the timer hits 20 seconds, at which time the game stops.

- The timer control tracks and displays the number of seconds elapsed since the game began. After the timer hits 20 seconds, the game stops and a caption with the player's score is displayed.
- The Play Again button takes the player back to the instructions screen.
- The Quit button unloads the movie. (Note that the Quit button works only when you open the .swf file directly. It will not work if you run the program from the Flash environment using Ctrl+Enter.)

Phase Two: Game Development and Coding

This phase includes placing the game pieces on the stage and writing the ActionScript that provides the navigation for the game, which corresponds to the story line. The new classes, events, and methods used in this game are the (a) timer class and (b) `hitTestObject()`.

A. Timer Class

The timer class is part of the `flash.utils` package. This package must be imported into the Flash game to access and use the timer class. This class expects one argument, which is the specified delay in milliseconds between `timer` events. The `timer` event can be used to make a function call at the specified interval. Other parameters for the timer class are `repeatCount` (which specifies the number of times you wish to repeat) and `Error` (which throws an exception if the delay is a negative number or not a finite number). The syntax for the timer object (where the second parameter is optional) is as follows:

```
public function Timer(delay:Number, repeatCount:int = 0)
```

B. hitTestObject()

The `hitTestObject()` method, another built-in function in Flash, detects when the two objects collide with each other. If they do collide, it returns the Boolean value true; if not, it returns the Boolean value false. The syntax of the function (where `mc1` and `mc2` are the two movie clips on the stage) is as follows:

```
mc1.hitTestObject(mc2)
```

Code Used in the Game

The rest of this section presents the objects and code to be inserted in various layers and frames used in the game. The code required for the game will be included in three frames: frame 1, frame 2, and frame 3.

Activity for Frame 1: Creating the Instructions Scene

This is the introduction scene to your game. It will have the title of your game, the instructions to the user on how to play the game, the rules of the game, and a button to start the game. Here are the instructions to create this scene:

1. If you have been following along the previous section, you should see layer 1 in the Flash document. If not, double-click on it and name it `Instructions`.
2. Choose any color you like for the background.
3. Use the Text tool and choose any font style that you like, and then type the following text to be displayed to the user:

```
The goal of this game is to fire missiles from the tank and shoot the enemy
ships falling vertically
Move the tanker to the left or right with your mouse
To fire a missile place your mouse on the tank and click the mouse

To win, your missiles should destroy at least 10 alien space ships in
30 seconds.
```

4. Create a button and name it `btn`. Drag an instance of it onto the stage and give it the instance name `mybutton_btn`. Type the word Start as static text on top of this button.Your screen should now be similar to Figure 5.10.

Code for the Instructions Screen

There are two blocks of code for this part of the game. Part A is to stop the scene from moving to the next frame, and part B is to place the code in the button to direct the user to move to the next scene.

1. Click on layer 1, frame 1 and open the Actions window.
2. Type the following code:

```
stop();
function buttonClick(myevent:MouseEvent): void {
gotoAndStop(2);
}
mybutton_btn.addEventListener(MouseEvent.CLICK,buttonClick);
```

Explanation of the Code

The `stop()` command ensures that the movie does not proceed to the next frame unless the movie is triggered by some other event, such as a button click. This is exactly what we want to do—we want the user to stop here, read the instructions, and then press the Start button to proceed to the next scene.

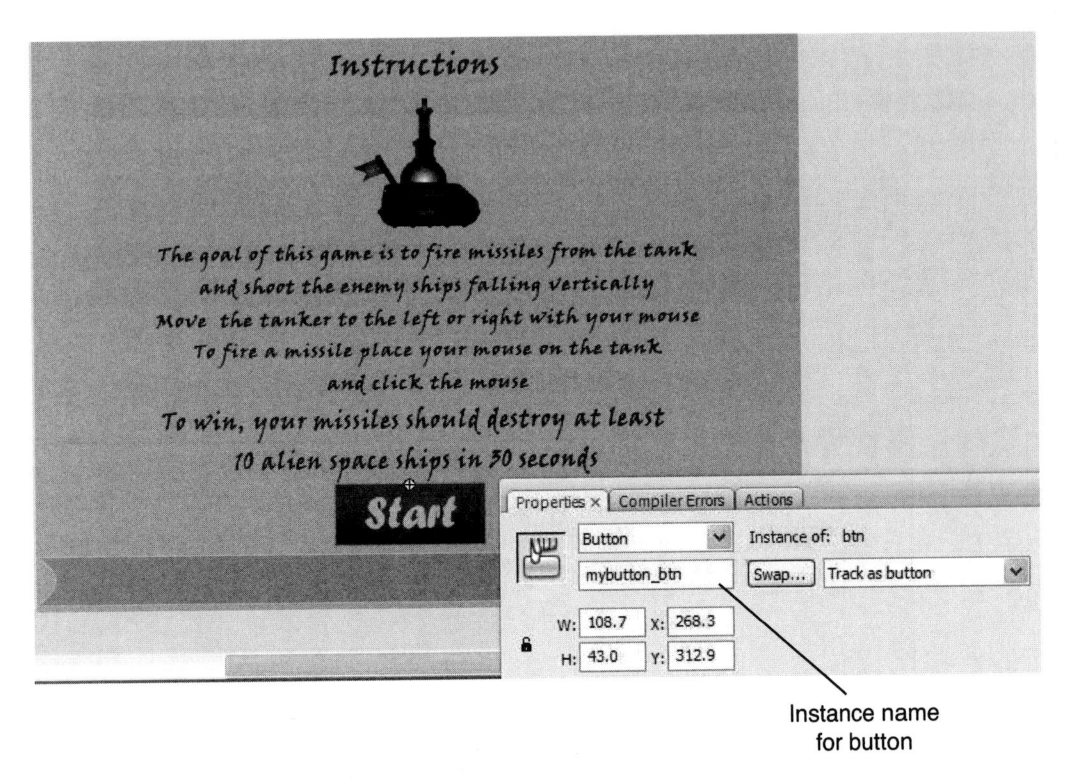

Figure 5.10
The instructions screen.

The next section of the code is a function called `buttonClick`, which takes the player to frame 2 when the button is clicked. An event listener is added to `mybutton_btn` that is triggered when the user clicks the button, and the function `buttonClick` is called.

Activity for Frame 2: Game Pieces

This is the scene where you place all your game pieces. You set up your stage with the tank, hovercrafts, alien spaceships, the timer, the scoreboard, and any required sound files. Instructions to set up the stage are given here:

1. Right-click on frame 2, and click on Insert Keyframe. This copies everything from frame 1 to frame 2. You can delete everything from the stage because you will be placing the game pieces here.

2. Place an instance of the tank, three instances of enemy spaceships, and three or four instances of hovercrafts on the stage. Give an instance name of `tank` to the tank on the stage. Name the enemy ships `enemy1`, `enemy2`, and `enemy3`.

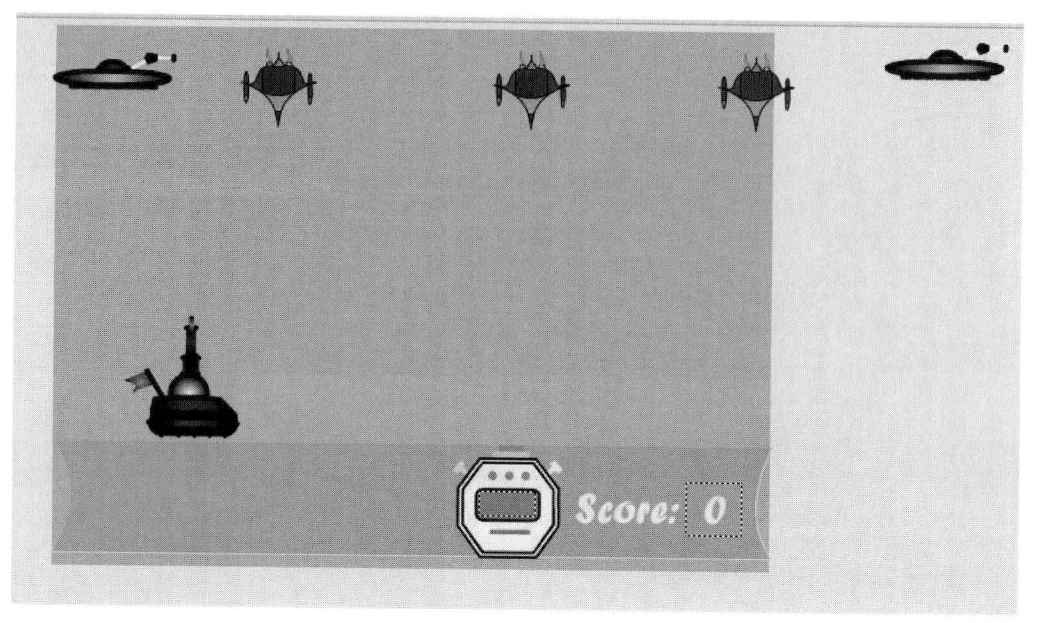

Figure 5.11
Game pieces.

3. If necessary, you can orient your hovercrafts to face in the right direction by clicking on the hovercraft and choosing Modify, Transform, or Flip Horizontal from the menu bar. Your stage should be similar to Figure 5.11.
4. Place an instance of the stopwatch at the bottom of the screen. The stopwatch is just an image. Place a dynamic text box on top of the stopwatch and type `cdTimer` in the Instance Name box. This text box should cover the area in the middle of the stopwatch where the time is displayed, as shown in Figure 5.12.
5. Place a static text box right next to the stopwatch. Type `Score` in the text box.
6. Create another dynamic text box and place it besides the static text box. Give it the instance name `score`.

Note

The use of dynamic text boxes in steps 4 and 6 is an important concept. Flash provides two types of text boxes: static and dynamic. A *static text box* contains text that will not change during execution of code. A *dynamic text box*, on the other hand, allows for its text to change during run time. An example is the value of a variable called *score*, which gets updated each time the player hits the enemy. This happens at run time, and the use of a dynamic text control is perfect here because we want the current value of the score displayed to the player at any given point of time. The dynamic text box can get the value of the variable called `score` and display it to the player.

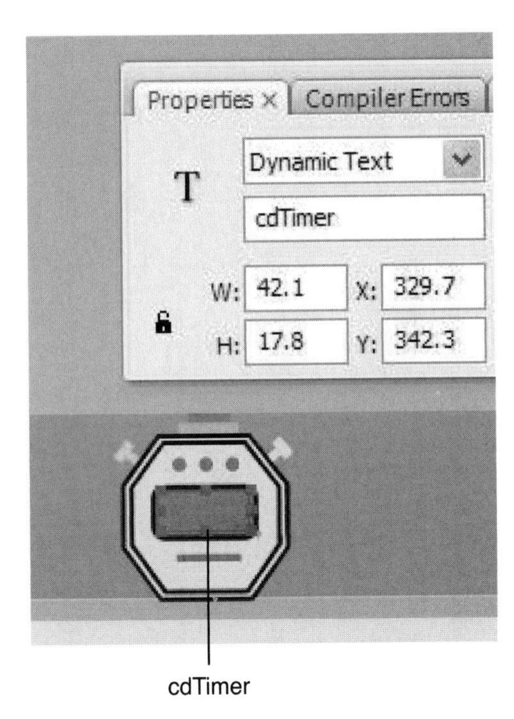

Figure 5.12
Stopwatch with time display area (`cdTimer`).

Code for the Game Pieces Scene

Click on frame 2 and choose Actions from the Window menu. Type the following code in the Actions panel for frame 2:

```
stop();
//import the flash.utils package
import flash.utils.*;

// Create a new Timer object with a delay of 1000 ms
var myTimer:Timer = new Timer(1000);

//add eventlistener timer to the Timer object and the function (timedFunction)
//to call after each delay
myTimer.addEventListener("timer", timedFunction);

//create a variable scr to record score
var scr:Number=0;

//create an instance(mySound) of the crash class
var mySound:crash = new crash();
```

```
// Start the timer
myTimer.start();

//create a variable msgText
var msgText:String;

// Function will be called every 1000 milliseconds
function timedFunction(eventArgs:TimerEvent) {
//variable tc to keep track of the number of ticks of the timer object
var tc:int= 21 - myTimer.currentCount;

// convert the numeric value to a string and display it in the //dynamic //text box
cdTimer
cdTimer.text = tc.toString();

if (myTimer.currentCount >20) {
            //conditional statement to check the value of score
            if (scr > 9) {
                 msgText = "Your score is" +scr + " You are a winner";
            } else {
                 msgText = "Your score is" +scr + " sorry try again";
            }
//reset timer, stop timer, remove all event listeners
//and go to frame 3
       myTimer.reset();
       myTimer.stop();
       enemy1.removeEventListener(Event.ENTER_FRAME, moveEnemy1);
       enemy2.removeEventListener(Event.ENTER_FRAME, moveEnemy2);
       enemy3.removeEventListener(Event.ENTER_FRAME, moveEnemy3);
       tank.removeEventListener(Event.ENTER_FRAME, moveTank);
       tank.removeEventListener(MouseEvent.MOUSE_DOWN, fireMissile);
       tank.removeEventListener(MouseEvent.MOUSE_UP, stopDragging);
       stage.removeEventListener(Event.ENTER_FRAME, detectCollision);
       gotoAndStop(3);
  }
}

//add event listener (ENTER_FRAME) to enemy1, move y position of enemy by 5
//pixels
enemy1.addEventListener(Event.ENTER_FRAME, moveEnemy1);
function moveEnemy1(myevent:Event):void {
enemy1.y += 5;
```

```
//if enemy1.y > 400, then reposition it at a random location on //the y //axis
        if (enemy1.y > 400) {
                enemy1.x = (Math.random()*450)+50;
                enemy1.y = Math.random()*-50;
        }
}

//add event listener (ENTER_FRAME) to enemy2, move y position of enemy //by 5
//pixels
enemy2.addEventListener(Event.ENTER_FRAME, moveEnemy2);
function moveEnemy2(myevent:Event):void {
enemy2.y += 5;
//if enemy2.y > 400, then reposition it at a random location on
//the y axis
        if (enemy2.y > 400) {
                enemy2.x = (Math.random()*450)+50;
                enemy2.y = Math.random()*-50;
        }
}

//add event listener (ENTER_FRAME) to enemy3, move y position of enemy
//by 5 pixels
enemy3.addEventListener(Event.ENTER_FRAME, moveEnemy3);
function moveEnemy3(myevent:Event):void {
enemy3.y += 5;
//if enemy3.y > 400, then reposition it at a random location on //the y //axis
        if (enemy3.y > 400) {
                enemy3.x = (Math.random()*450)+50;
                enemy3.y = Math.random()*-50;
        }
}

//add event listener (ENTER_FRAME) to tank
tank.addEventListener(Event.ENTER_FRAME, moveTank);
function moveTank(myevent:Event):void {
//if tank.x position is not equal to the root.mouseX (mouse's x
//position on the stage)
//and tank.x is < root.mouseX, increment x by 5 pixels and set the
//y position to 262
if (tank.x != root.mouseX && tank.x < root.mouseX) {
                tank.x += 5;
                tank.y = 262;
        }
```

```
//if tank.x position is not equal to the root.mouseX (mouse's x //position on
//the stage)
//and tank.x is > root.mouseX, increment x by 5 pixels and set the //y position
//to 262

if (tank.x != root.mouseX && tank.x > root.mouseX) {
                tank.x -= 5;
                tank.y = 262;
        }
}

//add an event listener (MOUSE_DOWN) to the tank which calls the fireMissile
//function
tank.addEventListener(MouseEvent.MOUSE_DOWN, fireMissile);

//function sets the visible property of the mc_missile to true
//The mc_missile is a nested movie clip within the tank movie clip
function fireMissile(myevent:MouseEvent):void {
tank.mc_missile._visible = true;
tank.mc_missile.gotoAndPlay(1);
}

// call stopdrag when the mouse is UP on the tank
tank.addEventListener(MouseEvent.MOUSE_UP, stopDragging);
function stopDragging(myevent:MouseEvent):void {
tank.stopDrag();
}
//set the stratdrag() on the tank to false
tank.startDrag(false);
//add an event listener to the stage to detect collision
stage.addEventListener(Event.ENTER_FRAME, detectCollision);


//function detectcollision checks if the enemy1, enemy2 or enemy3 collides with
//the tank
//if so it returns a true value, increments the score and positions the enemy
//at a random location
// the dynamic textbox score gets the value of the scr variable

function detectCollision(myevent:Event):void {

        if (enemy1.hitTestObject(tank)==true) {
             scr++;
```

```
            mySound.play();
            enemy1.y = Math.random()*-50;
            enemy1.x = Math.random()*450;
            score.text = scr.toString();
      }
      if (enemy2.hitTestObject(tank)==true) {
            scr++;
            mySound.play();
            enemy2.y = Math.random()*-50;
            enemy2.x = Math.random()*450;
            score.text = scr.toString();

      }
      if (enemy3.hitTestObject(tank)==true) {
            scr++;
            mySound.play();
            enemy3.y = Math.random()*-50;
            enemy3.x = Math.random()*450;
            score.text = scr.toString();
      }
}
```

Explanation of the Code

The `stop()` function is called to let the movie stop on this frame. Next, the `flash.utils` package is imported. This package contains classes like the timer class. A new timer object, `myTimer`, is created with a delay of 1,000 milliseconds, or one second. The timer class also has a timer event that can listen to the delay or timer tick and respond by calling a function. The timer event is added to the `myTimer` object, which calls the `timedFunction` every second. The variables created are `scr` to keep track of the score, `tc` to keep track of the timer ticks, and `msgText` (a string variable) to display a message to the user. The start method of the timer, called `myTimer.start()`, starts the timer.

The `timedFunction` has the code that will be executed every second (one second is the time delay set up earlier). The argument for this function is the `TimerEvent`, which is triggered every time the timer object reaches the specified delay interval. In this example, it is triggered every second, at which time the `timedFunction` is called. This function starts the `tc` (counter) at 21 and decrements it by `currentCount` of the timer. The `currentCount` is a read-only property of the timer, which gives the count of the number of times the timer has ticked since it started at 0. The variable `tc` has the number of seconds that have elapsed as the timer ticks down.

The first value that you will see is 20, which is the result of 21 minus myTimer .currentCount, where the value of currentCount is 1 after the first second and gets incremented by 1 every second thereafter. A conditional statement is used to check if the currentCount is greater than 20. If it is, then we check to see if the scr (variable for score) is greater than 9. If it is greater than 9, a congratulatory message is printed; if not, a message that says "try again" is printed. The rest of the code is the garbage-cleaning statements that remove all the event listeners, after which the code proceeds to frame 3 and stops. The next section of the code adds an event listener to the enemy movie clips. This event listener, ENTER_FRAME, calls the function moveEnemy(). This is done for all three enemy movie clips. The moveEnemy() function increments the y position of the movie clip by 5 pixels so it moves in a downward direction. An if condition is used to check if the y position is greater than 400; if so, it is positioned at a random x, y position as determined by the random number function. The tank movie clip has mouse event listeners, MOUSE_DOWN and MOUSE_UP, added to it. The MOUSE_DOWN event calls the fireMissile function. This function sets the tank.mc_missile to true and plays the animation of the mc_missile. When the MOUSE_UP event is triggered, the stopDrag() method is called, which disables the drag feature for the tank object.

The next segment of the code adds an event listener, ENTER_FRAME, to the stage and calls the detectCollision function when this event is triggered. The function detectCollision checks if enemy1 collides with the tank; if so, the variable scr is incremented, and enemy1 is placed at a random position determined by the random number generator. Next, the integer value of scr is converted to a string, and is displayed in the dynamic text box, score.text. The same sequence of code segments is repeated for enemy2 and enemy3. This completes the code for frame 2.

Activity for Frame 3: "Game Over" Scene

This is the last scene that you have to include in the game. This is the game over scene. In this game, we will display the score to the user, print a message to let the user know if he won or lost, and provide an option for the user to play again. Instructions to create this scene are given here:

1. Click on frame 3 and click on Insert Keyframe. This copies everything from frame 2 to frame 3.

2. Leave the score, the timer, and a couple of hovercrafts and delete everything else.

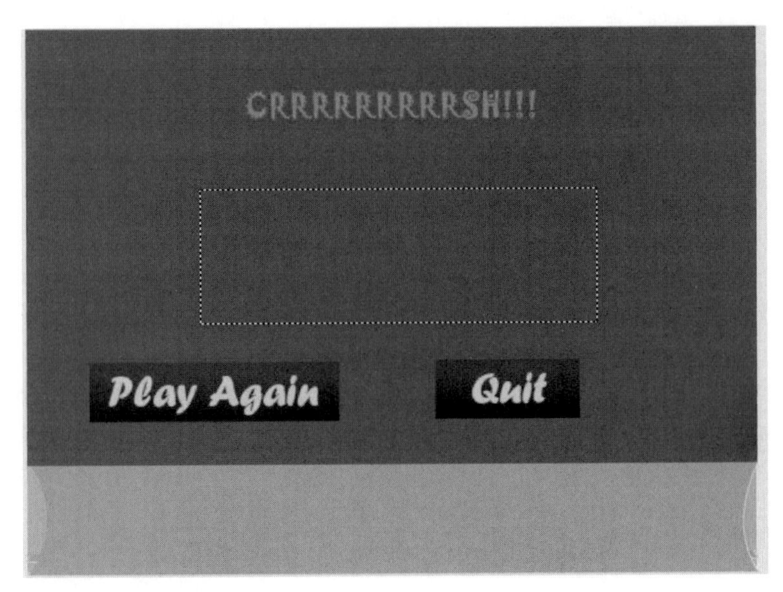

Figure 5.13
Game over.

3. Change the background color of the stage to any you like.
4. Add a static text box and type any text that you like. We used the word CRRRRRRRRSH.
5. Below this, choose the Text tool and add a dynamic text box. Type msg as the instance name for this dynamic text box.
6. Below this dynamic text box, create two buttons. On one of the buttons, use the Text tool and type the text Play Again. Give this button an instance name of pa_btn. On the second button, use the Text tool and type the text Quit. Give this button an instance name of quit_btn.

Your screen should look like Figure 5.13.

Code for Frame 3

Click on frame 3 and open the Actions window. Type the code given here:

```
msg.text = msgText;

function paClk(myevent:MouseEvent):void {
gotoAndStop(2);
}
pa_btn.addEventListener(MouseEvent.CLICK,paClk);
```

```
function qgame (myevent:MouseEvent):void {
  fscommand("quit");
}

quit_btn.addEventListener(MouseEvent.CLICK,qgame);
```

Explanation of the Code

The code in this frame displays a congratulatory or a play again message in the dynamic text box named `msg`. Next, it has two buttons, `Play Again` and `Quit`. The `Play Again` button has an event listener, `CLICK`, which responds when the button is clicked and calls the function `paClk`. The `paClk` function takes the player back to frame 2 to allow him to play again. Similarly, the `Quit` button has the event listener `CLICK`, which responds when the button is clicked and calls the function `qgame()`. The `qgame()` function calls a built-in JavaScript command, `fscommand`, to quit the game.

Note

The `fscommand` will work only if you open the .swf file, not if you test your game from Flash with Ctrl+Enter.

Phase Three: Testing Your Flash Movie

This phase includes running the Flash movie and checking its functionality and validating the output. If there are errors, then you debug your code to see where each error is, fix the error, and run the movie again. Sometimes this is a painful process, but once you succeed in fixing the errors, you'll experience immense satisfaction.

Press Ctrl+Enter to start the game.

Enjoy the game and try to fire missiles at as many alien spaceships as you can in 30 seconds.

Some Common Errors to Watch Out For

- Code typed in the frame when it should be placed in the instance of the movie clip.
- Code typed in the instance of the movie clip instead of the frame.
- Missing braces or semicolons or extra braces.

- Discrepancy between the instance or variable name and its reference in the code due to spelling errors and/or using the wrong case. (An example is to use the variable name `displayTime` in the code when it was named `displayTime`, the `var` name for this dynamic text box. Flash is case sensitive, so it treats these as two different words and gives you an error message.)

Summary

This chapter provided you with some tools and techniques to create a simple shooting game. We looked at ways to move objects across and/or vertically on the screen, provide an interface for the player, track the score for a player, and use a timer in a game. OK, now that you have some cool tools you can experiment with, have fun!

Review Questions

1. Describe the procedure to create a symbol of a movie clip of a racing car. Open a new Flash document to create this movie clip and name the symbol `mc_racingcar`.
2. What is the type of frame that must be used to write ActionScript in a frame?
3. What is the function that must be used in Flash to stop at a particular frame?
4. How many and what arguments does the `gotoandplay()` function take?
5. What is the function of the `hitTest()`? How does it work?
6. Write an ActionScript line of code to move a movie clip diagonally across the stage from the top left to the bottom right.
7. What is the difference between a static text box and a dynamic text box? When would you use a dynamic text box?

Project

Use the concepts discussed in this game to design a new game with the following requirements:

1. The theme is a forest with plenty of coconut or orange trees.
2. The fruit must fall randomly from the trees.

3. A farmer with a basket catches the fruit.
4. The timer control counts up to 30 seconds; once that time is up, the player must know how many coconuts or oranges were caught in the basket.
5. (Optional) Present an obstacle that the farmer will face while collecting the fruit. If the obstacle hits the basket, the farmer loses 1 fruit point. So the goal of the farmer is to catch the falling fruit while avoiding the obstacle.

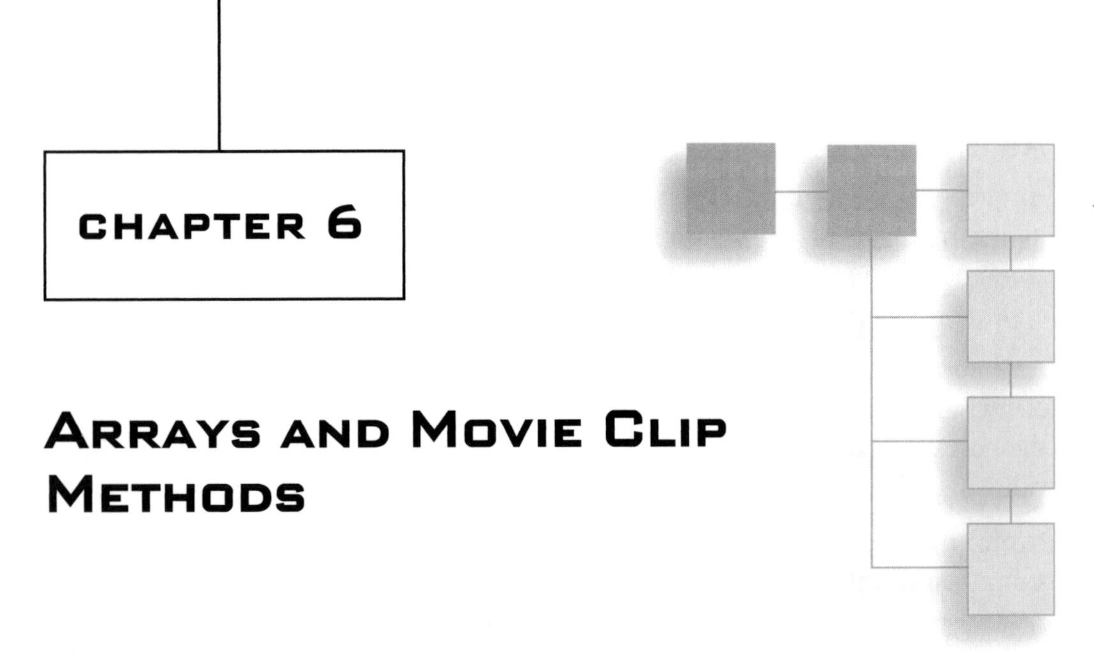

Chapter 6

Arrays and Movie Clip Methods

- Create and use arrays
- Use movie clip methods
- Add child
- Remove child
- Stop drag
- Use the `for` loop

Let's Make a Game!

In this chapter, we will look at designing a picture puzzle game. The main topics in this chapter are arrays, advanced methods of the movie clip object, and the `for` loop. Arrays are a type of structure that can hold a set of values. The movie clip object and its methods will be used in the design of this game. In Chapter 2, we already looked at creating a movie clip and manipulating its properties. This chapter will concentrate on the movie clip methods.

Before we proceed with the game design phase, we will look at the building blocks required for this game. These essentials include arrays and the movie clip methods.

Arrays

An array is special kind of data structure that can hold a set of data or values in the memory of your computer. An example is to think of an array as a container with slots where each slot holds one value. Such a structure is called a *single-dimensional array.*

An important point to remember is that array indices start from 0, so the first element in an array will be referenced to as the 0th element or will have a 0 index, the next element will have an index value of 1, the following will have an index value of 2, and so on. See Figure 6.1 for a single-dimensional array.

Notice that Figure 6.1 is an array with 11 elements because we started counting from 0, and 0 through 10 gives us 11 elements.

We also have multidimensional arrays. The most popular type of a multi-dimensional array is a two-dimensional array, which can basically be thought of as a structure with rows and columns or a matrix. An example of a two-dimensional array is to think of a matrix with student names in rows and their test scores in columns, as shown in Table 6.1.

So, if I need to access John's score for test 3, I would refer to the cell [0, 2] because John is in row 0, and the score for test 3 is in column 2 because we count both rows and columns starting from 0. Similarly, Kim's score for test 2 would be in cell [1, 1].

Multidimensional arrays also include three-dimensional arrays. Examples are 3D graphics, where you have x, y, and z coordinates.

0	1	2	3	4	5	6	7	8	9	10

Figure 6.1
A single-dimensional array.

Table 6.1 Multidimensional Array

Names	Test1	Test2	Test3
John	80	95	90
Kim	90	85	90
Ken	85	85	90

Arrays in ActionScript

Arrays play an extremely important role in game programming. For example, your game might require that you have multiple instances of an object, and you need to assign x and y coordinates for these objects or check the x and y coordinates of an object. In this case, arrays become very useful. Instead of setting the x and y properties for each object, you could just create an array object and use a `for` loop to access each individual array element and set its x and y properties. This is precisely what we will do in our game when we need to check the x and y coordinates for an instance of an array. There are several ways to create an array object in ActionScript.

```
myMusic = new Array ( );
myMusic = [4];
myMusic = ["song1", "song2", "song3", "song5", "song5"];
trace(myMusic);
```

OK, what did we do here? We first created an array object called `myMusic` with an undefined number of elements. Next we set the length of the array to five elements. Notice that even though we said `myMusic = [4];`, it actually means the array object has five elements because the array index starts from 0. The next line specified the actual data that will be stored in memory for each of the array index values. So we used a three-step procedure here to create an array, define its length, and specify the data values.

Let's look at the second block of code (given next). In this case, we have only two statements to create and populate the array. The first line creates an array with an undefined number of elements, the second line populates the array with five elements, and the third line prints the values.

```
myTemp = [];
myTemp = [1,2, 3, 4, 5];
trace(myTemp);
```

A third method to create an array is to create the array and assign values in the same line. Here is an example:

```
myTemp = new Array(1, 2, 3, 4,5);
```

We have seen many different ways to create and populate an array. However, it is important to remember that sometimes the array elements will be populated at run time, and at such times the the third method will not work, because we do not know what the data values are. The data values will be determined at run time. An example is to keep track of the x and y coordinates of a game piece when it collides with another object in the game. These coordinates will be determined only at run time. In such cases, we just create an array object as in line 1 and populate the array elements at run time. Array manipulations and operations will be discussed in Chapter 7.

Drag and Drop Methods

We will look at a couple more movie clip functions before we design the picture puzzle game in this chapter. The methods are `startDrag()` and `stopDrag()`.

startDrag()

The `startDrag()` method makes the *target* movie clip draggable at run time. Only one movie clip can be dragged at a time. After a `startDrag()` operation is executed, the movie clip remains draggable until it is explicitly stopped by `stopDrag()`.

stopDrag()

The `stopDrag` method ends a `MovieClip.startDrag()` method. A movie clip that was made draggable with that method remains draggable until a `stopDrag()` method is added or until another movie clip becomes draggable. At any given time in the movie, only one movie clip is draggable. Now that we have all the functions in place, we can create the picture puzzle game. Exercise 6.1 demonstrates the `startDrag()` and `stopDrag()` methods.

Linkage Identifier

The movie clip must be exported for ActionScript and assigned a unique linkage identifier before it can be used for dragging and dropping at run time. To do this, use the Linkage Properties dialog box.

Exercise 6.1

1. Open a new Flash document and create a simple movie clip with the Oval tool and call it `ball`. At this point, the circle should be added to the library. Click on Scene 1 to go back to the main Timeline.
2. Right-click the ball movie clip in the Library panel. Your screen should be similar to Figure 6.2.

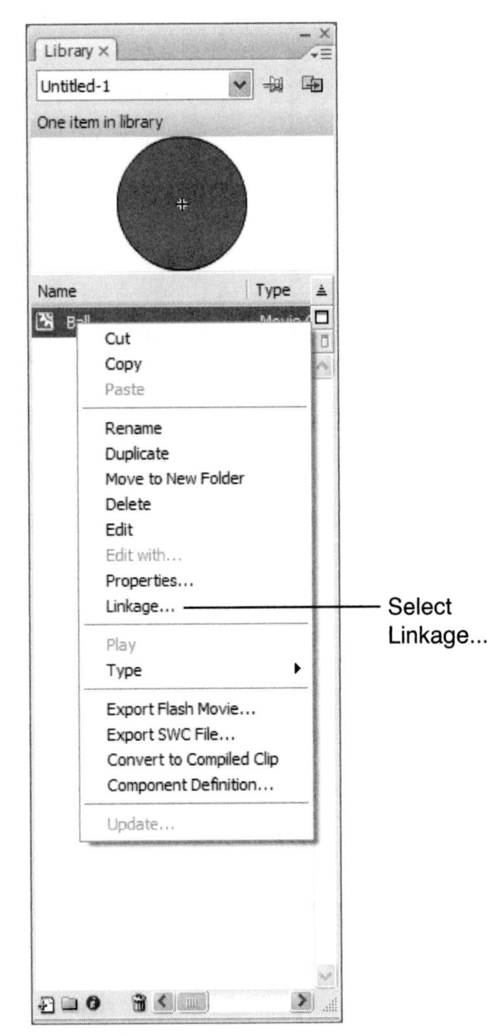

Figure 6.2
Pop-up on right-click.

3. Select Linkage from the Library panel pop-up menu, and you will have a pop-up window.

4. Check the Export for ActionScript box as shown in Figure 6.3.

5. You will find that the Class and Base Class boxes are filled in with the values `Ball` and `flash.display.MovieClip`. This means that the ball is a class that has certain properties and methods. In this case, it has all the properties and methods of a movie clip, which are available at run time.

6. Click OK to return to Scene 1.

7. Drag an instance of the movie clip ball to the stage.

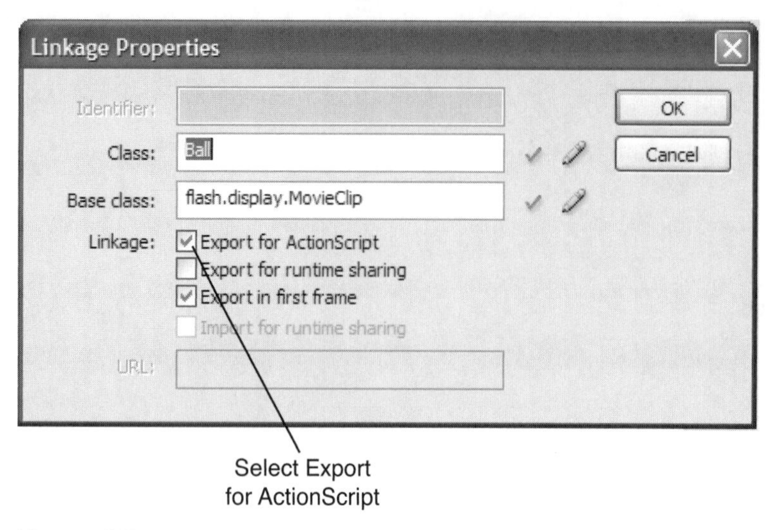

Figure 6.3
Linkage Properties.

8. Open the Properties window and give the ball an instance name, `ball1`.

9. Open the Actions window and type the following code:

```
ball1.addEventListener("mouseDown", pieceMove);
ball1.addEventListener("mouseUp", pieceMove);

function pieceMove(evt:Event):void {
        if (evt.type == "mouseDown") {
              evt.target.startDrag();
        }
        else if (evt.type == "mouseUp") {
              evt.target.stopDrag();
        }
}
```

10. Run the program and drag the ball around.

Explanation of the Code

An instance of the movie clip was added to the stage and was assigned the instance name `ball1`. Next, we add the event listener to `ball1` to be able to recognize when the `mouseDown` and `mouseUp` events are executed on this movie clip. The function `pieceMove` has the code that must be executed when the `mouseDown` and `mouseUp` events take place. The function takes the event as its argument; if the `evt` type is `mouseDown`, it enables the `startDrag` method, which allows `ball1` to be dragged, and if the `evt` type is `mouseUp`, it enables the `stopDrag` method.

Loops

A last concept to understand before we start the picture puzzle game is the notion of loops. Loops, or iterative structures, are extremely important in computer programming. They are used to repeat a set of code statements in your programming. Either the code can be repeated for a certain number of times decided by the programmer a priori (at design time) or it can be set to repeat until a condition is satisfied. When you decide the number of times a code is repeated a priori, you use a `for` loop; when the code has to be repeated until a condition is satisfied, you use a `while` loop. Chapter 7 offers more detailed information on loops. However, we will take a brief pass at a `for` loop here because we need it for the picture puzzle game.

The `for` loop has the following syntax:

```
for (k = 0, k < 4, k++){
        trace ("Hello");
}
```

In this code, `k` is the *loop counter variable.* The `for` loop has a start value, an end value when the iteration or looping should stop, and an increment value. In this example, we start with `k` equals 0 and check to see if `k` is less than 4; if it is less than 4, the value of `k` increments (increases) by 1 and executes the code, which is to trace the word *hello.*

In the next round of iteration, we start with `k` equals 1 (because it was just incremented by 1) and check to see if `k` is less than 4. It is less than 4, so the value of `k` increments by 1 to make it 2 and executes the code once again. This process repeats until `k` equals 4, once it is more than 4, the loop is terminated.

Exercise 6.2

Picture Puzzle Game

Picture puzzle games are very popular and interesting. In this exercise, we look at how to create such a game with Flash. We follow the game development process discussed in earlier chapters with the design phase, game development and coding, and, last, the testing phase.

Phase One: Design

The design phase consists of creating the story line, the storyboard, and the game pieces. These are discussed next.

Story Line

This game does not have a story line as such. The ultimate goal is to be able to assemble the puzzle. To maintain some interest, we have a scoreboard that keeps track of the number of pieces that were correctly assembled. And finally, after the puzzle is assembled, a congratulatory message with a smiley face is displayed.

Storyboard

The storyboard for this game is that we have a picture from which the puzzle will be created. The code must allow the user to drag the pieces of the puzzle and assemble the puzzle. The user must be given instructions to assemble the pieces together. After the puzzle is assembled, a congratulatory message is displayed to the player.

Game Pieces

The game pieces required for the game are the following:

1. Game assets—pieces for the puzzle (game design phase)
2. Game assets—sound files to be played when the piece of the puzzle fits (game design phase)
3. Instructions to the user (game development phase)
4. A scoreboard (game development phase)
5. Display message (game development phase)
6. Option to play again or quit (game development phase)

Phase Two: Game Development and Code

For this game, we will have four layers: the Instructions layer, Puzzle Pieces layer, Targets layer, and Actions layer.

Activities for Layer 1 (Creating the Instructions Scene), Frame 1:

This is the introduction scene to your game. It will have the title of your game, the instructions to the user on how to play the game, the rules of the game, and a button to start the game. Here are the instructions to create this scene:

1. Open a new Flash document. Double-click layer 1 and rename it `Instructions`.
2. Choose any color you like for the background.
3. Use the Text tool and choose any font style that you like, and then type the following text to be displayed to the user:

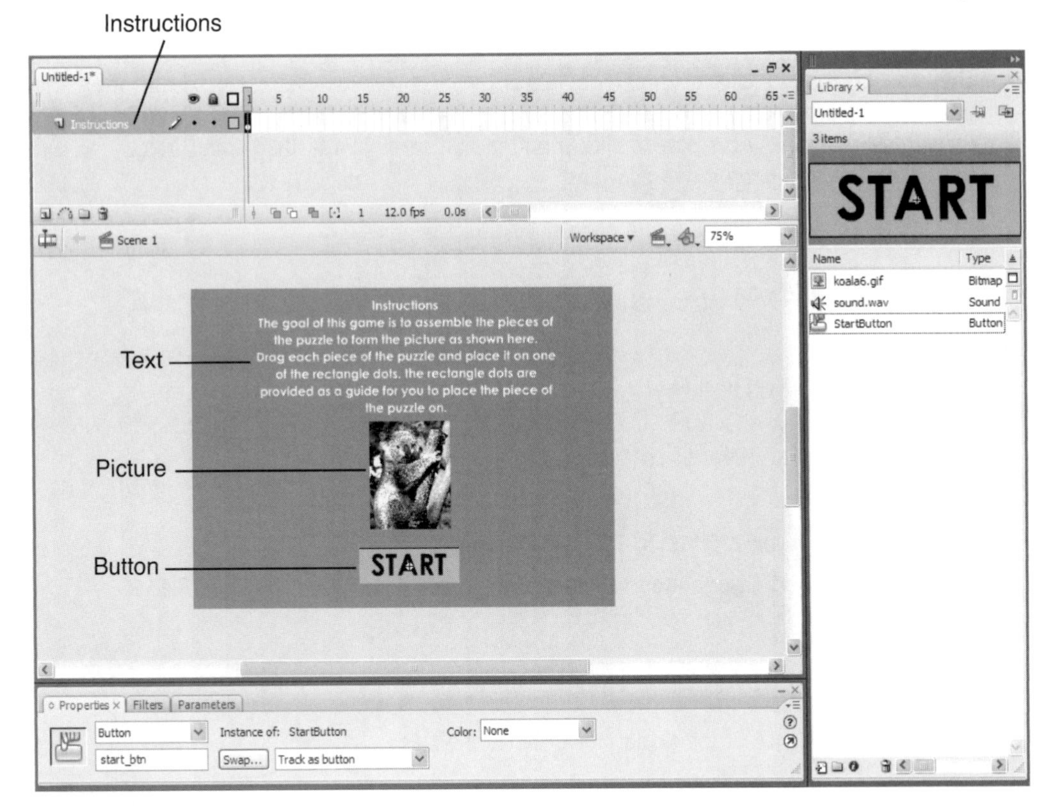

Figure 6.4
The Instructions scene.

```
Instructions
The goal of this game is to assemble the pieces of the puzzle to form the pic-
ture as shown in Figure 6.4.
Drag each piece of the puzzle and place it on one of the rectangular dots. The
rectangular dots are provided as a guide for where the puzzle should be placed.
```

4. Click on File, Import, Import to Library and import any .jpg or .gif file that you have in your computer or import the Koala image file from the chapter 6 folder from the CD accompanying this book.

5. Similarly import a sound file to the library.

6. Drag an instance of the Koala image onto the stage so the user knows that this will be the puzzle to be assembled.

7. Create a button and place a text box on it with the text `Start`. Name the button symbol as `start_btn`. Click Scene 1 to return to the main Timeline. Drag an instance of this button to the stage and give it an instance name of `start_btn`. Your screen should be similar to Figure 6.4.

Code for the Instructions Scene

The code in frame 1 accomplishes two tasks. The first task is to stop the Flash movie from automatically proceeding to the next frame. This is achieved with the `stop()` command. The second task is to allow the user to click a button that takes him to the second frame. The code that follows achieves these two activities.

1. Click on layer 1, frame 1 and open the Actions window.
2. Type the following code:

```
stop();
function playFunc (myEvent:MouseEvent):void{    gotoAndStop(2)
}
start_btn.addEventListener(MouseEvent.CLICK, playFunc);
```

Activities for Layer 2 (Puzzle Pieces), Frame 2

1. Click the Insert Layer button to insert a new layer, and rename it Puzzle Pieces. See Figure 6.5.
2. Right-click on layer 2 (Puzzle Pieces), frame 2 and insert a keyframe.
3. Drag an instance of the Koala image file to the stage.
4. While the image is selected, press Ctrl+B. This process will allow the image file to be broken up into pieces, which can be used as the pieces of the puzzle.
5. Use the Line tool and draw one line vertically and one line horizontally across the Koala image, as shown in Figure 6.6.

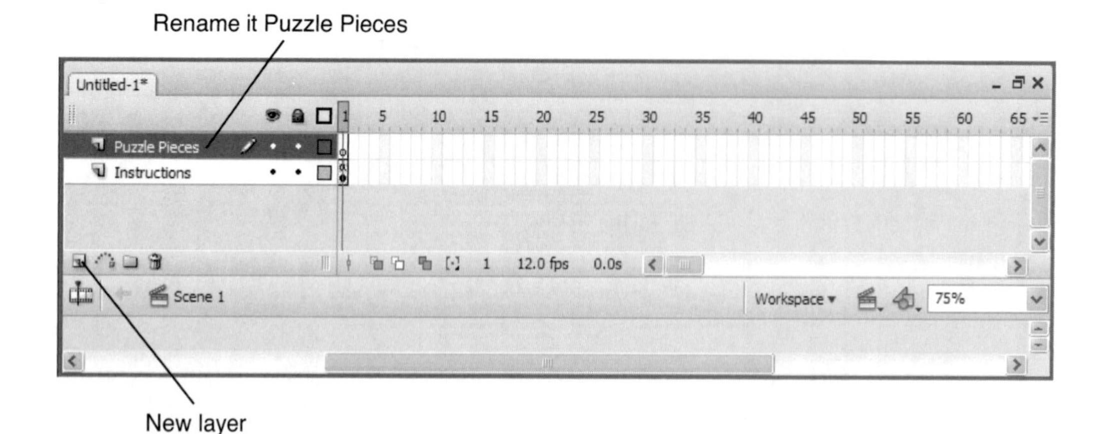

Figure 6.5
Insert a new layer.

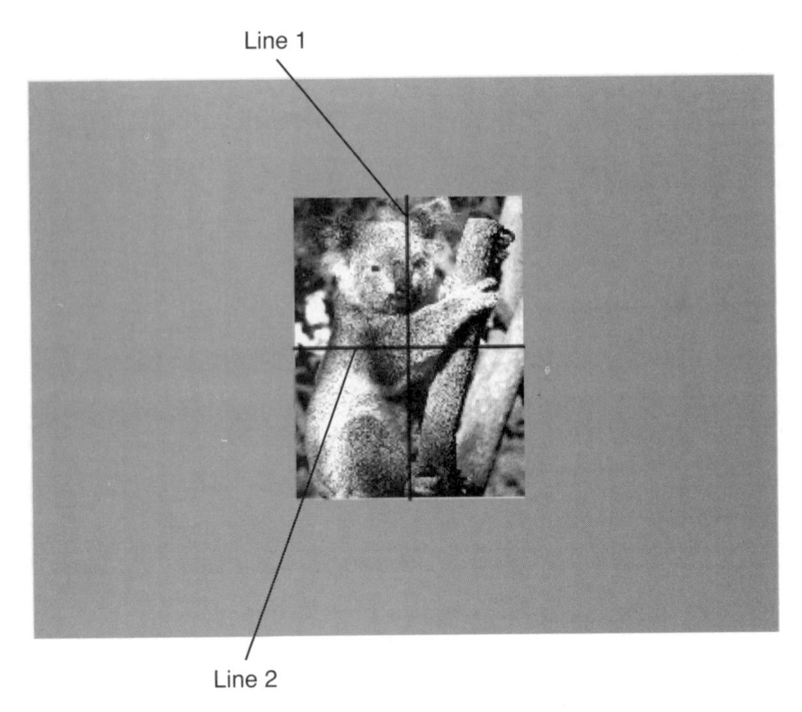

Figure 6.6
Breaking the image.

6. Use the Pointer or Selection tool and drag out each piece of the image. You should now have four separate parts. See Figure 6.7.
7. Right-click on the first piece (top left) and choose Convert to Symbol. You should get a Convert to Symbol pop-up box. See Figure 6.8. Type `a0` as the symbol name, and check the Export for ActionScript and the Export in First Frame boxes to enable the pieces to be available for ActionScript at run time.
8. Do this for all four pieces of the puzzle. Name the top right `a1`, the bottom left `a2`, and the bottom right `a3`. These are the names for the symbols.
9. Next, we have to give an instance name for each of these symbols on the stage. Left-click on a0 (the top left symbol) and, in the Properties tab, give it an instance name `tpg0_mc`. See Figure 6.9.
10. Do this for the other three symbols, naming a1 as `tpg1_mc`, a2 as `tpg2_mc`, and a3 as `tpg3_mc`.
11. Drag all the pieces back together to form the complete picture, and lock the layer by clicking on the lock symbol. See Figure 6.10.
12. This finishes activities for the Puzzle Pieces layer.

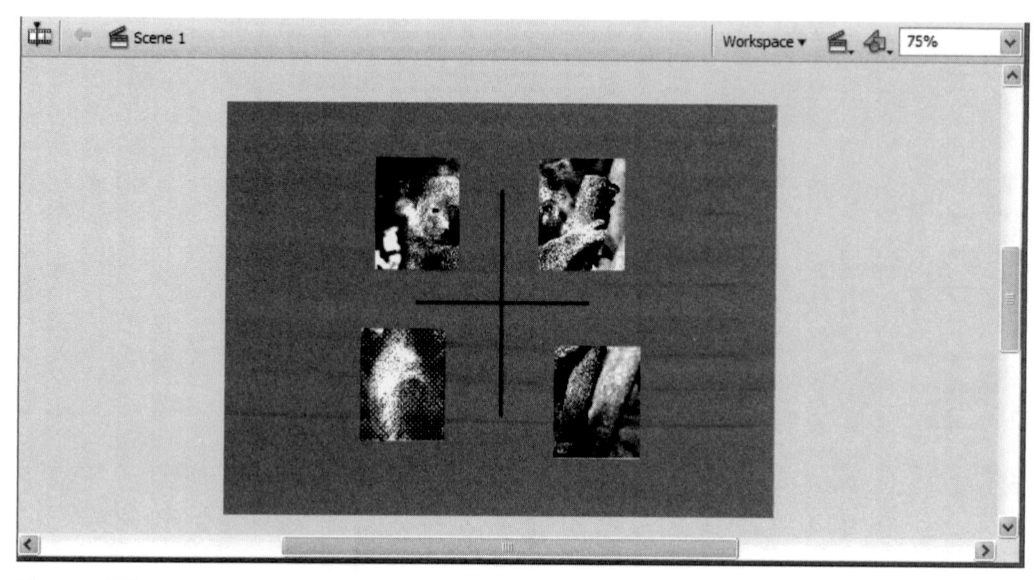

Figure 6.7
Picture pieces separated.

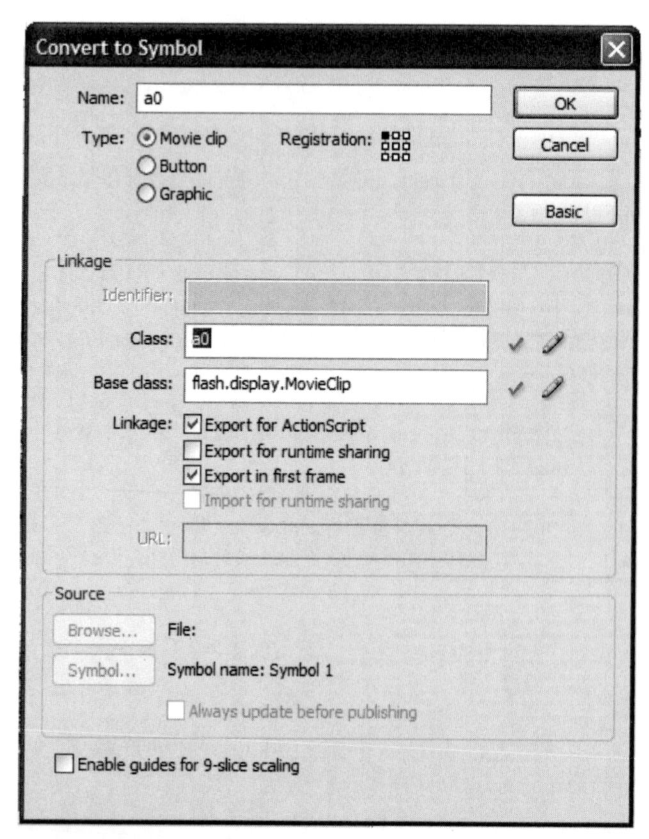

Figure 6.8
Convert to Symbol.

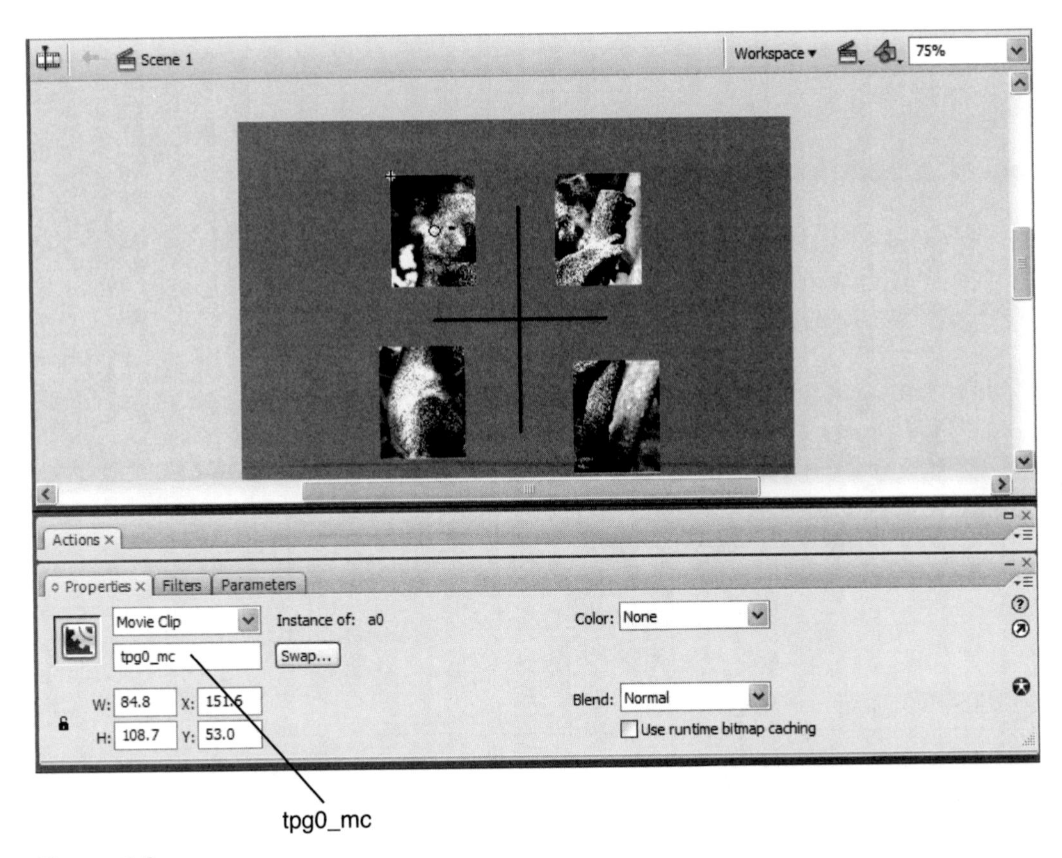

Figure 6.9
Instance name.

Activities for Layer 3 (Target Layer), Frame 2

The next step is to create an area where the player can drag and assemble the puzzle pieces. The game provides the player with specific target locations in the form of little rectangles where the puzzle pieces must be dragged and dropped.

1. Click on the Insert Layer button to create a new layer.
2. Double-click on the layer name and rename it `Target Location`.
3. Right-click on frame 2 and insert a keyframe.
4. The next step is to create some sort of a symbol to represent the target area. To do this, create a small rectangle movie clip and place an instance of it on each of the four pieces of the puzzle.
5. Create a new movie clip and name it `targetSymbol`. Draw a small rectangle and fill it with any color you like. See Figure 6.11.
6. Drag instances of the `targetSymbol` and place them on the four puzzle pieces. See Figure 6.12.

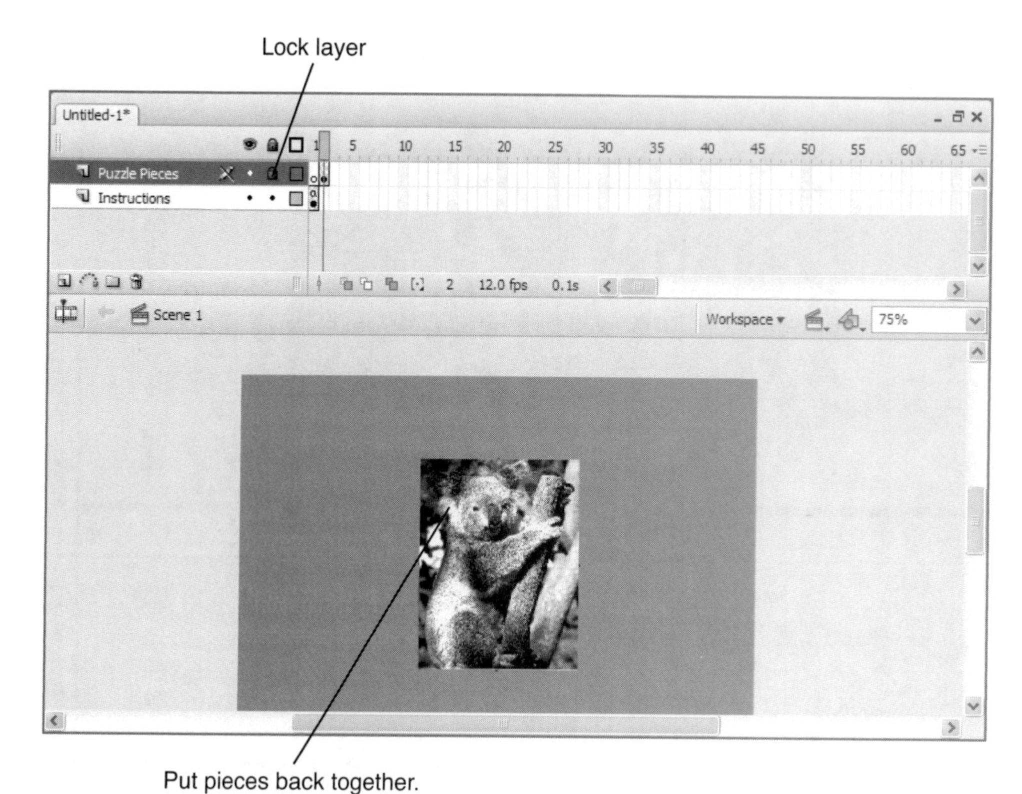

Figure 6.10
Lock layer.

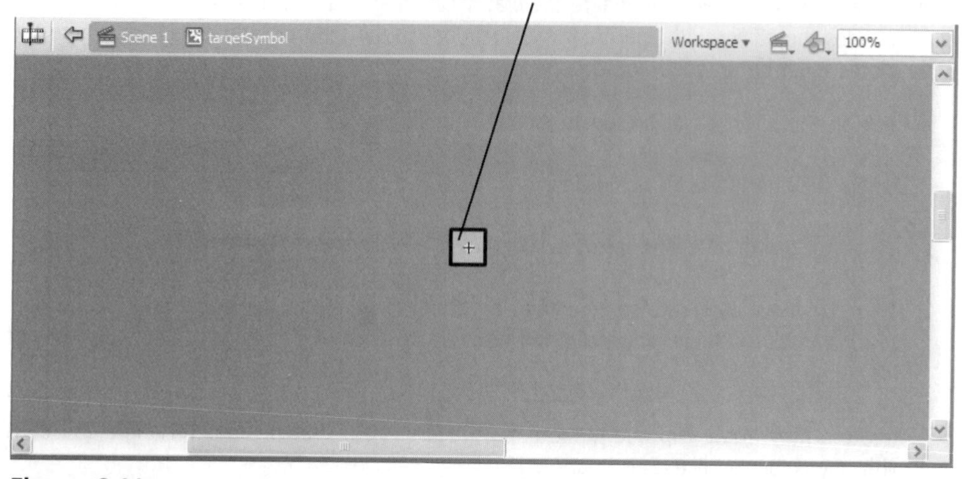

Figure 6.11
Create a target movie clip.

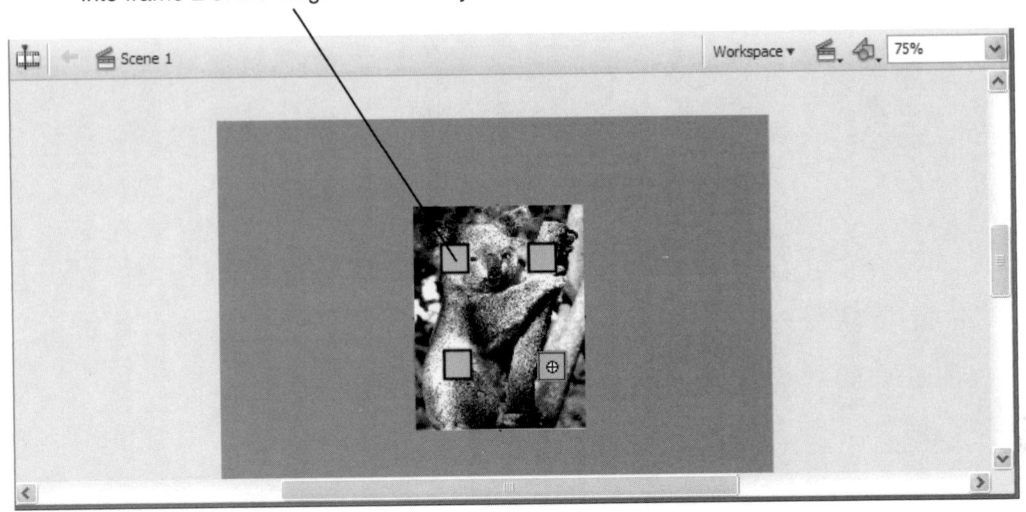
Make sure that you drag the instances into frame 2 of the Target Location layer.
Scene 1
Workspace
75%

Figure 6.12
Completed target locations.

7. Next, right-click on the rectangle (top left) and give it an instance name of nph0_mc.
8. Name the next three instances nph1_mc (top right), nph2_mc (bottom left), and nph3_mc (bottom right).
9. To make the puzzle pieces invisible, simply set the alpha setting for the pieces to 0. To do this, first, unlock the Puzzle Pieces layer. Click on the first puzzle piece (not the rectangle) outside the little rectangle. Then look at the properties for this movie clip and change the color from None to Alpha and make sure that the setting is 0%. See Figure 6.13. This should make that puzzle piece invisible. Do this for all the pieces of the puzzle.
10. The original puzzle pieces should now be invisible to the player. All he should see are the four rectangles, which indicate the target locations for the picture puzzle pieces to be dragged and dropped. Your screen should now match Figure 6.14.
11. The next part for this layer is to add a box to display the score. Draw a text box on the stage. Change the text type of the text box to Dynamic Text. Type scor in the Instance box for this text box. See Figure 6.15.
12. Drag another instance of the text box and place it above or next to the dynamic text box you just created, and type Score:. In the Properties tab, change the type of box to static. See Figure 6.16.

This completes the Target Location layer.

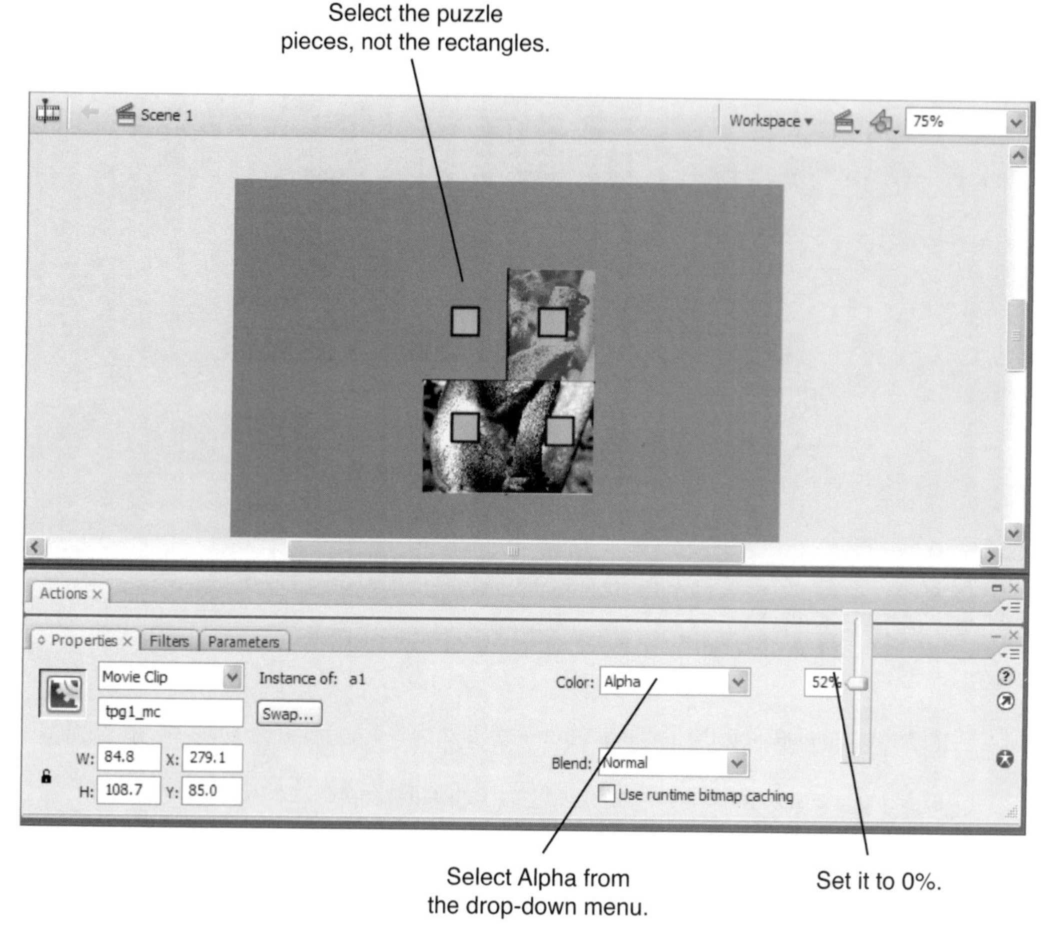

Figure 6.13
Alpha property.

Phase Three: Coding the Game

In this phase, we write the code to create the puzzle pieces with the `add child` method, we create an array of objects with these pieces, we use the `startDrag()` and `stopDrag()` methods to move the pieces around, and finally, we check to see if the correct piece was put in the correct spot with the `hitTestobject()` method we covered in Chapter 5. Instructions for this are given below.

1. Insert a new layer again and rename it `Actions`.
2. Move the code that you put in the Instructions layer, frame 1, into the Actions layer, frame 1, to more easily locate the ActionScript in this game. You can do this by selecting the code in the Instructions layer, cut it from there and paste it in the Actions layer, frame 1.
3. Right-click on frame 2 and choose Insert Keyframe.

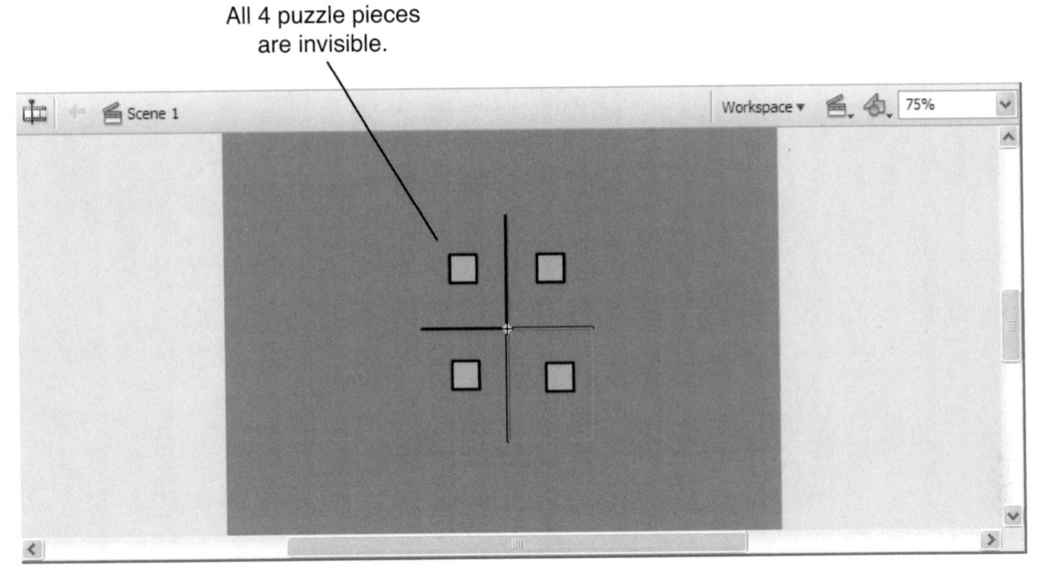
All 4 puzzle pieces are invisible.
Scene 1
Workspace
75%

Figure 6.14
Completed Alpha setting.

4. Insert a dynamic text box at the bottom of the workspace and give it an instance name of msgbox_txt.

5. Type the following code into the Actions tab:

```
var score:Number=0;
import flash.utils.*;
var numClips:Number=4;

//array to hold puzzle pieces that will be available to drag
var myClip = new Array(numClips);

// populate the myClip array with the movie clips from the library
myClip[0] = addChild(new a0());
myClip[1] = addChild(new a1());
myClip[2] = addChild(new a2());
myClip[3] = addChild(new a3());

//assign names to each element in the myClip array
myClip[0].name = "piece0";
myClip[1].name = "piece1";
myClip[2].name = "piece2";
myClip[3].name = "piece3";
```

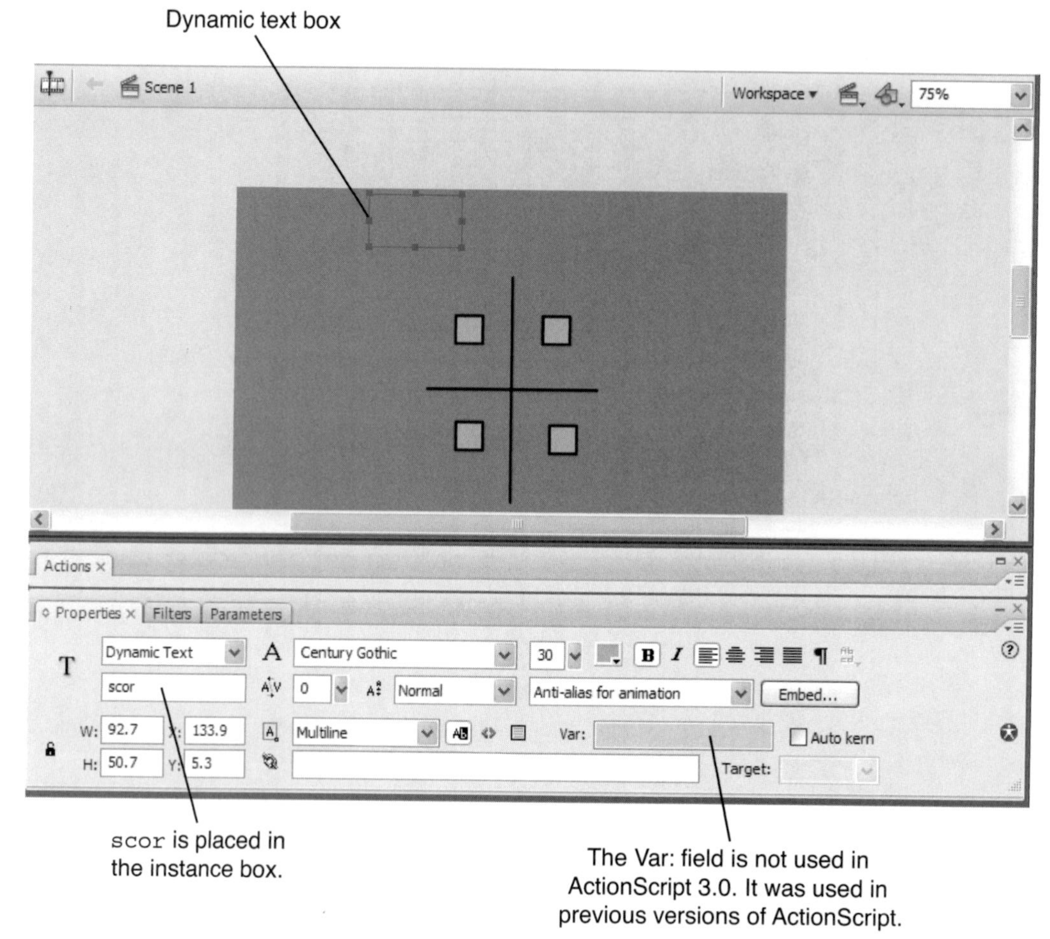

Figure 6.15
Dynamic text box.

```
//array to hold the locations (little rectangles) to drag the puzzle pieces
on //the stage
var nph = new Array(numClips);

//populate array with the locations (little rectangles) placed on the stage
nph[0] = nph0_mc;
nph[1] = nph1_mc;
nph[2] = nph2_mc;
nph[3] = nph3_mc;

//array to hold the original puzzle pieces on the stage
var tpg = new Array(numClips);
```

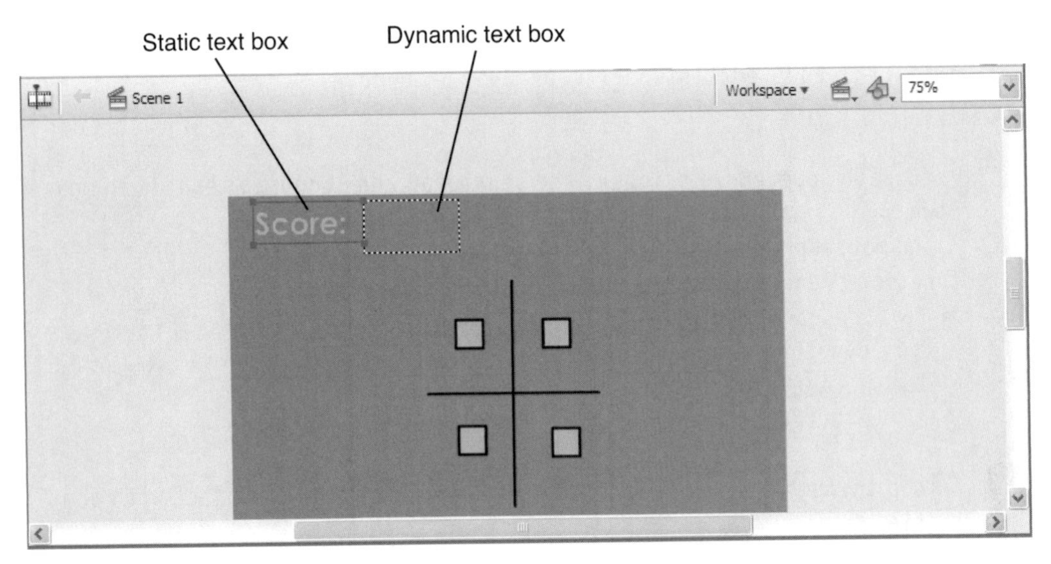

Figure 6.16
Static text box.

```
//populate the puzzle pieces array with the puzzle pieces on the stage
tpg[0] = tpg0_mc;
tpg[1] = tpg1_mc;
tpg[2] = tpg2_mc;
tpg[3] = tpg3_mc;

//generate random locations (x and y positions) for the movie clips to be
//dragged

var x0 = myClip[0].x = Math.random()*400+50;
var y0 = myClip[0].y = Math.random()*50+50;
var x1 = myClip[1].x = Math.random()*400+50;
var y1 = myClip[1].y = Math.random()*50+50;
var x2 = myClip[2].x = Math.random()*400+50;
var y2 = myClip[2].y = Math.random()*50+50;
var x3 = myClip[3].x = Math.random()*400+50;
var y3 = myClip[3].y = Math.random()*50+50;

var j:Number;

//use a "for loop" to loop through the movie clips created and add the
mouseDown //and mouseUp event listeners
//Call the function pieceMove on mouseUp and mouseDown
for (var k:Number=0; k<4; k++) {
```

```
myClip[k].addEventListener("mouseDown", pieceMove);
myClip[k].addEventListener("mouseUp", pieceMove);
}

//function pieceMove triggers the startDrag and stopDrag methods on mouse-
Down
//and mouseUp
function pieceMove(evt:Event):void {
if (evt.type == "mouseDown") {
       evt.target.startDrag();
} else if (evt.type == "mouseUp") {
       evt.target.stopDrag();

//loop through the four puzzle pieces, check for hitTestObject with the
little
//rectangle
// if true, increment the score, if not take the piece back to a random x, y
location
for (j = 0; j<4; j++){
if (evt.target.name == "piece" + j &&
evt.target.hitTestObject(nph[j])==true) {

              //remove the piece that was dragged
              removeChild(myClip[j]);

                            //set alpha of the little rectangle to 0
                            nph[j].alpha = 0;

//set alpha of the old puzzle piece in the locked layer to //100
                            tpg[j].alpha = 100;
                            score++;

       } else if (evt.target.name == "piece" + j) {
              evt.target.x = Math.random()*400+50;
                            evt.target.y = Math.random()*50+50;
              }
       }
// Display score in the dynamic text box scor
//Display Congratulations in the msgbox
scor.text = score.toString();
if (score == 4) {
       msgbox_txt.text = "Congratulations !";
       }
}
}
```

Explanation of the Code

The plan of action to write the code for this game is as follows. We create an array (`myClip`) of four elements to hold the puzzle pieces. We use the `addNewChild` method to populate the array with the puzzle pieces `a0`, `a1`, `a2`, and `a3`. Next, each of these pieces is given an instance name: `piece0`, `piece1`, etc. These are the pieces that the user will drag when the game starts. The elements of this `myClip` array are given a random x and y position to scatter them on the stage.

Another array (`nph[]`) with four elements is created to hold the little rectangles, which will be used as location indicators to drag and drop the puzzle pieces. This array is populated with the rectangles, and each element is given an instance name of `nph0_mc`, `nph1_mc`, etc.

The last array that we need is `tpg`, with four elements to hold the original puzzle pieces that we assembled on the stage. This array is populated by the puzzle pieces `tpg0_mc`, `tpg1_mc`, etc.

The next set of code statements uses a loop. A `for` loop is used to loop through the movie clips created and add the `mouseDown` and `mouseUp` event listeners to each of these movie clips.

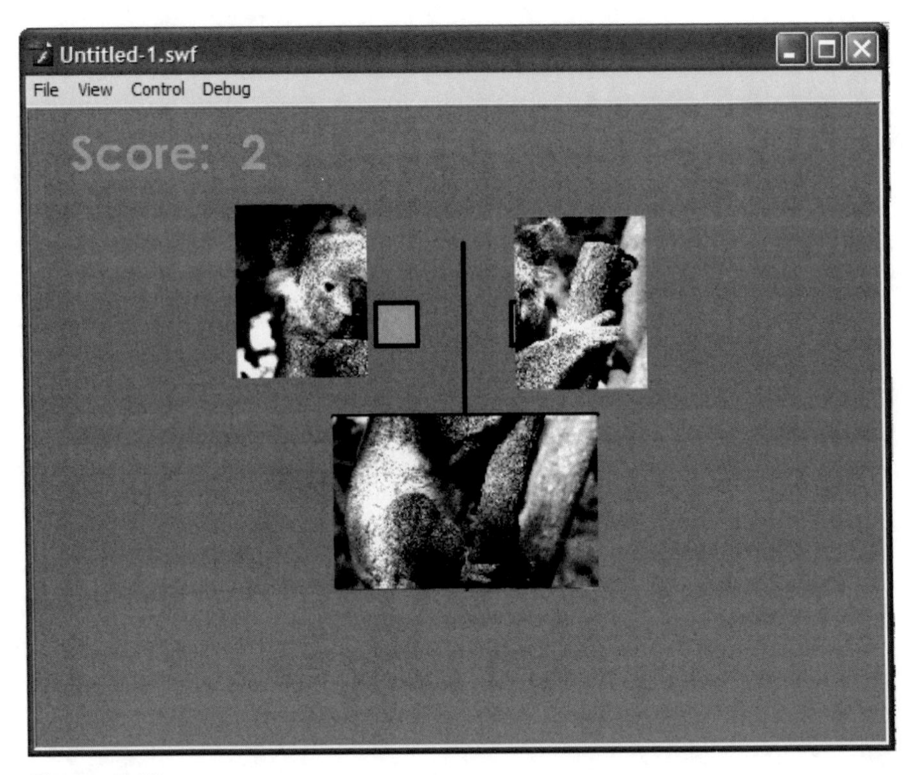

Figure 6.17
Picture puzzle at run time.

The function `pieceMove` is the crux of the code. It first calls the `startDrag` and `stopDrag` methods when the `mouseUp` and `mouseDown` events are triggered. Second, a `for` loop is used to loop through each of the puzzle pieces—`piece0`, `piece1`, `piece2`, and `piece3`—to check if these pieces collide with the little rectangles, elements of the array `nph[]`. Third, if this collision test returns a true value, then the movie clip that was dragged is removed from the movie, the original puzzle piece left on the stage with an alpha value of 0 is set to 100, the alpha value of the rectangle is set to 0, and the score is incremented. If the collision test returns false, the puzzle piece that was dragged is put back at a random location on the stage. This process repeats for all the pieces.

The last bit of code checks the final score. If it is equal to 4, a congratulatory message is displayed.

That's it! You have a picture puzzle game. Go ahead and run your Flash movie. You should see something similar to Figure 6.17. If you have errors, check that you named your game assets correctly, and check your code, block by block, for any accidental syntax and/or logic errors.

Summary

This chapter presented an introduction to arrays, `for` loops, and advanced movie clip methods. You created a picture puzzle game with an array of movie clip objects, used the `attachMovie` method to populate the array, and used the `for` loop to manipulate each movie clip object in the array. The next chapter will present a formal discussion on the notion of loops and their use in game programming.

End-of-Chapter Exercises

1. Write the ActionScript code to create an array of fruits, called `myFruits`, with five elements. Initialize this array with your choice of five fruits.
2. Write the ActionScript code to retrieve the third element in the `myFruits` array.
3. What do the `addChild()` and `removeChild()` methods do?
4. What are the methods available to drag and drop movie clips at run time?

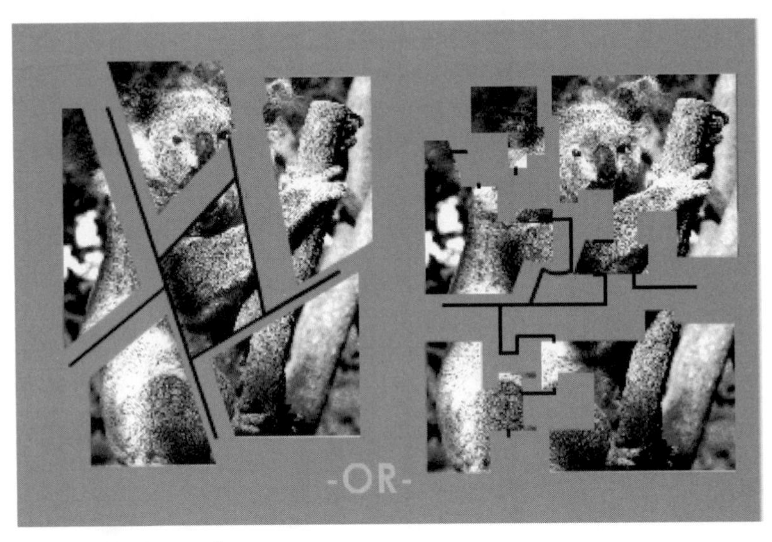

Figure 6.18
Sample shapes for picture puzzle pieces.

Project

Enhance your program by adding a sound file to your game. You can have the sound file play either all through the game or when the player finishes assembling all the puzzle pieces.

Create a picture puzzle with 9 or 12 pieces. You need not be restricted to using simple rectangle pieces; try using the Pencil tool or Line tool to create more interesting shapes for the puzzle pieces, similar to the pieces you see in regular picture puzzle board games. See Figure 6.18 for some ideas.

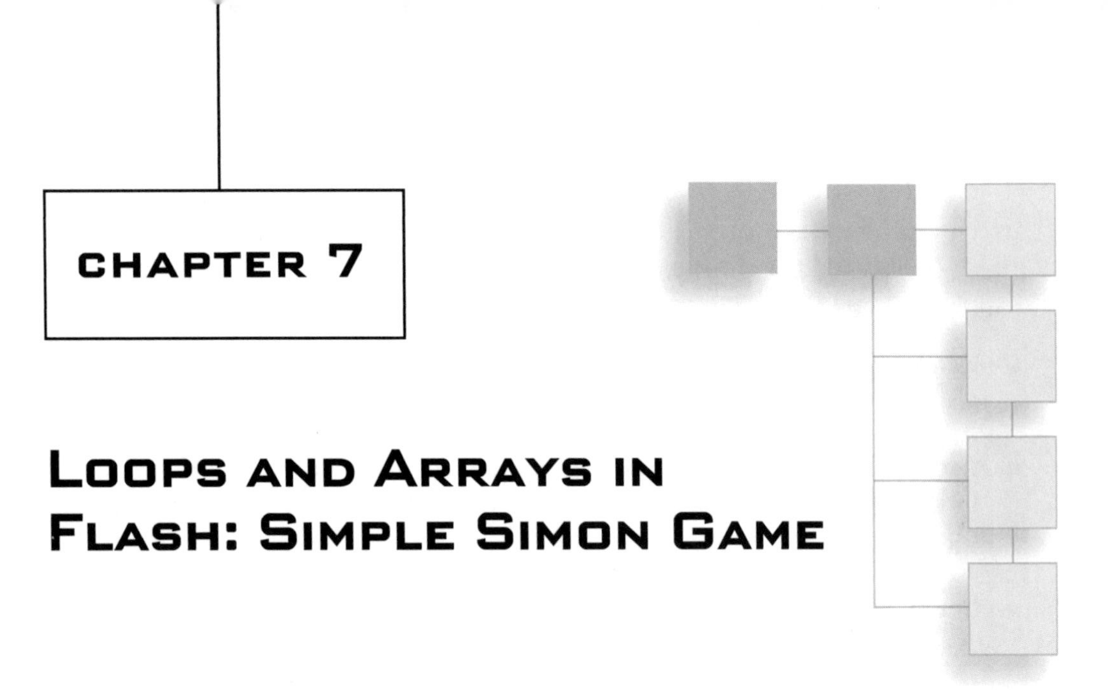

Chapter 7

Loops and Arrays in Flash: Simple Simon Game

- Understand the importance of loops
- Study basic types of loops in ActionScript
- Create and use loops
- Understand the use of arrays
- Create and use arrays

What Are Loops?

Loops, in computer programming, enable us to perform repetitive tasks quickly without any change in quality or speed. You might have a block of code that you need to perform five times. One way is to write the same code five times, while the alternative manner would be using loops.

In this chapter, we will learn about the three basic loops used in ActionScript:

- `for` loop
- `while` loop
- `do...while` loop

for Loops

This type of loop executes a block of code a fixed number of times. A loop variable behaves like a counter and changes value with each pass (or iteration) through the code block. The `for` loop statement is made up of three parts:

- A **counter variable** that is first set to an initial value. The counter is initialized only once, before the first iteration of the loop.
- A **conditional statement** that checks to see if the loop can execute or should end. This statement usually compares the counter variable with some value. This statement is executed before each iteration of the loop.
- An **expression** that changes the value of the counter variable. This executes after each iteration of the loop.

The following code loops five times. The value of `i` starts at 0 and ends at 9.

```
var i:int;
for (i=0; i<10; i++)
{
 trace(i);
}
```

When this `for` loop is executed, first the variable `i` is initialized to 0. Then the conditional statement `i<10` is checked. If `i` is less than 10, then the body of the loop executes. If `i` is greater than or equal to 10, then the loop terminates. For the next iteration, first the value of `i` is incremented by the expression `i++` before the condition is checked again.

while Loops

The `while` loop allows repeated execution of a block of code as long as some condition is true. The minute that condition is false, the `while` loop terminates. The following code produces the same output as the preceding `for` loop example.

```
var i:int = 0;
while (i < 10)
{
    trace(i);
    i++;
}
```

When this `while` loop is executed, first the value of `i` is checked against 10. If it is less than 10, then the body of the loop executes. If `i` is greater than or equal to 10, then the loop terminates. Note that the value of `i` is incremented within the body of the loop. If the value of `i` is not incremented, then the code will go into an infinite loop that will execute the body of the `while` loop an unlimited number of times. In the `for` loop, you cannot leave out the statement that increments the counter variable because it is part of the `for` loop structure.

do...while Loops

The `do...while` loop executes the loop body at least once. Because the condition is checked right at the end of the first iteration of the loop, this loop will execute once even if the condition is not met. The following code demonstrates the `do...while` loop:

```
var i:int = 10;
do
{
    trace(i);
    i++;
} while (i < 10);
```

The output of this code is 10, because a `do...while` loop checks the condition after the body is executed once. In an ordinary `while` loop, this code will not execute even once.

As you can see above, the `for` loop counts a particular number of times it will continue, the `while` loop adds more flexibility to how the value is incremented, and the `do...while` always performs the code at least once. These control structures are very important to understand.

What Are Arrays?

As you saw in Chapter 6, it is sometimes necessary to work with a list or set of items instead of a single item. For example, you might have 10 images to show one after the other. You should not create separate objects for each one. The images can be stored as elements of an array.

An array is like a table. You read about single- and multidimensional arrays in Chapter 6. To review, a single list of elements is called a *single-dimensional array*. A single-dimensional array is like a one-column table. *Multidimensional arrays* are arrays whose elements are themselves arrays that contain elements. A multi-dimensional array is like a multiple-column table.

Using an array, you can work with its elements by indexing them and accessing the elements through a single variable. Each item is stored in an indexed slot, and items are accessed using the index number (array index). The indices of an array start with 0 and increment by 1 for each subsequent array element. A single item in an array is called an *element*, and the address used to identify a single element in an array is called an *index*.

Creating an Array

Before you use an array you need to create a variable and declare it as an array. You can either use an array constructor or initialize the variable using an array literal. Both methods are explained below.

Using an Array Constructor

A new array is created by calling the Array class constructor using the `new` keyword. The constructor can be invoked with no parameters to create an empty array, as shown here:

```
var thisArray:Array = new Array();
```

Note that the length of an array that has been initialized with no parameters has length 0.

```
var names:Array = new Array();
trace(names.length); // output: 0
```

You can also invoke the constructor using an integer to tell the array its initial length.

```
var names:Array = new Array(3);
trace(names.length); // output: 3
```

Using an Array Literal

Another common way to create an array is by directly initializing it with an array literal (a set of elements), as you can see in the following code:

```
var thisArray:Array = ["red", "blue", "green"];
trace(thisArray); // output: red,blue,green
```

Array Methods

The Array class contains some properties and methods. Array methods do not modify the existing array. Instead, they return a new array. The following three array modification methods will be discussed here:

- inserting array elements
- deleting array elements
- sorting arrays
- querying arrays

Inserting Array Elements

There are three methods we can use to insert elements into an array. These are `push()`, `unshift()`, and `splice()`.

push()

The `push()` method appends elements to the end of an array. This method takes one argument: the value that needs to be inserted into the array. The return value is the length of the modified array.

```
var thisArray:Array = new Array();
thisArray.push("red");
thisArray.push("blue");
thisArray.push("green");
trace(thisArray); // output: red,blue,green
```

unshift()

The `unshift()` method inserts elements at the beginning of an array. This method takes one argument: the value that needs to be inserted into the beginning of the array. The return value is the length of the modified array.

```
var numberNames:Array = new Array();
numberNames.push("John");      // John
numberNames.unshift("Mary"); // Mary,John
```

splice()

The `splice()` method inserts elements at a specified location in the array. This method takes the following arguments:

- an integer that specifies the index at which to begin the insertion

- an integer that specifies how many items should be deleted at that point
- a list of items to be inserted

You can use the `splice()` method to insert elements into an array and also to remove elements from an array. When used to remove elements, the `splice()` method returns an array containing the elements removed.

```
var numberNames:Array = new Array();
numberNames.push("five");      // five
numberNames.unshift("one"); // one,five
numberNames.splice(1, 0, "two", "three", "four");
trace(numberNames);  // output: one,two,three,four,five
```

The above example creates an array of the names of numbers in ascending order. Initially, the array is empty. We use the `push()` method to add `five` to the end of the array. This element is now the first and last element in the array and has index 0. Now we can use the `unshift()` method to add `one` at the beginning of the array. Then we can use the `splice()` method to insert the items `two`, `three`, and `four` between the first and last elements in the array.

Deleting Array Elements

Three methods are used to remove elements from an array: `pop()`, `shift()`, and `splice()`.

pop()

The `pop()` method removes an element from the end of an array. It returns the item that was removed.

shift()

The `shift()` method removes an element from the beginning of an array. It returns the item that was removed.

splice()

The `splice()` method starts removing elements beginning with the index specified as the first argument sent to the method. It removes the number of elements as specified in the second argument sent to the method. It returns an array of the items that were removed. If no arguments are supplied to this method, it just copies over the original array.

The following example uses these methods to remove elements from an array. The array contains the names of flowers, as well as names of a few animals, which need to be removed.

First, the `splice()` method is used to remove the items `cat` and `dog` and insert the items `lily` and `poppy`. The first argument sent to `splice()` is 2, which indicates that the removal operation should start with the item that has the index 2 in the list—i.e., the third item. The second argument is 2, which indicates that two items should be removed. The remaining arguments, `lily` and `poppy`, are values to be inserted at index 2.

Then the `pop()` method is used to remove the last element in the array, `rat`. Lastly, the `shift()` method is used to remove the first item in the array, `ant`.

```
var flowers:Array = ["ant", "rose", "cat", "dog", "violet", "rat"];
flowers.splice(2, 2, "lily", "poppy"); // replaces cat and dog
flowers.pop();    // removes rat
flowers.shift(); // removes ant
trace(flowers);   // output: rose,lily,poppy,violet
```

You can change the `flowers` array example so that the call to `splice()` assigns the array to a new array variable, as shown in the following example:

```
var flowers:Array = ["ant", "rose", "cat", "dog", "violet", "rat"];
var animals:Array = flowers.splice(2, 2, "lily", "poppy");
trace(animals); // output: cat,dog
```

Delete Operator

An element's value can be deleted using the `delete()` operator. The element is still in the array with the value `undefined`. For example:

```
var flowers:Array = ["rose", "lily", "poppy", "violet"];
trace(flowers.length); // output: 4
delete flowers[2];
trace(flowers);          // output: rose,lily,,violet
trace(flowers[2]);       // output: undefined
trace(flowers.length); // output: 4
```

Note that the array length is unchanged with the `delete()` operator. Also note the double commas in the output of the second trace statement in the code to show that there is an undefined element in the array.

You can truncate an array by setting `length` to a value less than the actual length of the array, removing any elements stored at index numbers greater than or equal to the new length.

```
var flowers:Array = ["rose", "lily", "poppy", "violet"];
flowers.length = 2;
trace(flowers); // output: rose,lily
```

Sorting an Array

Sorting is arranging the elements of an array in ascending or descending order. There are two methods that can be used to sort an array: `reverse()` and `sort()`.

reverse()

The `reverse()` method reverses the order of elements in an array. It takes no parameters. It does not return any value. For example:

```
var flowers:Array = ["rose", "lily", "poppy", "violet"];
flowers.reverse();
trace(flowers); // output: violet,poppy,lily,rose
```

sort()

The `sort()` method sorts the elements of an array. The default sort is case sensitive in ascending order. Advanced sorting techniques are not covered in this book.

```
var flowers:Array = ["rose", "lily", "poppy", "violet"];
flowers.sort();
trace(flowers); // output: lily,poppy,rose,violet
```

Querying an Array

Sometimes we need to query or get some information about an array without making any modification to the array. This is used when we want to join or concatenate arrays. The four methods that query the array for information without modifying the array are `concat()`, `slice()`, `toString()`, and `join()`.

concat()

The `concat()` method takes a new array of elements as arguments and combines it with the existing array to return a new array.

slice()

The `slice()` method takes two parameters, `startIndex` and `endIndex`, and returns an array containing a copy of the elements taken from the existing array between the two index values. The element at `startIndex` is included in the resulting array, but the element at `endIndex` is not included in the resulting array.

The following example creates an array called `myColors` and calls both `concat()` and `slice()`:

```
var myColors:Array = ["blue", "green", "black"];
var yourColors:Array = ["red", "yellow", "white"];
var allColors:Array = myColors.concat(yourColors);
trace(allColors); // output: blue,green,black,red,yellow,white
var fewColors:Array = allColors.slice(2,5);
trace(fewColors); // output: black,red,yellow
```

toString()

The `toString()` method converts the specified object to a string and returns it. This method is further discussed under the `join()` method below.

join()

The `join()` method accepts a parameter named `delimiter`, which allows you to choose the symbol to use as a separator between each element in the returned string. If no parameter is used, the `join()` and `toString()` methods behave the same way.

The following example creates an array named `states` and calls both `join()` and `toString()` to return the values in the array as a string. The `toString()` method is used to return comma-separated values, `statesComma`, while the `join()` method is used to return values separated by the + character, `statesPlus`.

```
var states:Array = ["California", "Florida", "Georgia", "Arizona"];
var statesComma:String = states.toString();
trace(statesComma); // output: California,Florida,Georgia,Arizona
var statesPlus:String = states.join("+");
trace(statesPlus);  // output: California+Florida+Georgia+Arizona
```

Simple Simon Piano Game

This Flash game plays a series of musical notes with light and sound. Players follow the pattern for as long as they can remember it.

Exercise 7.1

Creation of the Simple Simon Game

Activities for the Background Layer

1. Open Flash CS3 and create a new Flash document.
2. Rename the default layer `Background` and import the background image for the piano from the Assets folder or from the library.
3. Drag the image onto the stage and change the background color to whatever you like.
4. Lock the layer.

Activities for the MovieClips Layer

1. Create a new layer and name it `MovieClips`.

Figure 7.1
Background layer.

2. Now use your drawing tools and skills to create shapes that exactly overlay on the piano keys. Convert each one into a movie clip and name them `mc0`, `mc1`, `mc2`, `mc3`, `mc4`, `mc5`, `mc6`, and `mc7`.

3. It is time now to edit these movie clips. Starting with the first movie clip, create a glow effect by brightening the color in its second frame. You can do this in the Properties panel by selecting the Brightness option for Color and increasing the percentage until it looks bright. Press F5 at the 10th frame of the movie clip to show the effect for a few milliseconds. Add a new layer, and in the first frame, open the Actions panel and add the code `stop();`. Repeat this for the remaining seven movie clips for the other seven notes.

4. In the main Timeline, give each of these movie clips instance names in the Properties tab, from `mc0` to `mc7` for the eight movie clip instances.

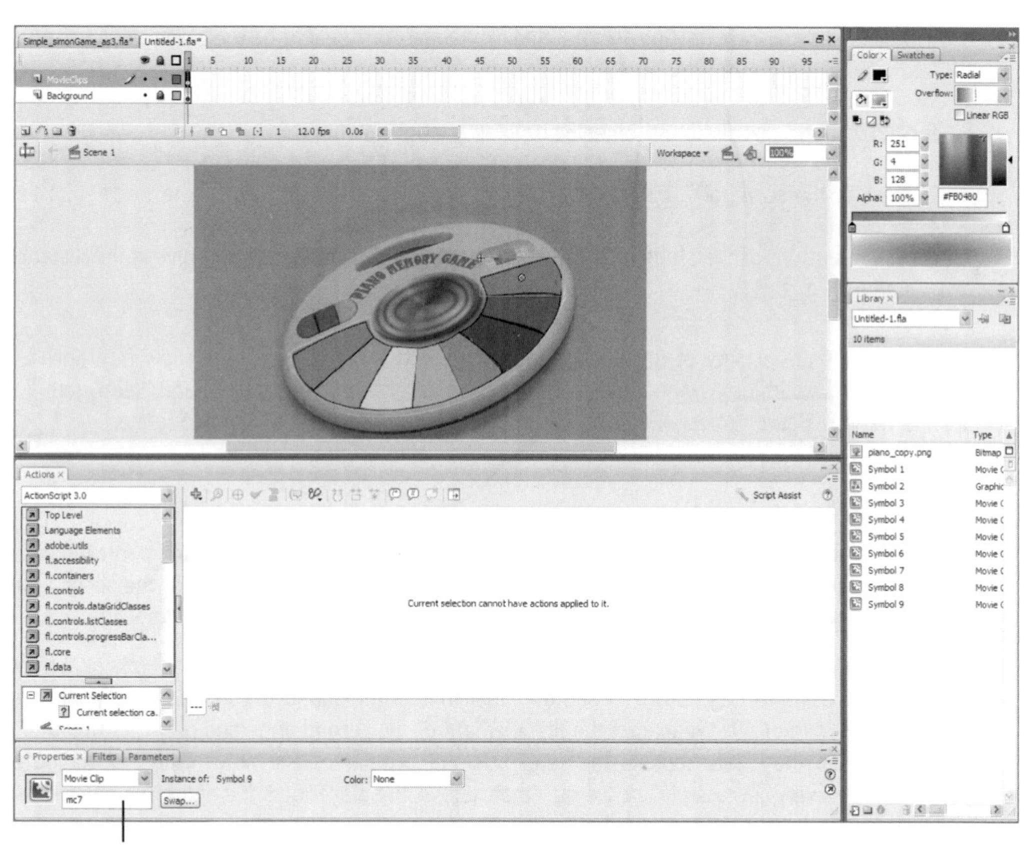

The instance names should be `mc0` through `mc7`.

Figure 7.2
MovieClips layer.

Activities for the Buttons Layer

1. In the main Timeline, create a new layer and name it `Buttons`.

2. Repeat the same procedure of creating a vector shape with drawing tools to create eight separate shapes that fit exactly on the piano keys like we did in the MovieClips layer.

3. Select each shape and convert it into a button. Make each an invisible button by dragging the keyframe in the Up state and dropping it to the Hit state of the button. In the main Timeline, give each button an instance name in the Properties tab, from `c0_btn` *to* `c7_btn` for the eight buttons. Repeat this step for all the shapes.

4. Now create an invisible button on the green rectangle switch and enter the static text `Start` on the button in the first frame. Give this button the instance name `start_btn`.

5. Add the game caption title `Piano Memory Game` on the top of the stage in the main Timeline.

6. Add a static text field and enter `Score` as a label for the score.

7. Next to the score, add a dynamic text field and give it the instance name `score_txt`.

8. At the bottom of the stage, add a dynamic text field for messages and give it the instance name `msg_txt`.

This completes the activity of the Buttons layer. The next three screen shots show how the Buttons layer should look when we select the keyframe of the layer on the stage. See Figure 7.3 for the design, Figure 7.4 for the score setting, and Figure 7.5 for the running game.

Game Logic Explanation

Now we need to develop the logic for the program. Before we start, remember to import the eight sound files for the notes into the library. Name the sound for the first button `s0`, the second `s1`, the third `s2`, and so on. Import the sound for the wrong keys and name it `Lose`.

We need to define two arrays: one to maintain the original array and append randomly generated numbers to it using `array.push()` and the other to hold the duplicate copy of the original array using `array.slice()`. We extract the first element of the second array and play the computer's sequence. Then the player repeats the sequence. We compare these notes with the computer notes, and for every successful click we play that note. If the player gets the entire sequence right, then we create a new random number and append it to the actual original sequence and then duplicate it using `array.slice()`. Then we play the computer's turn and wait for the player to complete his turn. This goes on until the player doesn't commit an error. We use the code on the last frame (43) `gotoAndPlay("Loop");` to loop the playhead until it plays the entire computer sequence and then stops at frame 32 for the player to complete his turn. These frame numbers could be different in your version of the game.

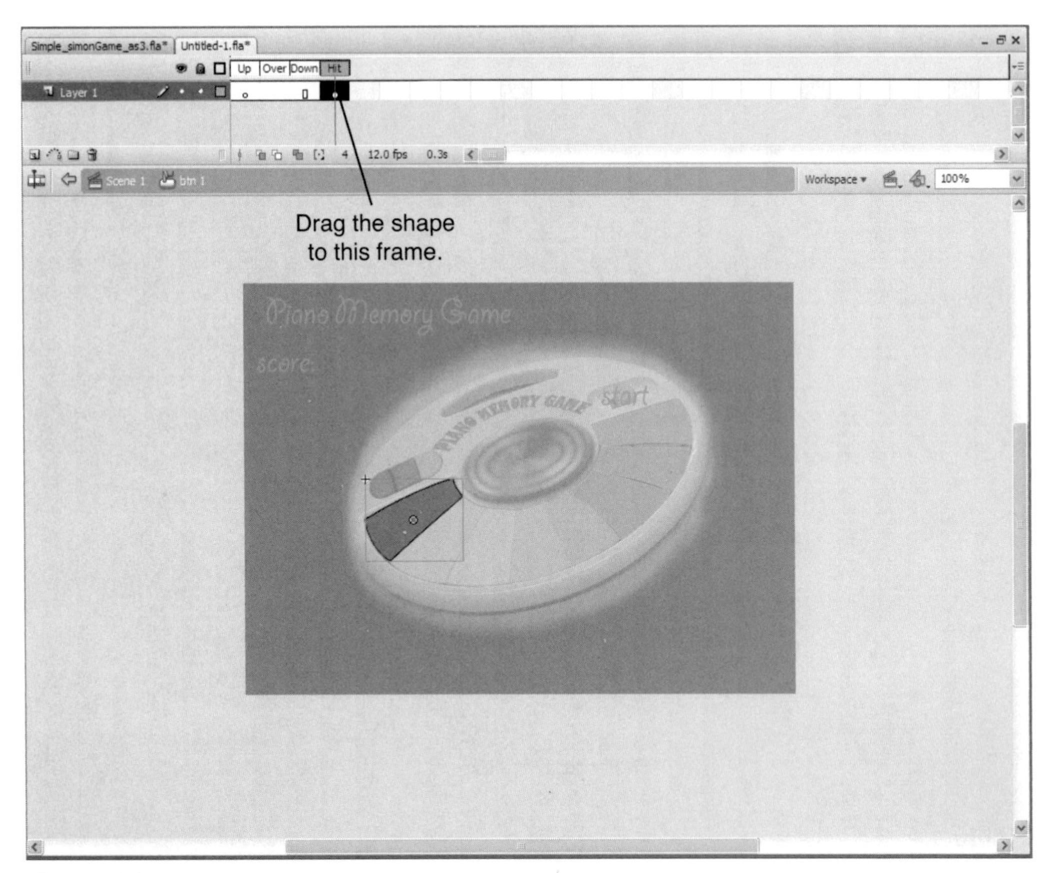

Figure 7.3
Simple Simon game design.

When we click on the Start button, the playhead goes to the frame with the label Loop, and the playhead goes to the else part of the if condition, as we have initialized the compTurn Boolean variable to false in the first frame, and it creates a random number and populates the seq array. Then we duplicate that array into the tempSeq array, so that each time we can extract the first element of the array to play the entire original sequence if it is the computer's turn. Using tempSeq, we can also check whether the player is correctly clicking when it is the player's turn. Then we can decide whether to continue the game or to stop because the player lost. The compTurn Boolean variable is set to true in order to play the computer's turn. After the computer plays its turn, it waits for the player to play his turn, and we use the tempSeq array, as already noted, to check to see if the player's clicks match the actual sequence. If the player clicks correctly, then the computer increases the score and again goes to the else part of the if condition on frame 32 and generates the next random number and carries the game forward. If the player clicks incorrectly, then the playhead goes to the frame labeled Lose and plays the note, reinitializes all the game variables, and stops the game.

Activities for the Actions Layer

Create a new layer and name it Actions. Follow the steps given below for different frames.

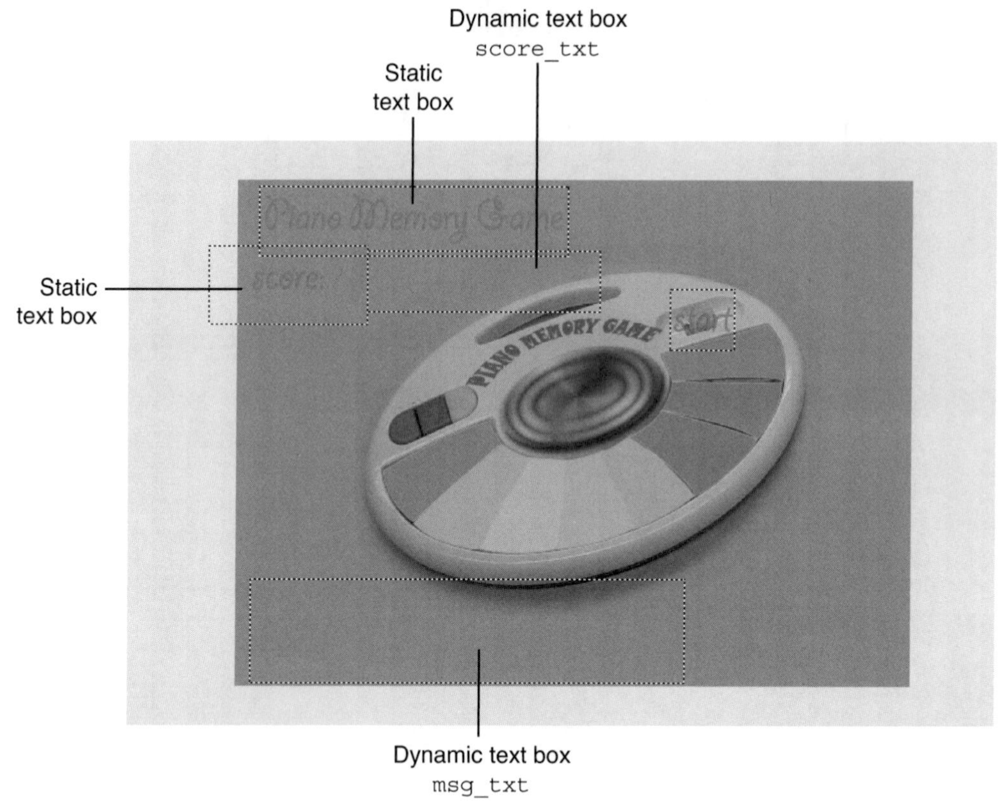

Figure 7.4
Simple Simon game scoreboard.

ActionScript for Frame 1

In the first frame, add the following code:

```
//to stop the playhead at first frame
stop();
// Score Variable
var score:Number = 0;
// Array to hold the original sequence
var seq:Array = new Array();
// Array to hold the temp sequence from which we extract first element every
time using shift()
var tempSeq:Array = new Array();
// Boolean variable to switch turns between computer and player
var compTurn:Boolean = false;
//variables for Sound notes objects instances for 8 notes
var s0Snd:s0 = new s0();
var s1Snd:s1 = new s1();
```

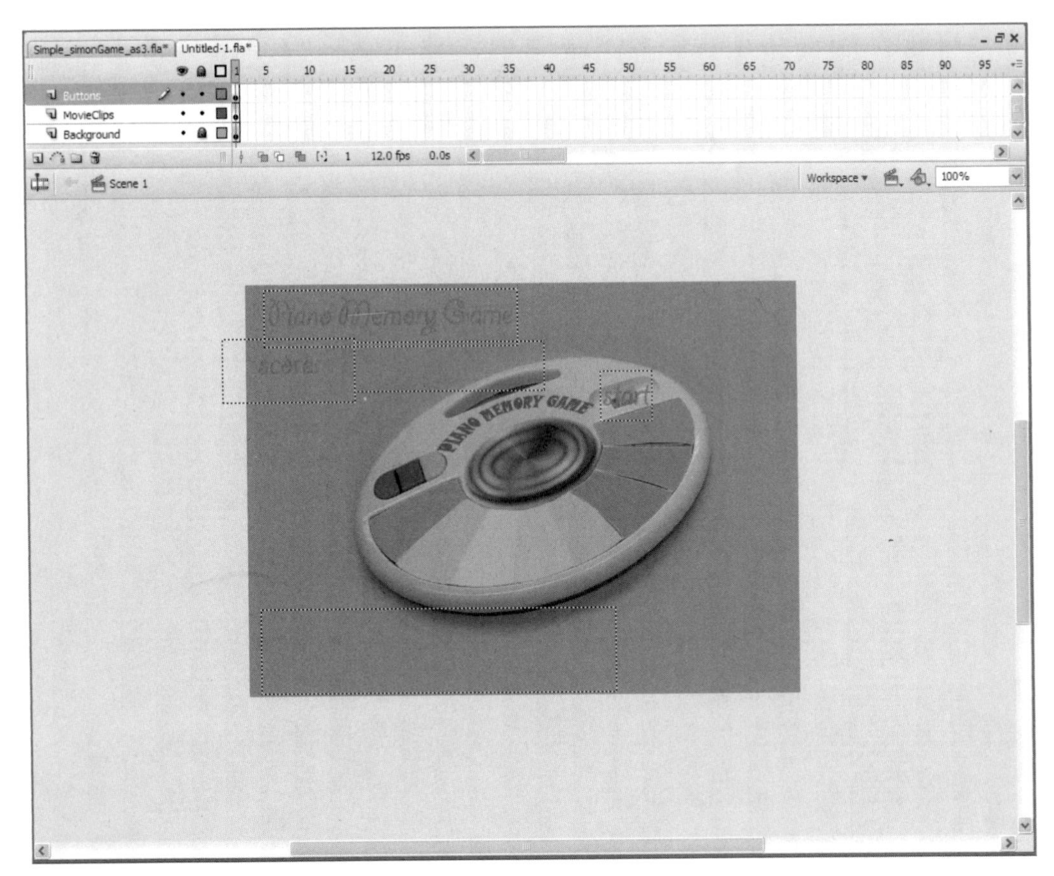

Figure 7.5
Simple Simon game.

```
var s2Snd:s2 = new s2();
var s3Snd:s3 = new s3();
var s4Snd:s4 = new s4();
var s5Snd:s5 = new s5();
var s6Snd:s6 = new s6();
var s7Snd:s7 = new s7();
//variable for sound note of lose situation
var loseSnd:Lose = new Lose();
//initial start message
msg_txt.text = "Click on Green Button to Start";
//start button
start_btn.addEventListener(MouseEvent.CLICK, startGame);
//start button function
function startGame(evt:MouseEvent):void {
        gotoAndPlay("Loop");
}
```

```
//Disable all buttons so that they can be enabled when it's the player's turn
btnsDisable();
// function to enable all buttons only if it's the player's turn
function btnsEnable() {
        c0_btn.enabled = true;
        c1_btn.enabled = true;
        c2_btn.enabled = true;
        c3_btn.enabled = true;
        c4_btn.enabled = true;
        c5_btn.enabled = true;
        c6_btn.enabled = true;
        c7_btn.enabled = true;
}

// function to disable all buttons
function btnsDisable() {
        c0_btn.enabled = false;
        c1_btn.enabled = false;
        c2_btn.enabled = false;
        c3_btn.enabled = false;
        c4_btn.enabled = false;
        c5_btn.enabled = false;
        c6_btn.enabled = false;
        c7_btn.enabled = false;
}

// function to play computer or the player sequence function playSeq(seqNum) {
 switch (seqNum) {
                case 0 :
                        mc0.play();
                        s0Snd.play();
                        break;
                case 1 :
                        mc1.play();
                        s1Snd.play();
                        break;
                case 2 :
                        mc2.play();
                        s2Snd.play();
                        break;
                case 3 :
                        mc3.play();
                        s3Snd.play();
                        break;
```

```
            case 4 :
                  mc4.play();
                  s4Snd.play();
                  break;
            case 5 :
                  mc5.play();
                  s5Snd.play();
                  break;
            case 6 :
                  mc6.play();
                  s6Snd.play();
                  break;
            case 7 :
                  mc7.play();
                  s7Snd.play();
                  break;
      }
}
/* function to check whether the player clicked the correct button notes se-
quence order*/
function checkClick(num) {
 // getting the first element(Number) from an array using shift
 var thisNum:Number = Number(tempSeq.shift());
/* condition to check if the player click button number tallies with the computer
sequence number. If the player click is not equal to the sequence number */
      if (thisNum != num) {
                        // Wrong move, start again
                        btnsDisable();
             var correctOne:Number = Number(thisNum+1);
             score_txt.text = "0";
             gotoAndPlay("Lose");
/* For correct display of button numbers from 1 to 8 (as we use from 0 in an
array) to check if it is Not a Number */
      if (!isNaN(correctOne)) {
              msg_txt.text = "Wrong Click. The Correct Click was Button"
              + correctOne + ". Click Start to Try Again";
             }
             // Re-initializing Array variables
             seq = new Array();
       tempSeq = new Array();
       compTurn = false;
       score = 0;
       playSeq(thisNum);
```

```
        loseSnd.play();
        return;
}

/*if the player click number matches with the actual sequence and the tempSeq
array length is not zero then it plays the sequence calling the playSeq fun-
ction. If it is 0 then it disables the buttons, increments the score and plays
the else part of if condition on frame 32. It then generates the next random
number and so on. */
else if (tempSeq.length == 0) {
                // Right move, play on
                btnsDisable();
        score++;
        score_txt.text = score.toString();
        gotoAndPlay("Loop");
}
playSeq(num);
}
//Button Event Listeners for all eight buttons ( 0 - 7)
c0_btn.addEventListener(MouseEvent.CLICK, cA0);
c1_btn.addEventListener(MouseEvent.CLICK, cA1);
c2_btn.addEventListener(MouseEvent.CLICK, cA2);
c3_btn.addEventListener(MouseEvent.CLICK, cA3);
c4_btn.addEventListener(MouseEvent.CLICK, cA4);
c5_btn.addEventListener(MouseEvent.CLICK, cA5);
c6_btn.addEventListener(MouseEvent.CLICK, cA6);
c7_btn.addEventListener(MouseEvent.CLICK, cA7);
//functions to call when the buttons are clicked....
function cA0(evt:MouseEvent):void {
        checkClick(0);
}
function cA1(evt:MouseEvent):void {
        checkClick(1);
}
function cA2(evt:MouseEvent):void {
        checkClick(2);
}
function cA3(evt:MouseEvent):void {
        checkClick(3);
}
function cA4(evt:MouseEvent):void {
        checkClick(4);
}
```

```
function cA5(evt:MouseEvent):void {
        checkClick(5);
}
function cA6(evt:MouseEvent):void {
        checkClick(6);
}
function cA7(evt:MouseEvent):void {
        checkClick(7);
}
```

ActionScript for Frame 2

We need frames 2 through 30 to be empty to give it time to play the sound for the correct and wrong answers: correct and lose. Create a keyframe and in the Properties panel give it a frame label `Lose`. Also give it visibility up to frame 30 by copying and pasting the frame just created to frame 30.

ActionScript for Frame 31

Create a keyframe at frame 31 and add the following code:

```
/* Reset the score and make all movie clips move back to their initial positions on a lose situation. Wait here so that the player can click on the start button to start the game.*/
score = 0;
mc0.gotoAndStop(1);
mc1.gotoAndStop(1);
mc2.gotoAndStop(1);
mc3.gotoAndStop(1);
mc4.gotoAndStop(1);
mc5.gotoAndStop(1);
mc6.gotoAndStop(1);
mc7.gotoAndStop(1);
stop();
```

ActionScript for Frame 32

Add the following code at frame 32.

```
if (compTurn) {
    btnsDisable();
if (tempSeq.length) {
            var thisNumC:Number = Number(tempSeq.shift());
            playSeq(thisNumC);
    } else {
            msg_txt.text = "Player Turn";
            compTurn = false;
            tempSeq = seq.slice();
```

```
                stop();
                btnsEnable();
        }
    } else {
            btnsDisable();
            seq.push(Math.floor(8*Math.random()));
            tempSeq = seq.slice();
            compTurn = true;
            msg_txt.text = "Computer Turn";
    }
```

Until the `tempSeq` array is not empty, we have to loop and play each note from the `tempSeq` array. We use the `tempSeq.shift()` method, which returns the first array element and reduces the array by one element every time. This enables us to retrieve and play all notes until the end. Once the length of the array `tempSeq.length` is empty, it returns false and thereby goes to the `else` part of the condition and makes it the player's turn. The same sequence follows for the player, too. Every time the player clicks the correct note, the next array element is extracted using `tempSeq.shift()` in the function `checkClick(num)` and then the flow follows.

ActionScript for Frame 33

Here we need to add some empty frames up to frame 43, so that we have some time to hear the sound of the note play and we can keep the playhead looping until all notes are played. Create a keyframe and add the frame label `Loop`.

ActionScript for Frame 43

Here we just need one line of code to repeat the loop.

```
gotoAndPlay("Loop");
```

Summary

In this chapter, you expanded your knowledge about arrays and loops and their application. We learned about single- and two-dimensional arrays and also three different types of loops in ActionScript and went over some example code. Finally, we developed a Simple Simon game using arrays to hold the sequence of notes.

Review Questions

1. Describe the purpose of using arrays.
2. Why do we need loops?
3. When would we use `for` loops and when would we use `while` loops?

4. What is the difference between a `while` loop and a `do...while` loop?
5. Write an ActionScript block of code to create a single-dimensional array of numbers. Then sort that array in ascending order.
6. Write an ActionScript block of code to initialize a counter to 0. Then display your name 10 times. Use a `for` loop.
7. Rewrite #6 using a `while` loop.

Project

Create four colored blocks on the screen. Use the same theme as the Simple Simon game but with four blocks. Allow the player to win if he gets the sequence correct five times in a row.

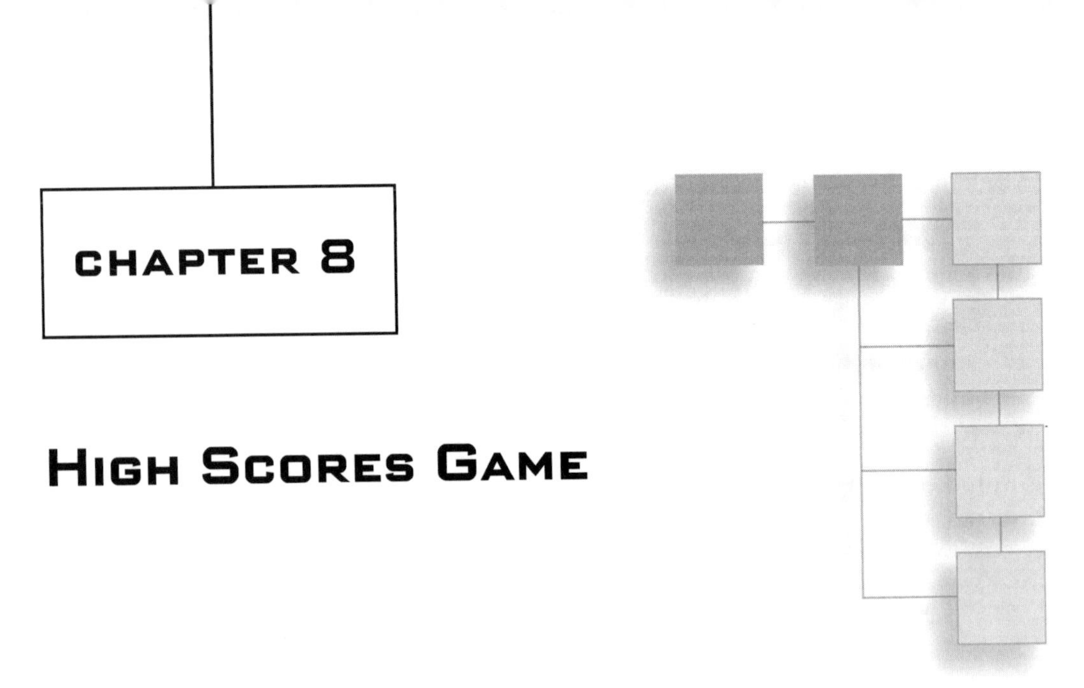

Chapter 8

High Scores Game

- Use a SharedObject
- Use arrays
- Use a timer

What Is a SharedObject?

The SharedObject class available in the Flash environment is used to store small amounts of data on the client machine. It is very similar to a cookie, which is set on your local machine and whose value can be retrieved at a later time. The SharedObject is one way to have *persistent data,* which means the value saved in this object continues to be accessible even after the program is closed, unlike variables in a program whose value is alive only as long as the program is open.

Uses of a SharedObject

There are many uses for a SharedObject. Some of these uses are:

- A SharedObject can be used as a cookie to store data on the local machine. This data that is saved is accessible only to that single machine.
- A SharedObject can be used to save data on a server. This data can be seen by many clients at one time. An example is a high-scores game where

you can see the scores of different people and compare your score to their scores.

- A SharedObject can be used to provide real-time data sharing among many clients. An example is where all the airline reservation agents can see the same number of seats available for any given flight, and once a ticket is booked everybody has the updated data reflecting the total available seats.

Limitations of the SharedObject include the following:

- Sometimes .swf files are not allowed to write data to local SharedObjects.
- Sometimes the local SharedObject may be deleted without your knowledge.

For more information on SharedObjects, visit Adobe livedocs at http://livedocs.adobe.com/flash/9.0/ActionScriptLangRefV3/flash/net/SharedObject.html.

In this chapter, we will only be looking at the first type of use, which is to save data on your local machine. We will design a high scores game to show a SharedObject in action.

Exercise 8.1

Story Line

The main theme of this game is to mimic a high score feature, which is common in games. The game keeps track of scores of 10 individuals playing on the same machine. The scores are ranked from highest to lowest. The game requires that the player be able to click on an object that appears at random places. The goal is for the player to click on the object as many times as possible within 20 seconds. The number of clicks is saved in the SharedObject and is displayed the next time the player opens the game.

Storyboard

This phase includes the logical flow of your game depicted pictorially. Figure 8.1 shows this process.

Game Assets

The graphics you need for this game are all going to be button symbols. You will need a Start button, an object (also a button type) that will be placed randomly at different positions, a Clear Scores button, and a Play Again button. Use your imagination and create the three buttons (Start, Clear All, and Play Again). For the object, create a button with a fancy shape, such as a teddy bear, a rabbit, an orange, or whatever you fancy. In this game, a dog biscuit will be used as the clickable object. Make sure you choose button type for these game assets when you create the new symbols.

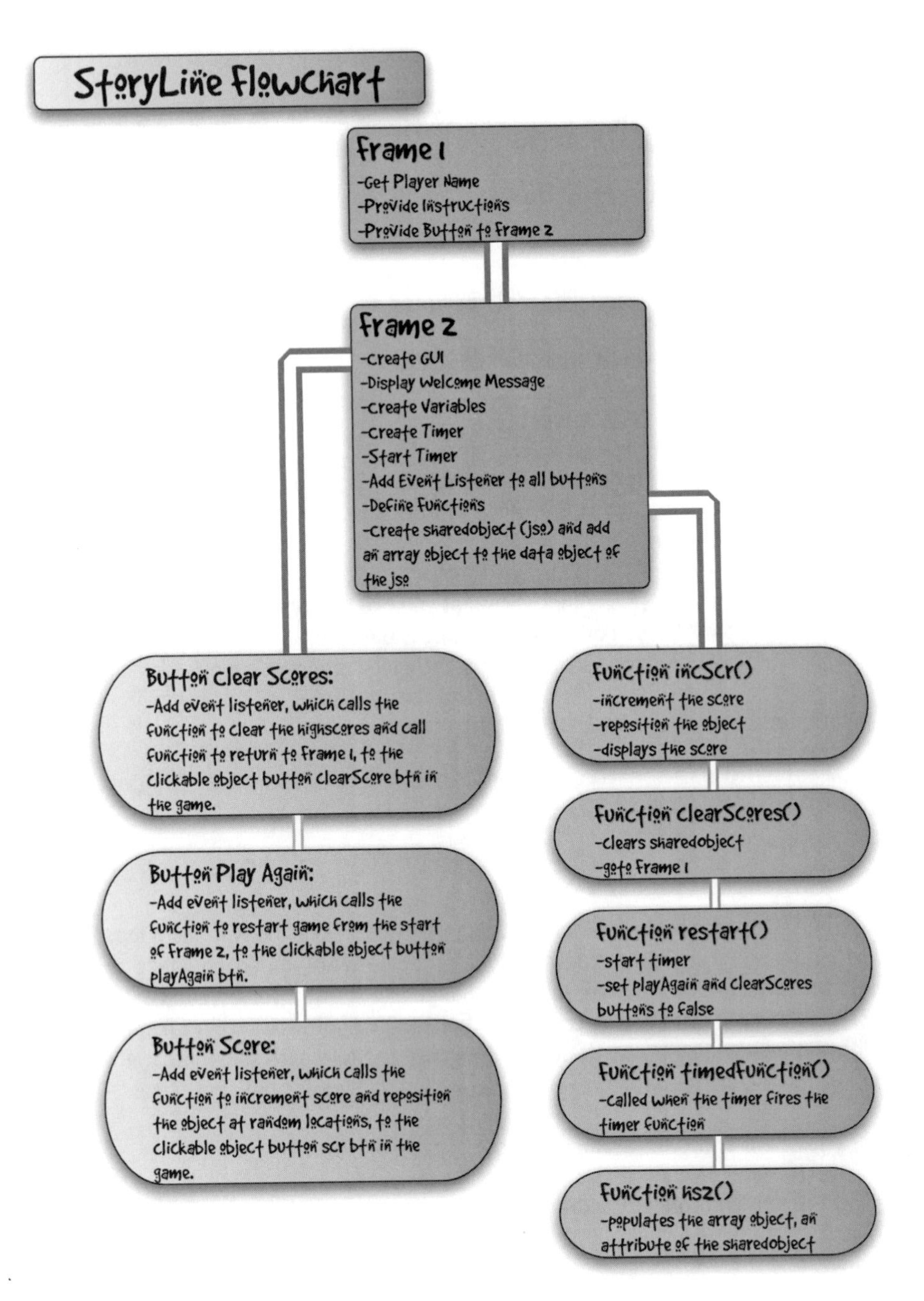

Figure 8.1
Storyboard flowchart.

Code Used in the Game

This section presents the objects and code to be inserted in various layers and frames used in the game. The code required for the game will be included in two frames, frame 1 and frame 2.

Activity for Frame 1: Creating the Instructions Scene

1. Create a new Flash document.
2. Import (to the library) a few graphics you would like to use in the game. This book and the accompanying CD have used graphics for a garden, a puppy, and a dog biscuit. Of course, if you are creative, you can instead draw your own graphics in Photoshop or Flash.
3. Select frame 1 and click on the stage.
4. Choose any color you like for the background. You can also import any image to the library and use that as a background, as was done in this game. An image of a garden was imported and then used as a background. See Figure 8.2.
5. Use the Text tool and choose any font style that you like and type the following text to be displayed to the user. (Please note that you can customize the text to follow the theme of your game. In the figures provided, the game is themed around a puppy collecting treats.)

   ```
   Instructions:

   The goal of this game is to click on as many randomly appearing dog bones
   as you can in 20 seconds.

   The top 10 high scores will be displayed.
   ```

6. Create a button of any shape. See Figure 8.3 for a sample. In keeping with the puppy theme, call the button `btn_Fetch` and type the word `Fetch`. Draw or import an image of a puppy paw. This is a fancy button, in that it has different colors for different states (you saw how to assign different colors to different states of a button in Chapter 2). The different colors for different states are intended just to create some visual effects. If you like to keep it simple, you needn't use different colors for different states.
7. Drag the Text tool and draw a static text box. Type `Please name your dog:`.
8. Drag the Text tool and draw a text box on the stage. Change the type of the text box to Dynamic. Name this instance `playerName_txt`. Your screen should be similar to Figure 8.4.

Code for the Instructions Scene

Click on frame 1 and type the following code:

```
stop();
var pNam:String;
enter_btn.addEventListener(MouseEvent.CLICK, enterGame);
```

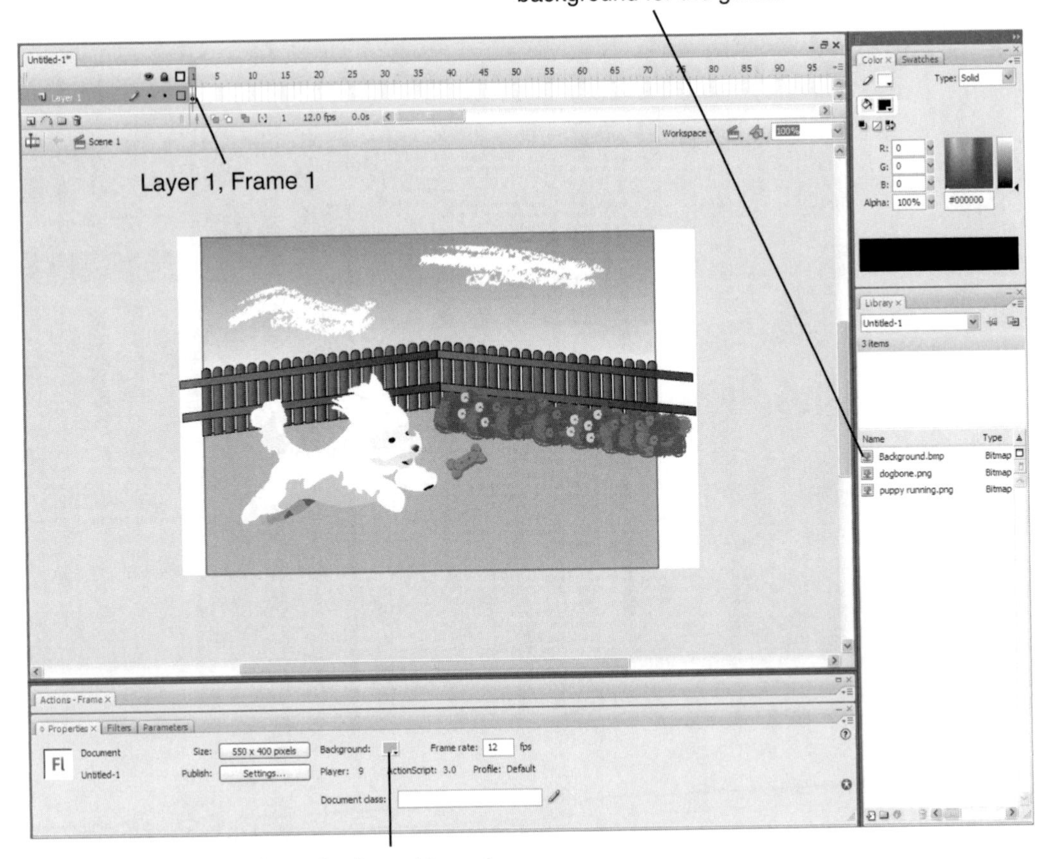

These files were imported to the library and then dragged onto the stage. All three will make up the background for the game.
Layer 1, Frame 1
If you don't want to make a custom background, that's OK. You can still set up a default color as your background here.

Figure 8.2
Puppy game background.

```
function enterGame(evt:MouseEvent) {
pNam = playerName_txt.text;
if (playerName_txt.text !="" && playerName_txt.text!="Enter Your Name") {
        nextFrame();
} else {
        playerName_txt.text = "Enter Your Name";
}


}
```

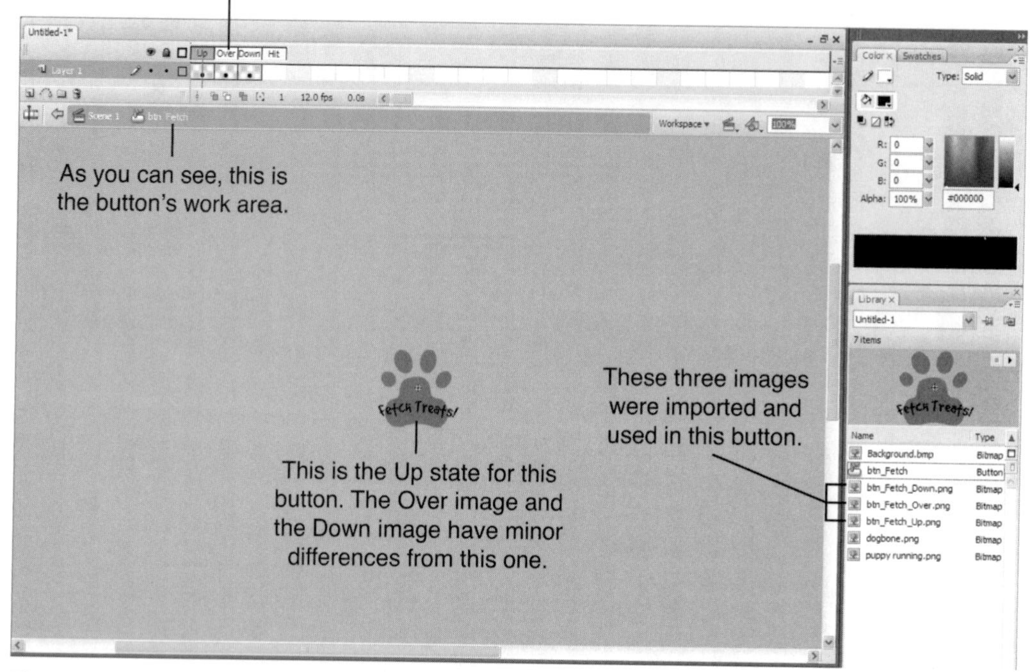
Buttons have four states: Up, Over, Down, and Hit. Add a keyframe if you want to add an image to a button frame.
As you can see, this is the button's work area.
These three images were imported and used in this button.
This is the Up state for this button. The Over image and the Down image have minor differences from this one.
Fetch Treats!
Background.bmp
btn_Fetch
btn_Fetch_Down.png
btn_Fetch_Over.png
btn_Fetch_Up.png
dogbone.png
puppy running.png

Figure 8.3
The Start button.

Explanation of the Code

This code has the usual `stop()` function. Next, the variable `pNam` is created to capture the value of the text typed into the dynamic text box `playerName_txt` when the player clicks on the Start button. An event listener is added to the Start button to recognize the mouse click event. The mouse click event then calls the function `enterGame`. The `enterGame` function assigns the value of the text in `playerName_txt` to the variable `pNam`. This function also checks to see if `playerName_txt` is not equal to an empty string and does not contain the string `Please name your dog:`. If the player entered a satisfactory name, the player is directed to frame 2. If not, a box displays the string `Please name your dog:` to alert the player to type a name for the puppy.

Activity for Frame 2: Creating the Game Pieces Scene

See Figure 8.5 before you start creating this scene so you have an idea of the stage layout.

This frame is the actual frame where the game will be played. This frame also displays the score at the end of the game.

1. Click on frame 2 and insert a keyframe.

2. Delete the text boxes and button from frame 1. In the puppy game, the picture of the puppy and the dog bone were also removed. These images were then replaced with a new image

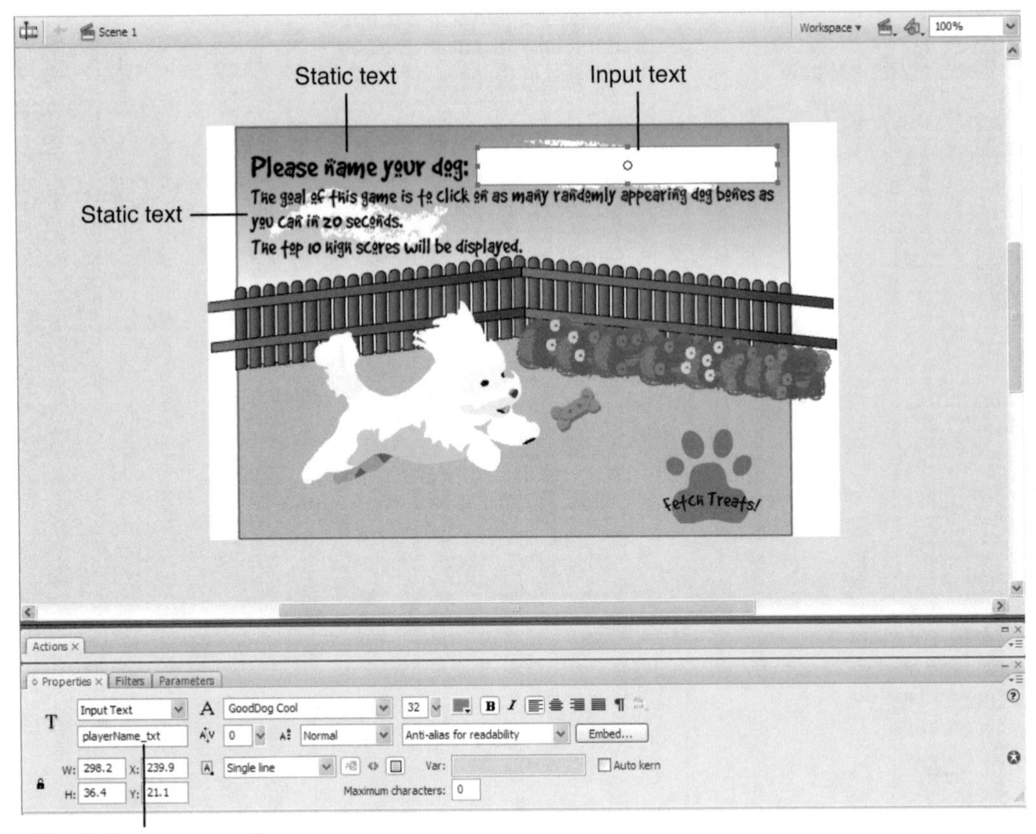

Figure 8.4
Frame 1 completed.

of a puppy and three instances of a bone pile. Again, these don't affect the game. They are just there to make the game more interesting.

3. Drag the Text tool and draw a static text box. Type `Go Fetch`.
4. Drag the Text tool and draw a dynamic text box. Give it the instance name `pName_txt`. See Figure 8.6.
5. Drag the Text tool and draw a static text box. Type `Score`.
6. Drag the Text tool and draw a dynamic text box. Give it the instance name `pScore_txt`. See Figure 8.7.
7. Drag the Text tool and draw a static text box. Type `Time`.

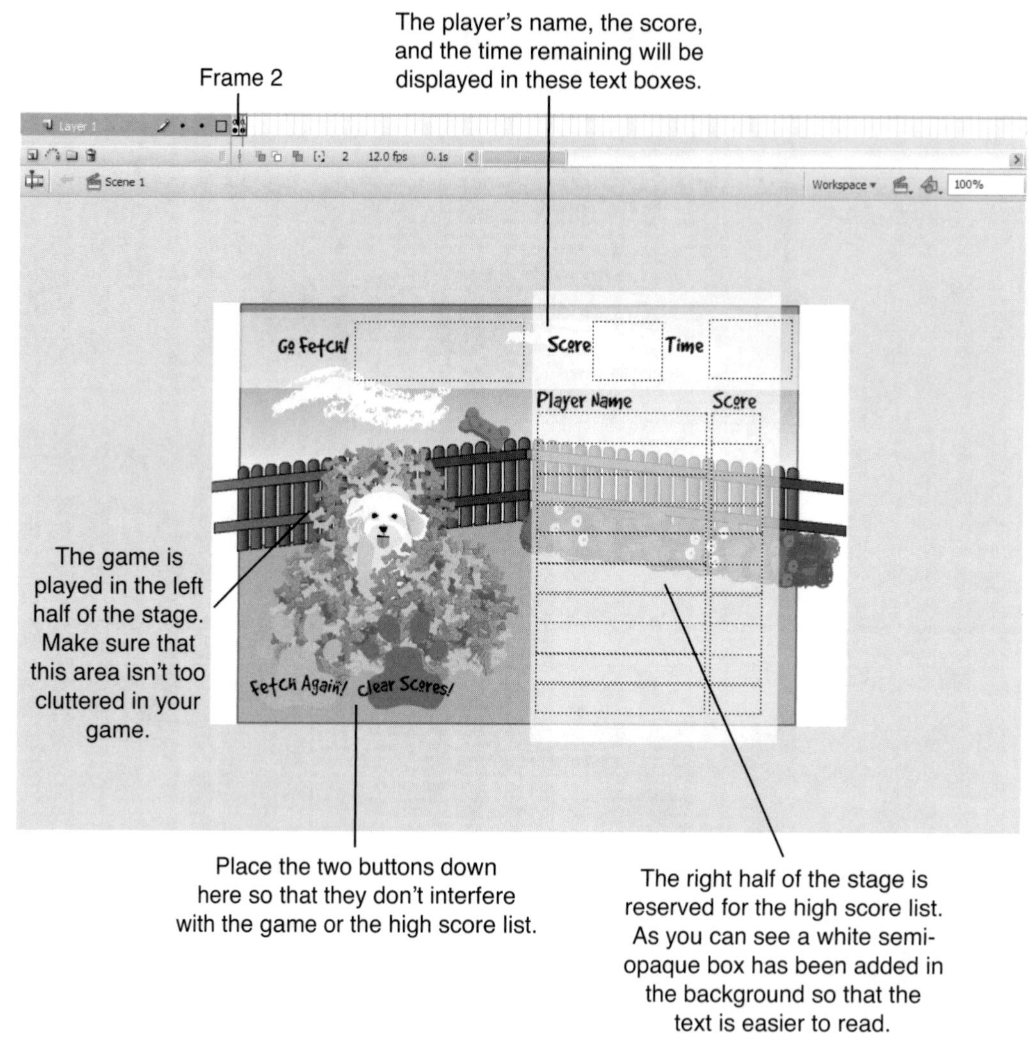
Frame 2
The player's name, the score, and the time remaining will be displayed in these text boxes.
Scene 1
Workspace
100%
Go Fetch!
Score
Time
Player Name
Score
The game is played in the left half of the stage. Make sure that this area isn't too cluttered in your game.
Fetch Again!
Clear Scores!
Place the two buttons down here so that they don't interfere with the game or the high score list.
The right half of the stage is reserved for the high score list. As you can see a white semi-opaque box has been added in the background so that the text is easier to read.

Figure 8.5
Frame 2 layout.

8. Drag the Text tool and draw a dynamic text box. Give it the instance name `pTime_txt`. See Figure 8.8.

9. Now we want to create two buttons for frame 2. Create a button called `btn_Again` and another button called `btn_Clear`. Use any shape you like for these buttons, or use the previously imported images from the library.

10. The `btn_Again` button should include a text box with the text `Fetch Again!` in it.

11. The `btn_Clear` button should include a text box with the text `Clear Scores!` in it.

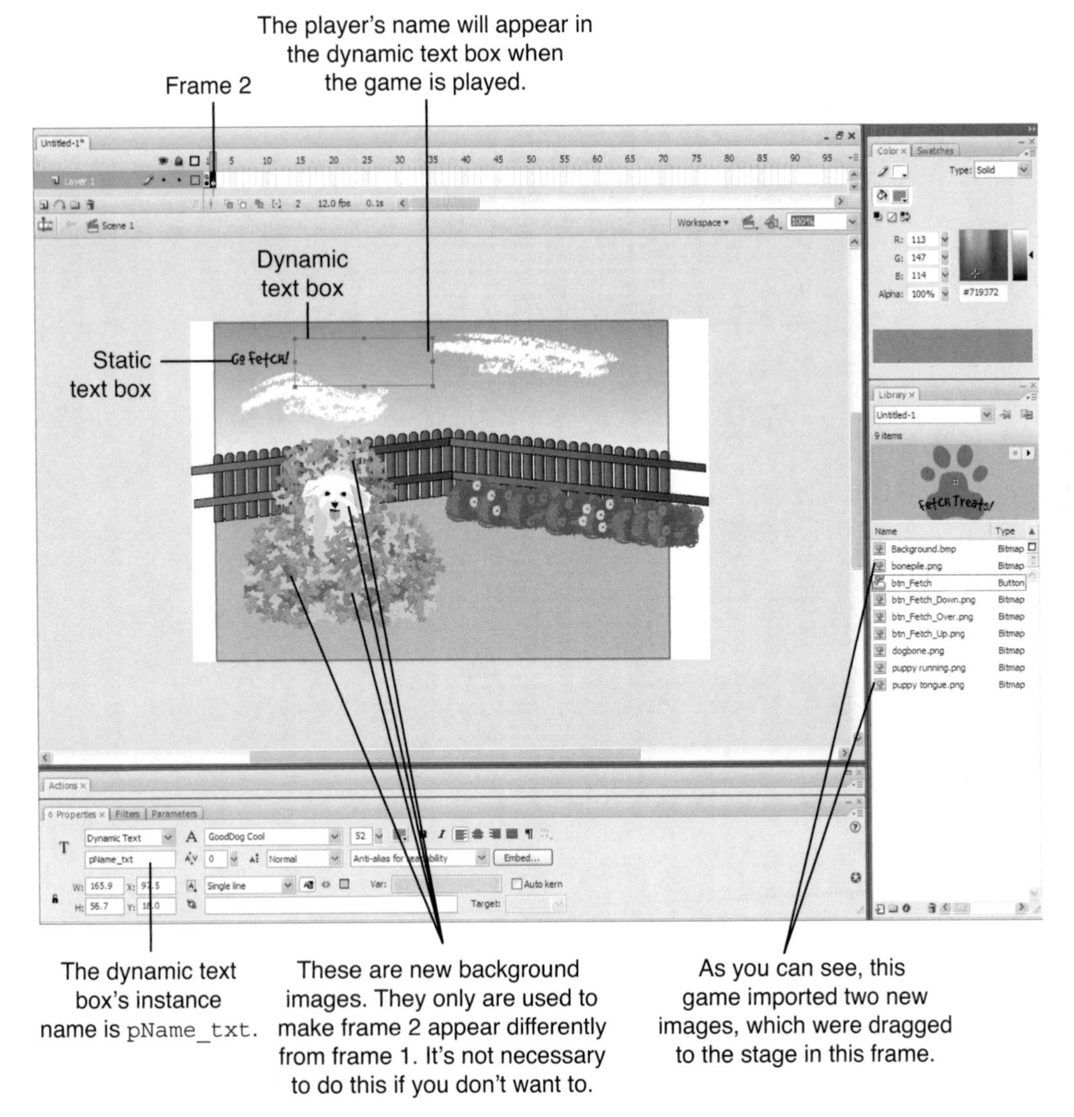
The player's name will appear in the dynamic text box when the game is played.
Frame 2
Dynamic text box
Static text box
Go Fetch!
Fetch Treats!
The dynamic text box's instance name is pName_txt.
These are new background images. They only are used to make frame 2 appear differently from frame 1. It's not necessary to do this if you don't want to.
As you can see, this game imported two new images, which were dragged to the stage in this frame.

Figure 8.6
Dynamic text box for Puppy Name.

12. Drag an instance of the `btn_Again` button to the stage. Give it the instance name `pa_btn`. See Figure 8.9.

13. Drag an instance of the `btn_Clear` button to the stage. Give it the instance name `cls_btn`. See Figure 8.10.

14. The last set of text boxes to be drawn on the stage will show the scores for the last 10 players with their names. Drag the Text tool and draw a static text box and type `Player Name` in it.

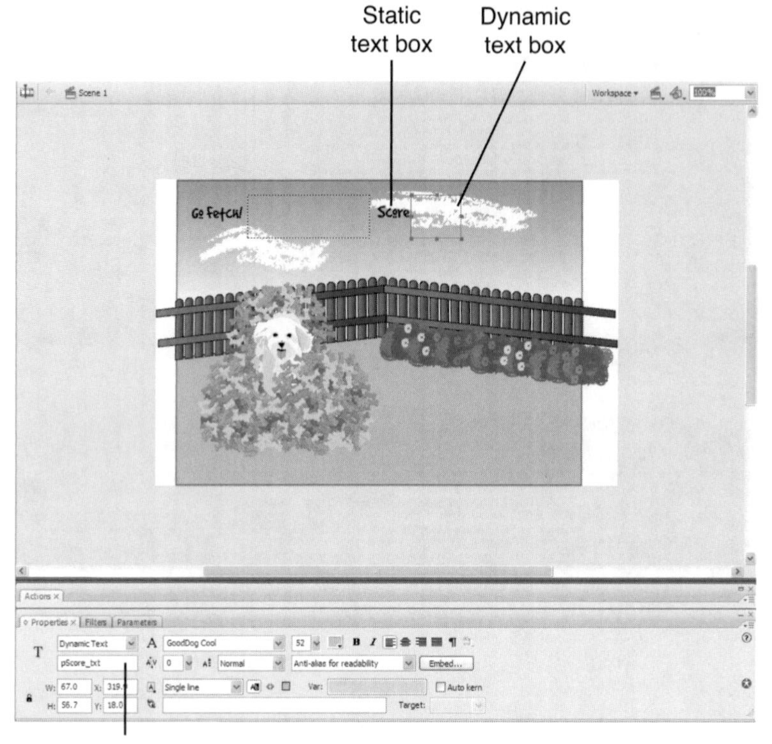

Figure 8.7
Score.

15. Drag the Text tool and draw a static text box and type `Score` in it. See Figure 8.11.

16. The next set of text boxes are the dynamic text boxes to display the names and scores of the players. Drag the Text tool and draw a dynamic text box below the Name static text box. Give it the instance name `pn0`.

17. Repeat step 16 nine more times each time incrementing the instance name number by 1. The last text box you add will have `pn9` for its instance name. You will now have created a total of 10 dynamic text boxes for names. See Figure 8.12.

18. Drag the Text tool and draw a dynamic text box below the Score static text box. Give it the instance name `ps0`.

19. Repeat step 18 nine more times. The last text box you add will have `ps9` for its instance name. You will now have created a total of 10 dynamic text boxes for scores. See Figure 8.13.

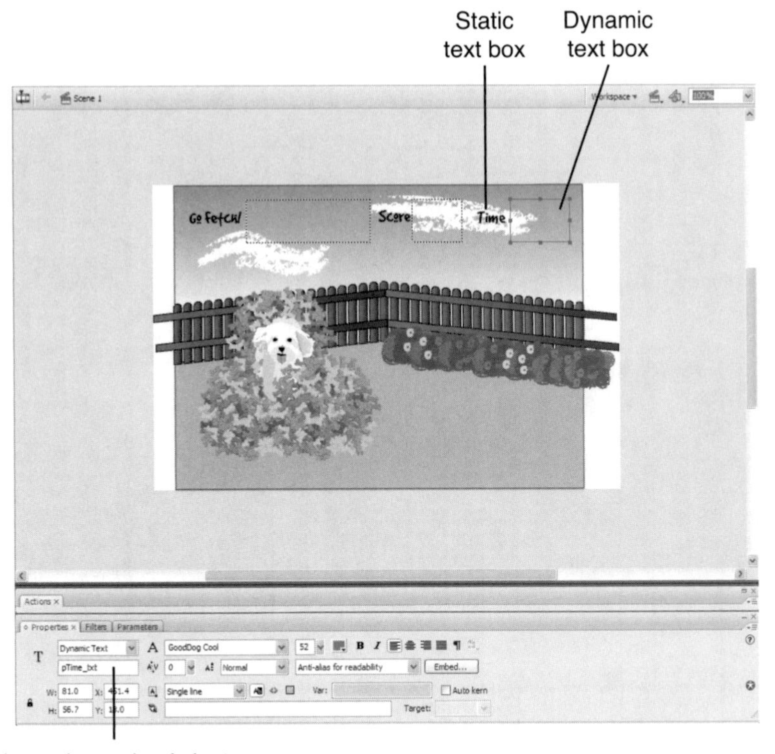

Figure 8.8
Time.

20. Select Insert, New Symbol. This symbol is going to be the game piece that will be clicked on during the game. Name this symbol `btn_Bone` and make sure it is of type Button.

21. Draw some kind of object resembling a bone or a dog biscuit.

22. Return to Scene 1 and drag one instance of `btn_Bone` to somewhere on the left half of the stage.

23. Name this Instance `scr_btn`. See Figure 8.14. The caption for Figure 8.14 is The Target Object because this is the target that should be clicked on to increment the score.

Code for Frame 2 Click on Actions for frame 2 and type the following code:

```
var score:Number=0;

var rec_array:Array = new Array();

var myTimer:Timer = new Timer(1000);
```

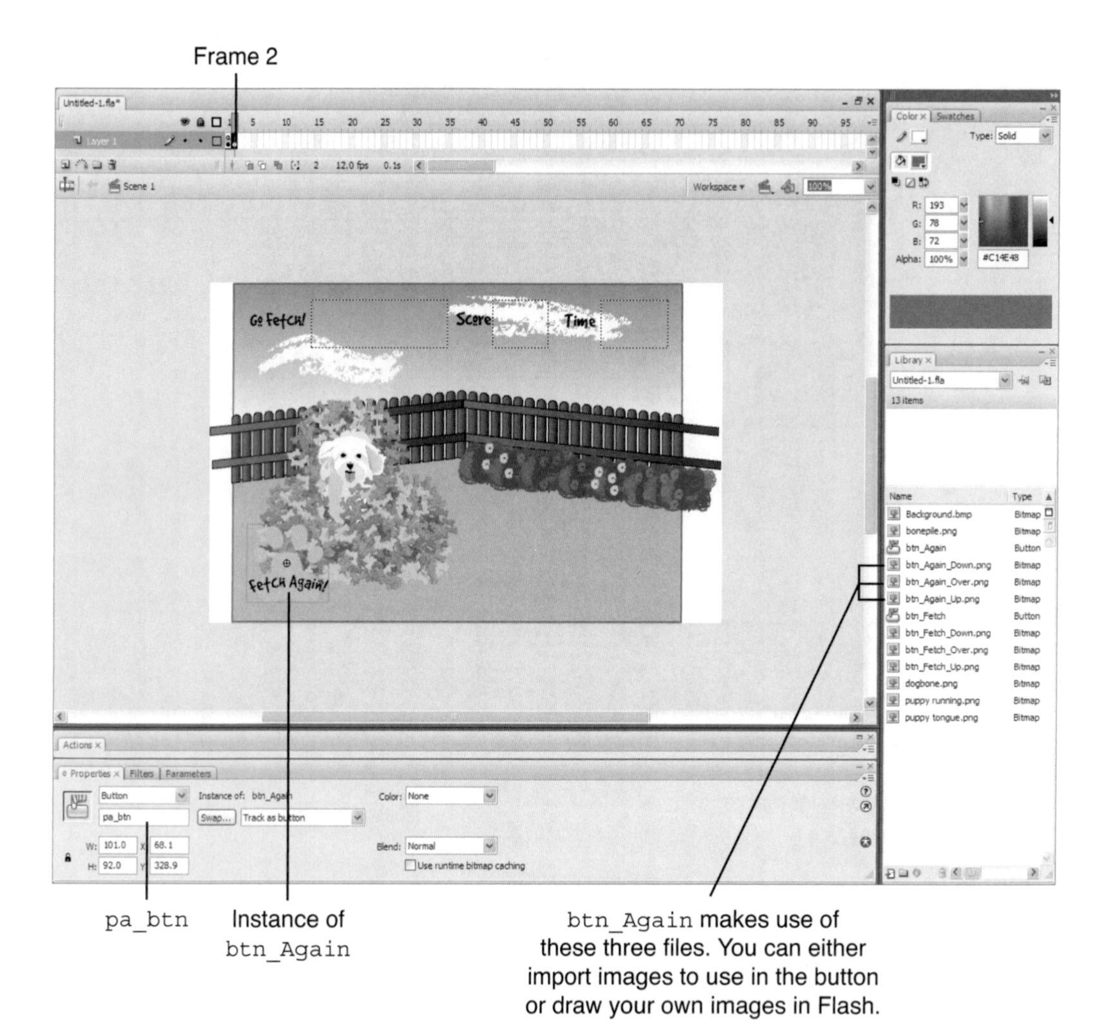

Frame 2
pa_btn
Instance of btn_Again
btn_Again makes use of these three files. You can either import images to use in the button or draw your own images in Flash.

Figure 8.9
The Play Again button.

```
myTimer.addEventListener("timer", timedFunction);

myTimer.start();

pa_btn.visible = false;

cls_btn.visible = false;

pName_txt.text = pNam;

cls_btn.addEventListener(MouseEvent.CLICK, clearScores);
```

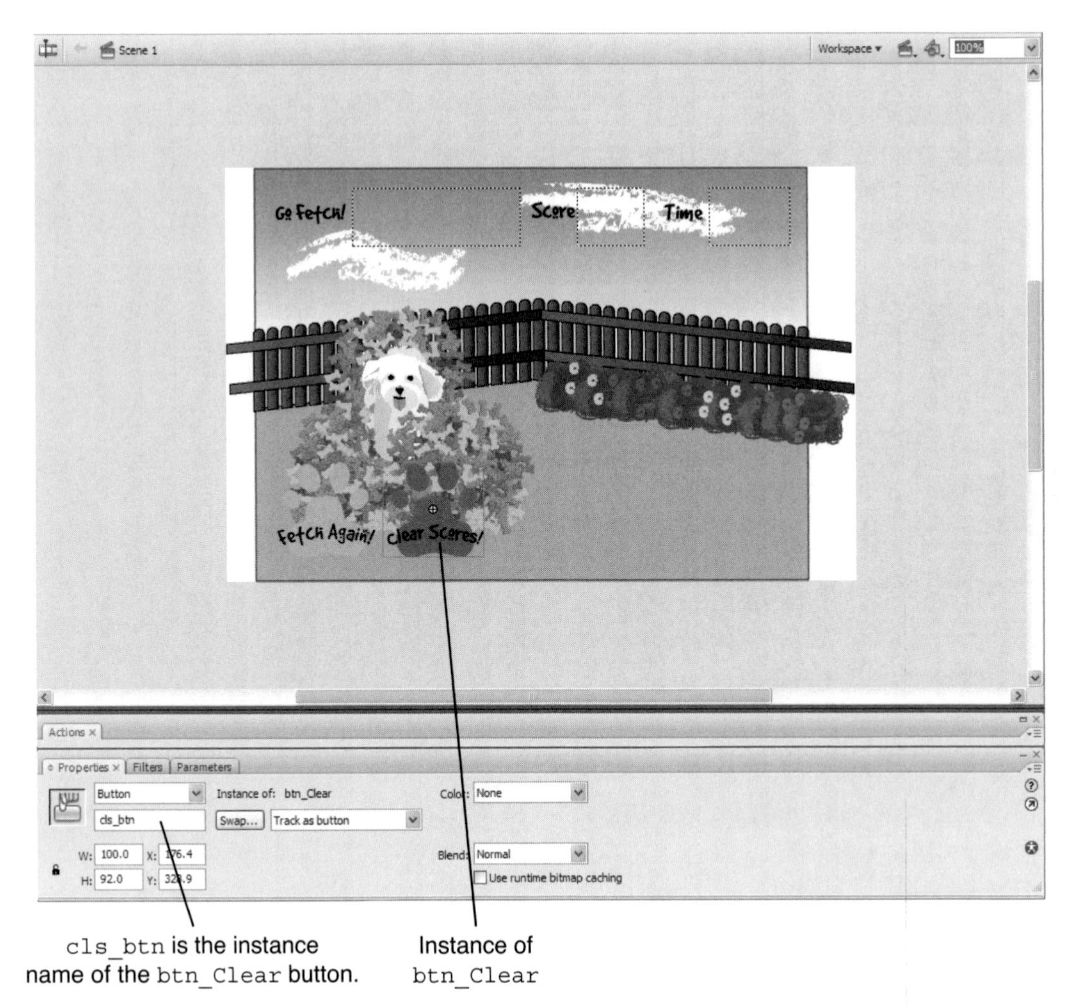

Figure 8.10
The Clear Scores button.

```
function clearScores(evt:MouseEvent):void {
 jso2.clear();
 gotoAndStop(1);
}


pa_btn.addEventListener(MouseEvent.CLICK, restart);

function restart(evt:MouseEvent):void {

 myTimer.start();
```

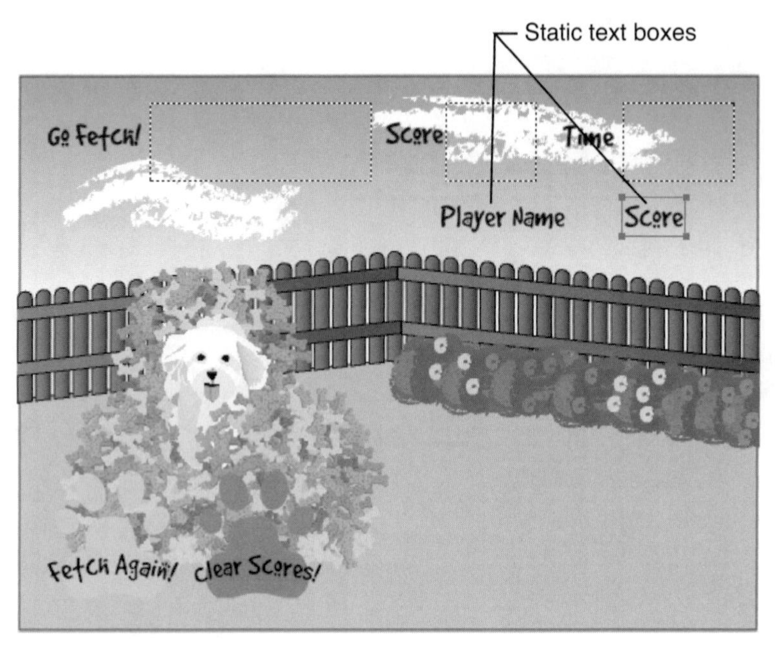

Figure 8.11
Player name and score.

```
  scr_btn.addEventListener(MouseEvent.CLICK, incScr);
  pa_btn.visible = false;
  cls_btn.visible = false;
}

scr_btn.addEventListener(MouseEvent.CLICK, incScr);

function incScr(evt:MouseEvent):void {
  scr_btn.x = 50+(Math.random()*200);
  scr_btn.y = 100+(Math.random()*200);
  pScore_txt.text = String(score++);
}


var jso2:SharedObject = SharedObject.getLocal("hsr");

if (jso2.data.scrz!=null) {
  rec_array = jso2.data.scrz;
}

function hs2() {
```

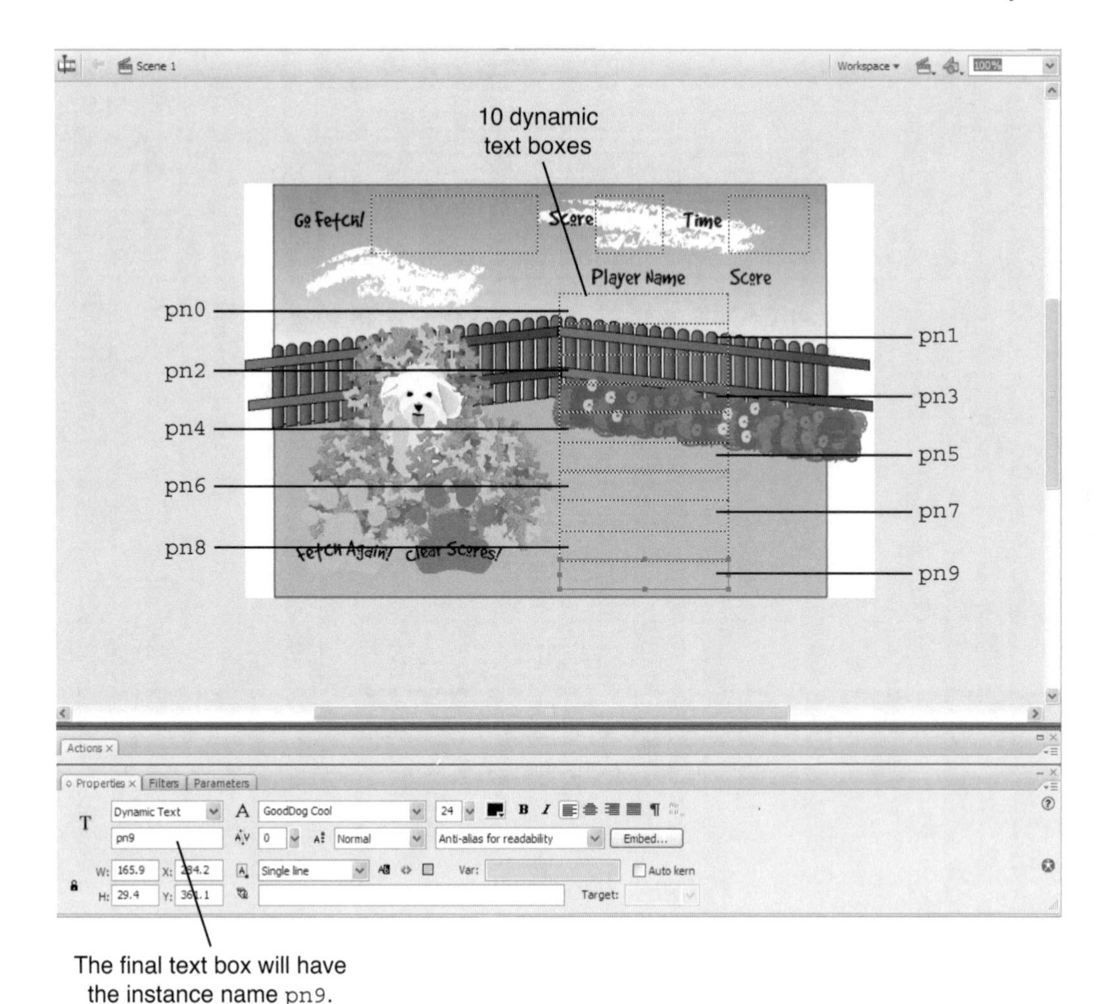

Figure 8.12
Name list.

```
rec_array.push({pN: pName_txt.text, pS: Number(pScore_txt.text)});
jso2.data.scrz = rec_array;
jso2.flush();
rec_array.sortOn("pS", Array.DESCENDING | Array.NUMERIC);

if ( rec_array[0]!=null) {
      pn0.text = rec_array[0].pN;
      ps0.text = rec_array[0].pS;
}
if ( rec_array[1]!=null) {
      pn1.text = rec_array[1].pN;
```

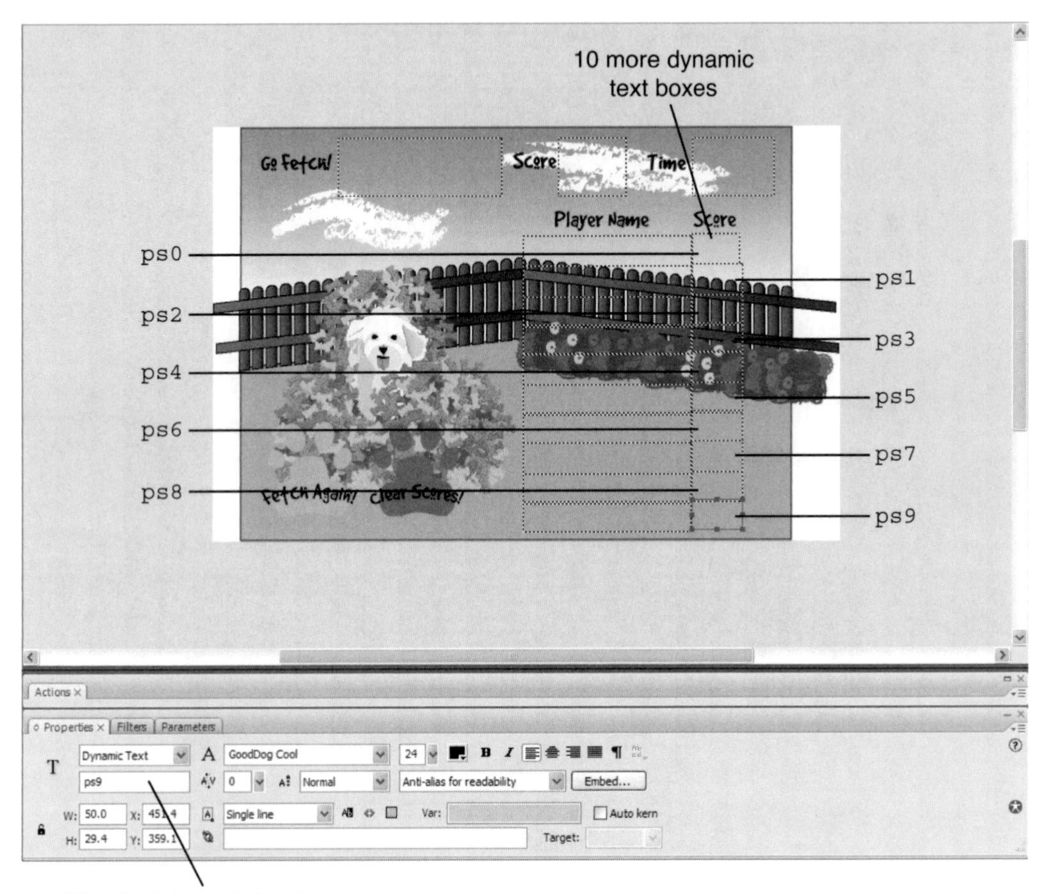

Figure 8.13
The score list.

```
        ps1.text = rec_array[1].pS;
    }
    if ( rec_array[2]!=null) {
        pn2.text = rec_array[2].pN;
        ps2.text = rec_array[2].pS;
    }
    if ( rec_array[3]!=null) {
        pn3.text = rec_array[3].pN;
        ps3.text = rec_array[3].pS;
    }
    if ( rec_array[4]!=null) {
        pn4.text = rec_array[4].pN;
        ps4.text = rec_array[4].pS;
```

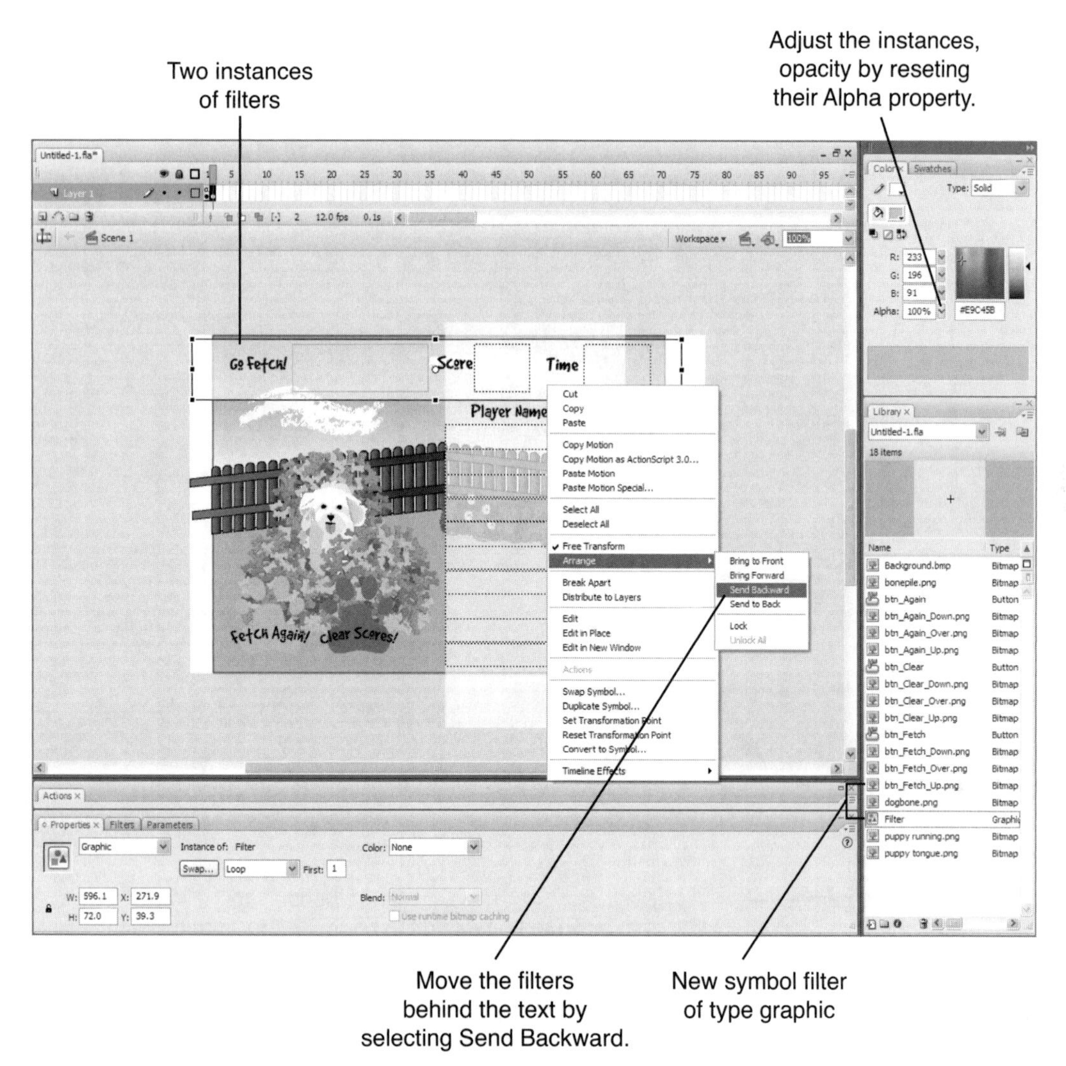
Two instances of filters
Adjust the instances, opacity by reseting their Alpha property.
Move the filters behind the text by selecting Send Backward.
New symbol filter of type graphic

Figure 8.14
The target object.

```
}
if ( rec_array[5]!=null) {
        pn5.text = rec_array[5].pN;
        ps5.text = rec_array[5].pS;
}
if ( rec_array[6]!=null) {
        pn6.text = rec_array[6].pN;
        ps6.text = rec_array[6].pS;
}
if ( rec_array[7]!=null) {
```

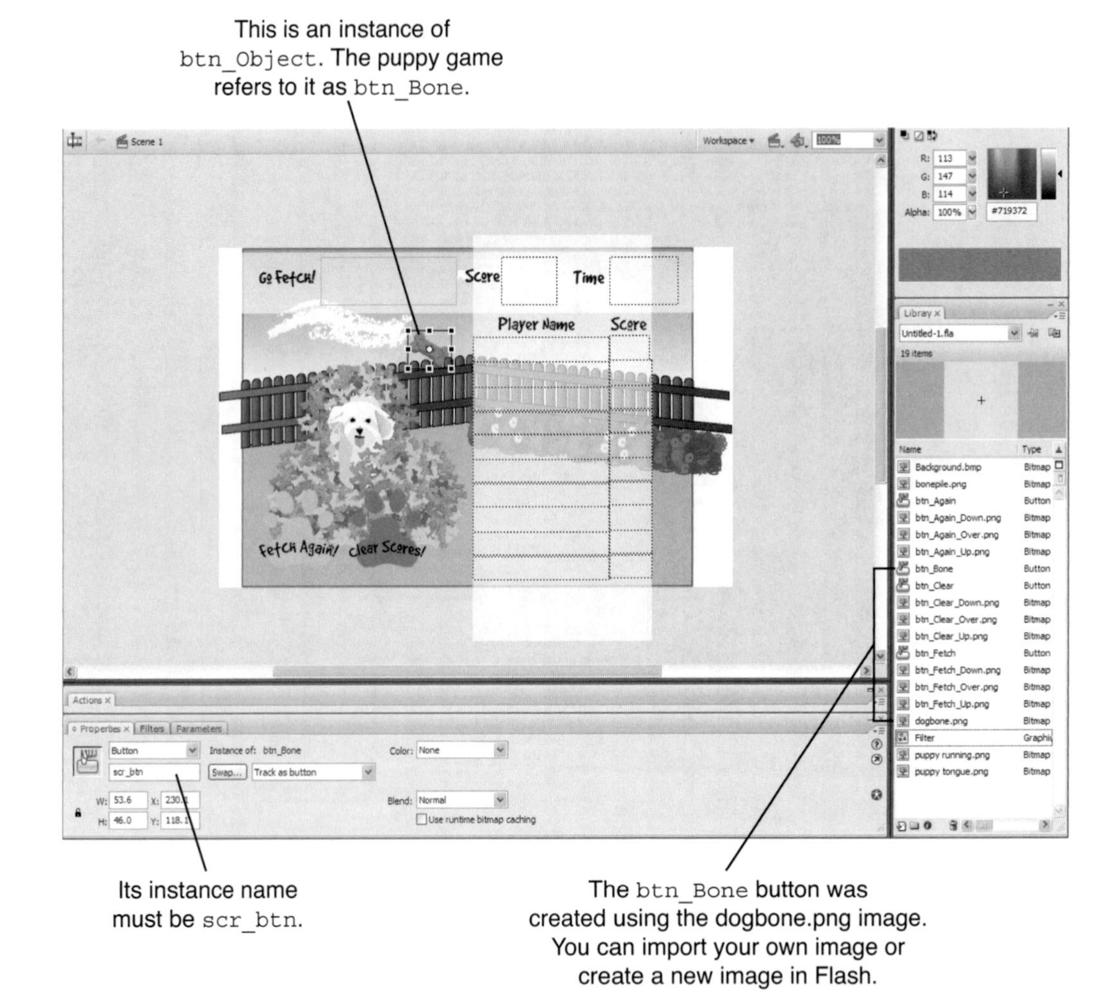

This is an instance of btn_Object. The puppy game refers to it as btn_Bone.
Go Fetch!
Score
Time
Player Name
Score
Fetch Again!
Clear Scores!
Its instance name must be scr_btn.
The btn_Bone button was created using the dogbone.png image. You can import your own image or create a new image in Flash.

Figure 8.15

```
        pn7.text = rec_array[7].pN;
        ps7.text = rec_array[7].pS;
}
if ( rec_array[8]!=null) {
        pn8.text = rec_array[7].pN;
        ps8.text = rec_array[8].pS;
}
if ( rec_array[9]!=null) {
        pn9.text = rec_array[9].pN;
        ps9.text = rec_array[9].pS;
}
```

```
}

function timedFunction(eventArgs:TimerEvent) {
 var tc:int= 31 - myTimer.currentCount;
 pTime_txt.text = tc.toString();
 if (myTimer.currentCount >30) {
        scr_btn.removeEventListener(MouseEvent.CLICK, incScr);
        myTimer.reset();
        myTimer.stop();
        hs2();
        pa_btn.visible = true;
        cls_btn.visible = true;
        score=0;
        pScore_txt.text = "0";

 }
}
```

Explanation of the Code We first create variables for score, an array (rec_array) to hold the individual scores, and a timer that ticks every 1,000 milliseconds and add an event listener to the timer, which calls a function (timedFunction) at every tick. The timer is started. The visible property of the two buttons (pa_btn and cls_btn) is set to false. The dynamic text box pName_txt is assigned the value from the variable pNam.

The rest of the code is set up as function calls upon button click events. A mouse click event handler is added to the cls_btn, which calls the clearScores function. The clearScores function clears the SharedObject jso2 and takes the player to frame 1.

A mouse click event handler is added to the pa_btn that calls the function restart(). The restart() function starts the timer. It also adds a mouse click event listener to the scr_btn, which in turn calls the incScr function. Finally, the restart() function sets the visible property of the pa_btn and cls_btn to false.

A mouse click event handler is added to the scr_btn (the object that will be clicked), which calls the function incrScr(). The incrScr function positions the object at random x and y positions, which were generated by the random position. The value of the variable score is assigned to the text box pScore_txt.

A variable jso of type SharedObject is created and is assigned the value saved in the local shared object hscr. The shared object has a data property to which objects of type Array, Number, Boolean, ByteArray, or XML can be assigned. In our example jso.data.scrz, the scrz is an array that keeps track of the names and scores of the players. This scrz array is assigned to the variable rec_array.

The function hs2 basically populates the rec_array elements with values and sorts the array in descending order of numeric values. Each element of the rec_array has two fields, name (pN) and score (pS). The push method of the array is used to send the values from the pName._text and pScore_txt text boxes to the pN and pS fields. The jso.flush method is used to write the content of the SharedObject to the local file, which in this case is the array object. An `if` condition is used to check if each element of the array is not equal to null, and the data contained in that element is written to the corresponding text boxes, `pn0` and `ps0`. This process is repeated until the last elements of the array, `[rec_array9].ps` and `rec_array[9].ps`, have been checked, and the data is written to the corresponding text boxes, `pn9` and `ps9`.

The last function is the `timedFunction`, which will be called by the `myTimer` every 1,000 milliseconds, which is the same as one second. This function has the variable `tc` set to 31, which gets decremented every second, the numeric value provided by the `currentCount` (gives the total number of times the timer has fired starting at 0) method of the timer object. This value is displayed to the player in `pTime_txt`, which is a dynamic text box. An `if` condition is used to check if the value of `currentCount` is greater than 30; if true, it does the following tasks: `MouseEventevent.CLICK` is removed from the object so it cannot be clicked anymore, the timer is reset, the timer is stopped, and the `hs2` function is called. The Play Again (`pa_btn`) and Clear Scores (`cls_btn`) buttons are set to false, the score is set to 0, and the text box used to display the score (`pScore_txt`) is also set to 0. That finishes the design and explanation of the code for your high scores game. Test your game, save it, and enjoy it.

Summary

In this chapter we looked at the SharedObject, its purposes, and limitations. We also looked at managing persistent data through a SharedObject. Finally we looked at how to use the SharedObject for keeping track of high scores on an individual computer.

Review Questions

1. What are the purposes of a SharedObject?
2. What are the limitations of a SharedObject?
3. How can you use a SharedObject in a game?
4. What are some types of objects that can be added to the data object in a SharedObject?

Project

1. Use the concepts presented in this chapter and add a SharedObject feature to the game in Chapter 5.
2. Display the high scores for five players.

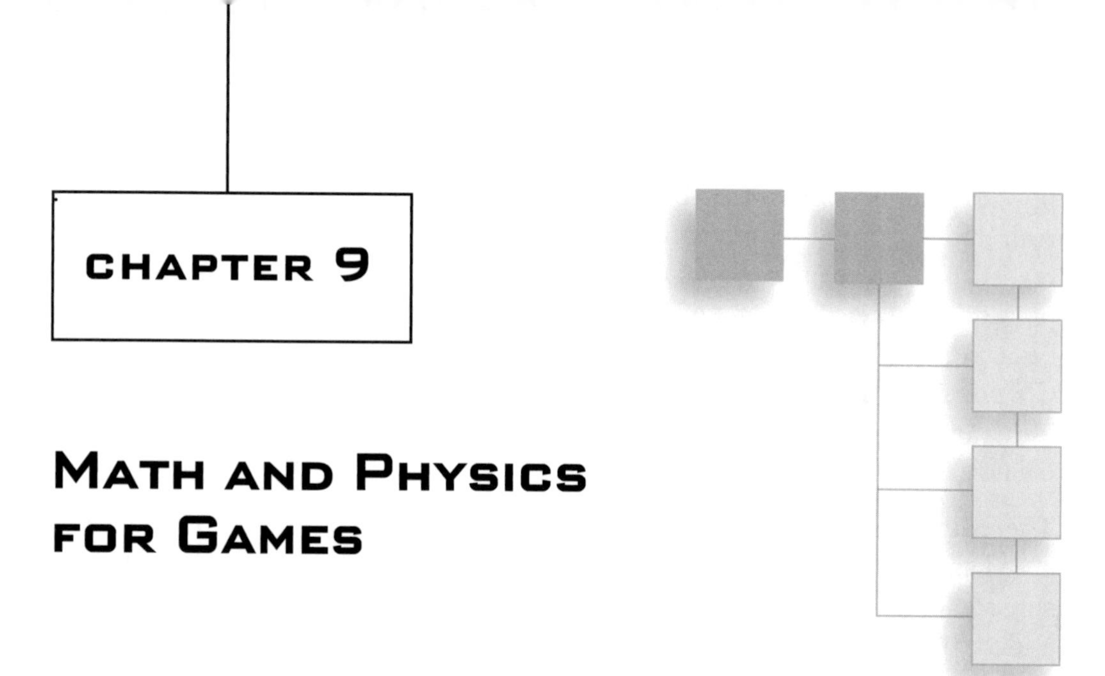

Math and Physics for Games

- Motion
- Displacement
- Speed and Velocity
- Acceleration
- Friction
- Angles
- Trigonometric functions (sine and cosine)
- Detection of keyboard events
- Mouse keys
- Collision with `hitTestPoint`

Realistic Movement

In this chapter, we will design a car racing game. But before we plunge into the design of the game, let us consider a very important aspect of any game. If you have moving objects in a game, they have to move according to the laws of physics and mathematics. If you move them arbitrarily, the motion will not look real, and the game player will quickly catch on to it. The motion has to be realistic, which requires that the design of the motion has to follow the laws of physics. Another requirement is a bit of elementary mathematics, primarily the basics of trigonometry and algebra, to calculate the required quantities. In Chapter 2, we used the most basic ideas of motion. This chapter will extend these ideas to cover the basic concepts in physics and mathematics necessary to calculate elementary aspects of motion.

The main topics that will be discussed in this chapter are motion, displacement, speed and velocity, acceleration, friction, angles, and trigonometric functions of sine and cosine, including how to use these. We will also discuss techniques such as detection of keyboard events, the use of mouse keys to control movie clips, and collision detection with the `hitTestPoint()` function.

How Do Objects Move on the Stage?

Depending on the application, you will need to move objects in different directions and with different speeds. You may want to rotate an object, and you may also want to change the speed of the object (this is called *acceleration*).

In Chapter 2, you learned how to move an object horizontally and vertically on the stage. We will briefly review those concepts and then see how to move the object in any direction.

Position

First, you need to know how you can specify the position of an object on the stage. Movement is then just a change in position.

The position of an object is specified by two numbers. We will use the symbols x and y for these two numbers. In standard notation, this pair of numbers is written (x, y). The meaning of these two numbers is the following:

- Starting from 0 at the left edge of the stage, count how many pixels to the right the object is. This is the number x.
- Starting from 0 at the top edge of the stage, count how many pixels down the object is. This is the number y.

Figure 9.1 shows an example of the position of an object.

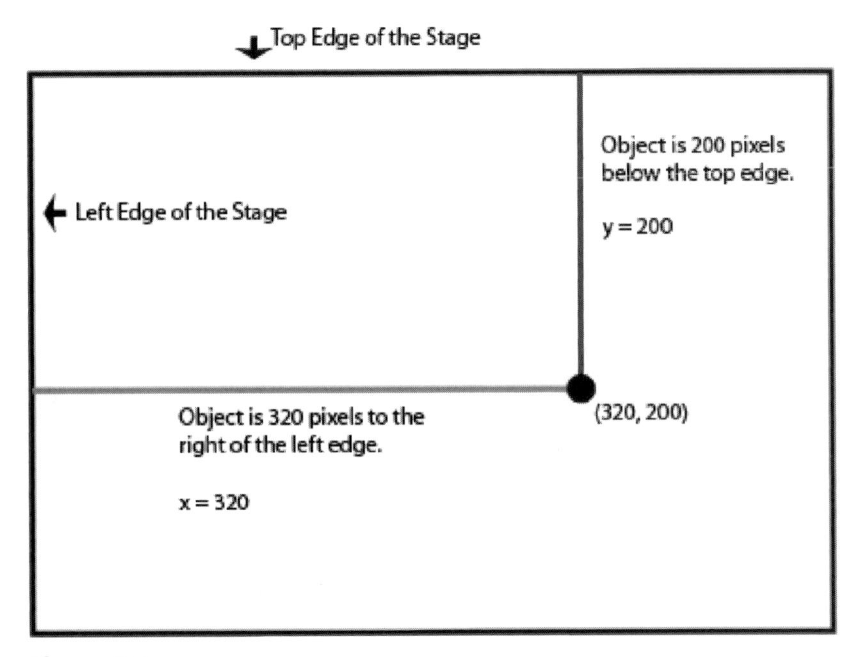

Figure 9.1
Position of an object.

In this example, the position of the object is (320, 200).

Exercise 9.1 will help you to become familiar with the concept of position. This program allows the user to enter the x and y values and move the ball to that position.

Exercise 9.1

1. Open a new Flash document. Create a new symbol of type movie clip. Name it `Ball_MC`. This movie clip should be in the shape of a ball. Drag an instance of the ball to the stage. Give it the instance name `mc_ball`.

2. Add two text boxes of type Input Text. Give one of the boxes an instance name of `getValuex` and the second `getValuey`.

3. Add two static text boxes to serve as labels next to the two input boxes. Type `Enter position X.` and `Enter position Y.` as captions for these boxes.

4. Create a button symbol and name it `Submit_Btn`. Design it however you like. Drag an instance of it to the stage. Give it the instance name `btn_x`. Create a static text box on top of the button instance and type `Submit.` as its caption.

5. In frame 1, open the Actions window and type the following code:

```
function buttonmove(myevent:MouseEvent): void {
```

```
mc_ball.x=Number(getValuex.text);
mc_ball.y=Number(getValuey.text);
}
btn_x.addEventListener(MouseEvent.CLICK,buttonmove);
```

Explanation

Run the movie and observe the position of the ball on the stage, depending on the values entered in the text boxes. You should also enter values outside the stage dimensions. For example, try entering the values -10 for position x and 200 for position y. As in earlier examples, an event listener is added to the button, which when clicked triggers the function `buttonmove()`. The function takes the values for x and y from the text boxes and places the ball in that position. See Figures 9.2 and 9.3 for examples of how this program works. This program will be used in Exercise 9.2, so you should save your work here.

Displacement

To change the position of the object and move it on the stage, you increment (or decrement) the x and y values. Such a change in position is called a *displacement* and will be an x_displacement or a y_displacement, or a combination of both, depending on the direction.

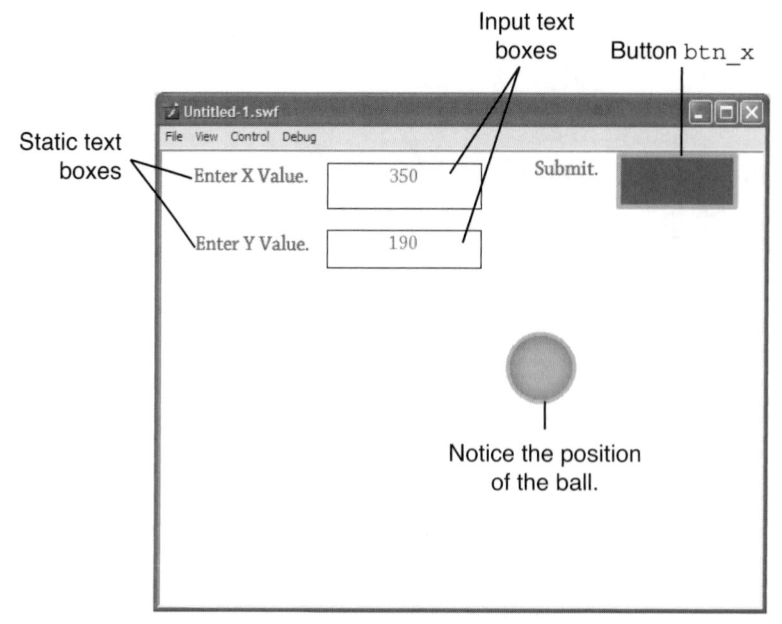

Figure 9.2
Run program.

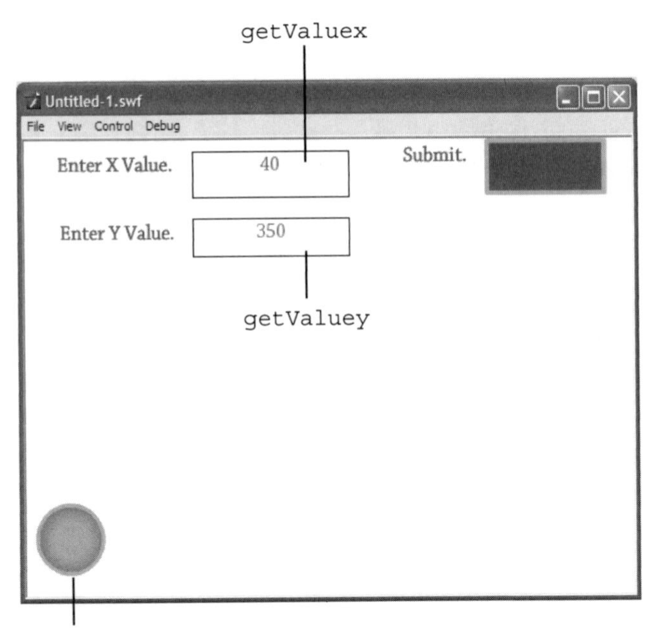

Figure 9.3
Rerun program.

So lines of code like

```
object.x + = 5;
```

move the object to the right by 5 pixels. The x_displacement is 5.

Code like

```
object.x - = 3;
```

moves the object to the left by 3 pixels. The x_displacement is −3.

Code like

```
object.y + = 4;
```

moves the object down by 4 pixels. Remember that y increases downward, starting from 0 at the top of the stage. The y_displacement is 4.

And finally, code like

```
object.y - = 2;
```

moves the object up by 2 pixels. The y_displacement is −2.

Exercise 9.2

ballDisp.fla

For this exercise, we will continue with Exercise 9.1 and extend it. Here, you will enter the displacement of the ball. The ball will move through that displacement, and the new position is displayed.

Change the text of the two static text boxes serving as labels for the input boxes to "Enter X Displacement" and "Enter Y Displacement." Add two dynamic text boxes called posX and posY. Beside these, add static text boxes to serve as labels, with captions "Position X" and "Position Y." The "Submit" button in Exercise 9.1 should be relabeled; the caption on the static text box on the button should read "Displace." Rename the button itself as **btnPos.** At this time, your screen should be similar to Figure 9.4.

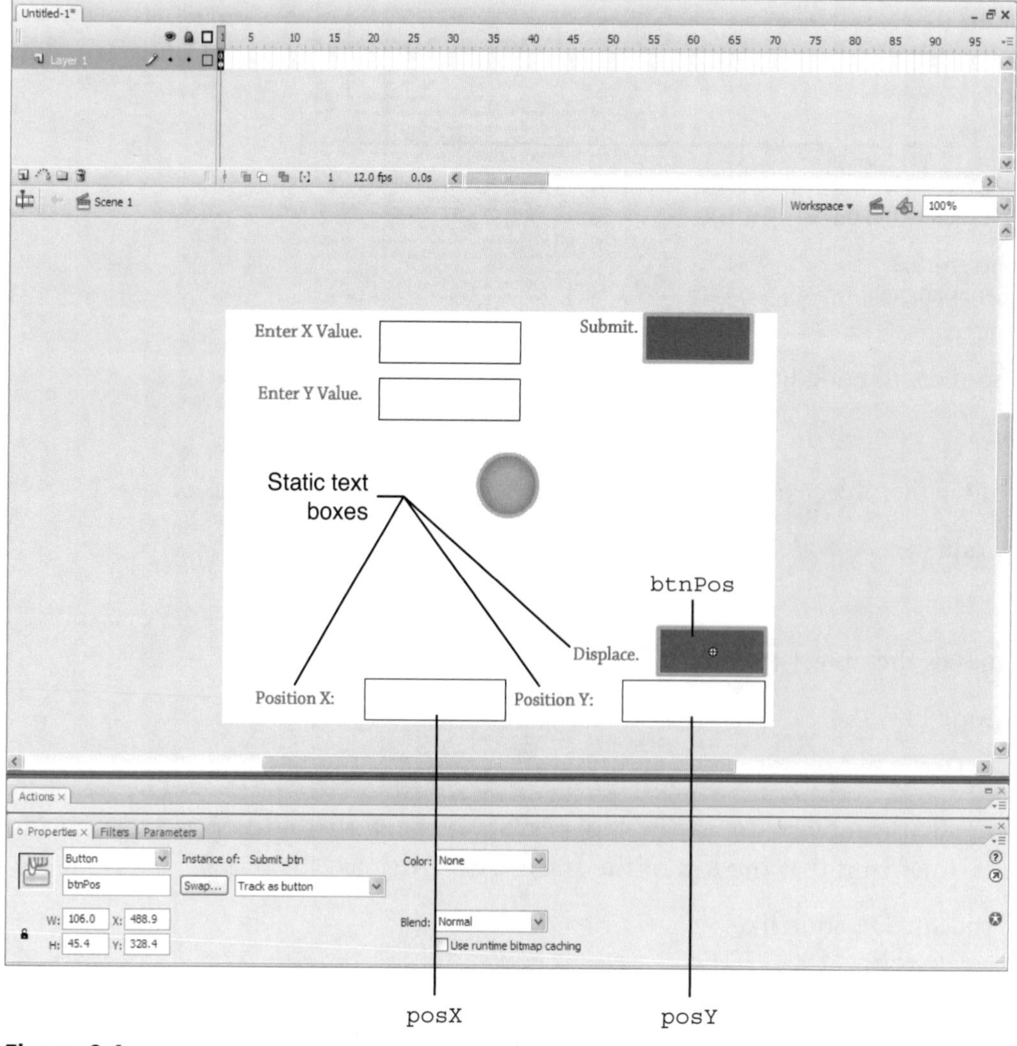

Figure 9.4
Stage with the ball, input boxes, and buttons.

Open the Actions window and type the following code after the previously entered code:

```
function ballPos(myevent:MouseEvent): void {
mc_ball.x += Number(getValuex.text);
mc_ball.y += Number(getValuey.text);
posX.text=String(mc_ball.x);
posY.text=String(mc_ball.y);
}
btnPos.addEventListener(MouseEvent.CLICK, ballPos);
```

Explanation

This example is an extension of Exercise 9.1. It has the addition of two dynamic text boxes, posX and posY. The user inputs displacements. Try it! Start off by entering a small number, such as 10. Press the Displace button. Without changing the value, press the Displace button again. Now experiment with negative numbers. See what happens if you input zero in one or both boxes, and if you enter large numbers such as 500. The program takes these values and moves the ball from its current position according to the displacements entered. Depending on the current position, the ball may not be on the stage!

Moving the Object in Any Direction

So now the question is, if we want to move the object by, say, 5 pixels in a slanted direction, as shown in Figure 9.5, how do we do it?

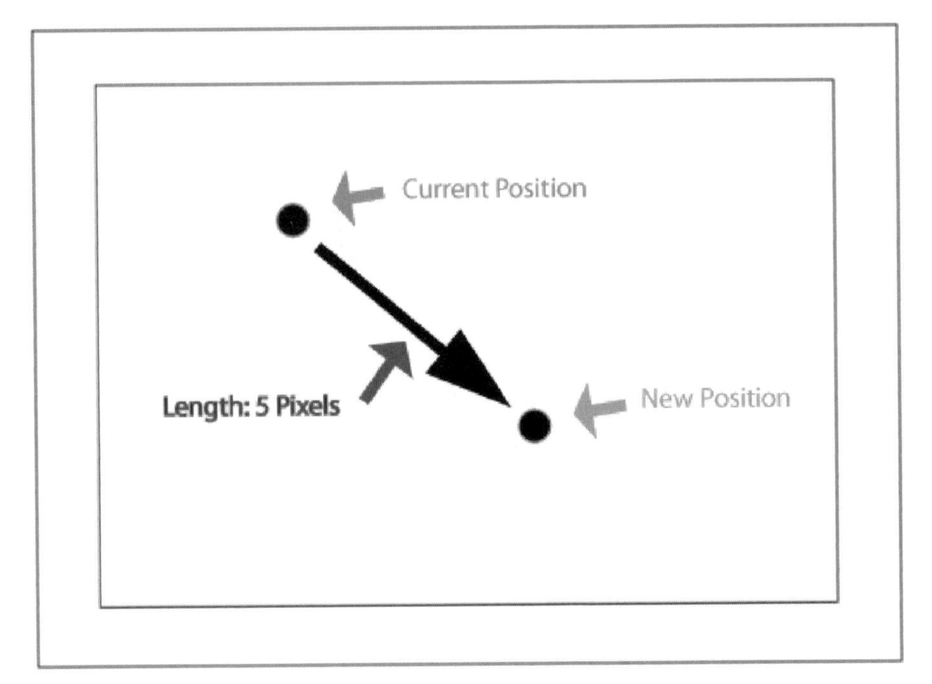

Figure 9.5
Slanted movement.

Once we answer this question, we will be able to simulate different types of motion of objects. If we want to simulate continuous movement of objects, these displacements should occur in every frame of a movie. The concepts of speed and velocity, which are fundamental concepts in physics used to describe motion, are critical at this stage.

Speed

The speed of an object is simply how fast it moves. Continuous movement on the stage is simulated by moving the object a certain number of pixels per frame. So the x_ and y_ displacements that we looked at in the previous section can be used to specify the speed. You use the same code in the `onEnterFrame()` event.

Relation Between Speed and Frames per Second (fps): Suppose you want to move an object in the horizontal (x) direction at a speed of 100 pixels per second (pps). Depending on the fps, you will need to displace the object a certain number of pixels per frame (ppf). If the fps is 20, then a ppf of 5 will produce the desired result. If the fps is 10, then you need 10 ppf. In general then, the speed of the object in pps is related to the ppf, and the fps is:

$$\text{pps} = \text{ppf} \times \text{fps}$$

Once the fps is fixed, the ppf becomes the measure of the speed.

Velocity

The velocity of an object is its speed along with the direction. For example, if we say that an object is moving 5 pixels per frame, we have specified the speed. We have not stated the direction of movement. If we state the direction also and say, for example, that the object is moving 3 pixels per frame in the downward (or +y) direction, we specify the velocity. In the parlance of physics and mathematics, velocity is a vector quantity, which needs both magnitude (how fast) and direction (which way) to be specified completely. Speed is a scalar, the specification of which requires only the magnitude (how fast) of the velocity, without the information of direction.

Velocity in any direction is a combination of velocities in the x and y directions. In our discussions, we will use `vel_x` for velocity in the horizontal (x) direction and `vel_y` for velocity in the vertical (y) direction. `vel_x` is called the x-component, and `vel_y` is called the y-component of the velocity. If the value of `vel_x` is positive,

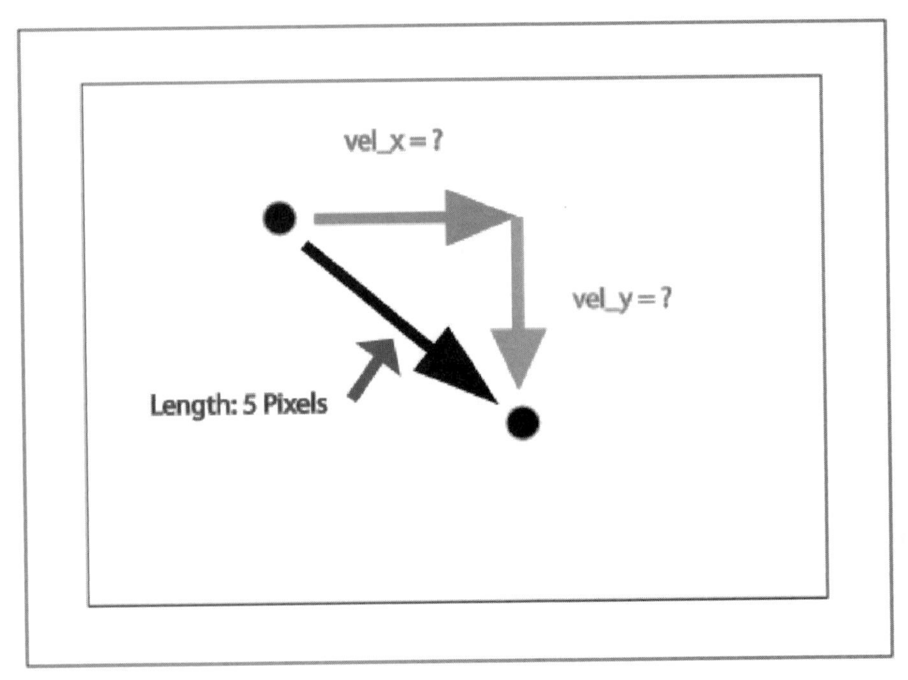

Figure 9.6
Finding the distance.

the object will move to the right. If it is negative, it will move to the left. If the value of `vel_y` is positive, the object will move down. If it is negative, it will move up.

What we should do is to figure out how many pixels in the horizontal direction (`vel_x`) and how many pixels in the vertical direction (`vel_y`) together make up the 5 pixels in the slanted direction. See Figure 9.6.

We need the following pieces of information to be able to calculate the x_ and y_ velocities:

1. How many pixels is the movement? In the example in Figure 9.6, this is 5 pixels.
2. What is the direction of the movement? This raises the question, how do we specify the direction?

Figure 9.7 shows one way to specify the direction of movement, by giving the angle between the line of motion and the vertical. The angle is positive if the line

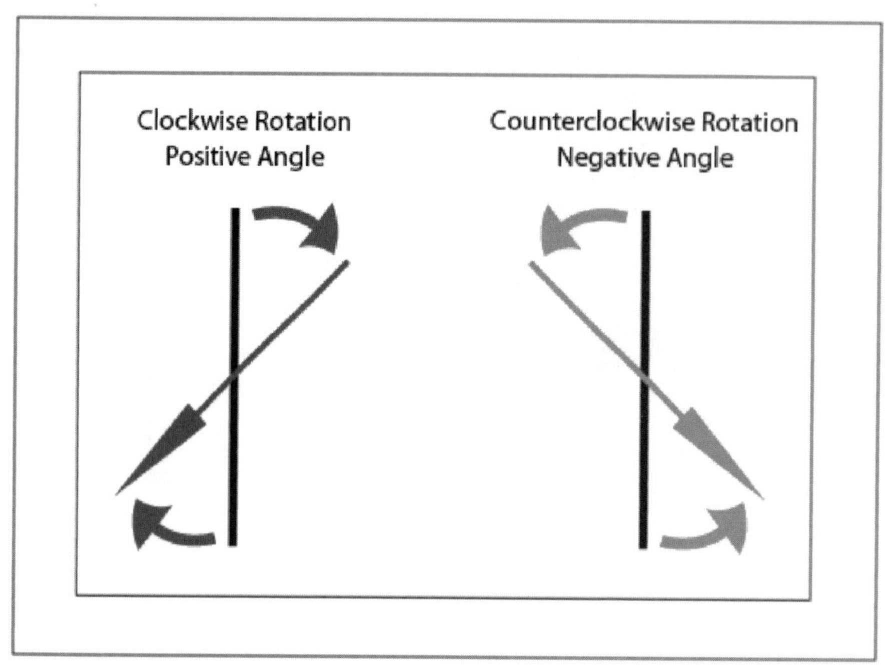

Figure 9.7
Finding the angle.

of motion is rotated clockwise from the vertical and negative if it is rotated counterclockwise from the vertical. This is how it is done in Flash. The vertical direction is taken as zero degrees, and any other direction is specified by the angle it makes with the vertical.

So, supposing we say that we want the object to move 5 pixels in a direction given by -12 degrees (that is along the dotted line rotated 12° counterclockwise from the vertical), how do we calculate `vel_x` and `vel_y`, which results in such a slanted velocity?

A Bit of Trigonometry In order to deal with the calculations, we need to know a little bit about right triangles:

- A right triangle is a triangle with one of its interior angles equal to 90 degrees.
- The side opposite the right angle is called the hypotenuse.
- The Pythagorean theorem: The square of the length of the hypotenuse is equal to the sum of the squares of the lengths of the other two sides.

For example, supposing the two sides forming the right angle are 3 units and 4 units (the units could be inches, miles, or pixels, it does not matter). It follows from the Pythagorean theorem that the hypotenuse must be of length 5 units, since

$$3^2 + 4^2 = 5^2$$

Our use of the properties of right triangles depends on the following property of all vector quantities:

- A vector and its x- and y-components can be represented by the sides of a right triangle. The length of each side is proportional to the magnitude of the corresponding vector.

Let us look at a particular example of a velocity vector. Suppose `vel_x` is 4 ppf, and `vel_y` is 3 ppf. The three vectors, velocity, `vel_x`, and `vel_y` (remember, each has a magnitude and direction, and is therefore a vector) are represented by the sides of a right triangle. The horizontal side of the triangle could be chosen to be 40 pixels on the screen, or 40 mm on a piece of pape, the vertical side 30 pixels on the screen or 30 mm on paper. The third side of the triangle (by the Pythagorean theorem) will be 50 pixels on the screen or 50 mm on pape, and will represent, in magnitude and direction, the 5 ppf velocity in the correct slanted direction. The proportionality between the length of each side and the magnitude of the velocity in that direction is very important. (Remember that the magnitude of the velocity is the speed.)

Now back to figures 9.6 and 9.7 where we have a velocity of 5 ppf (or a displacement of 5 pixels), slanted at – 12 degrees to the vertical. We again represent the velocity, `vel_x`, and `vel_y` by the sides of a right triangle.

Caution: Every 5 ppf velocity will not be equal to the combination of a `vel_x` = 4 ppf and a `vel_y` = 3 ppf! That is so only for a particular direction.

This is important and worth repeating: The velocity is the side of the triangle that is opposite the right angle; it is called the *hypotenuse* of the triangle. The length of the hypotenuse is proportional to the speed (so many pixels per frame).

`vel_y` is along the vertical, so the angle of –12 degrees that we specified is the angle between the `vel_y` and the hypotenuse. We will call this the *rotation angle.* Note carefully the correspondence between the sides of the triangle and the velocities:

- The hypotenuse represents the velocity. Its length is proportional to the magnitude of the velocity (which is the speed).

- The side of the triangle *opposite* the rotation angle represents `vel_x`.
- The side *adjacent* to the rotation angle represents `vel_y`.

Trigonometry is a subject that relates the lengths of the sides of a right triangle to the angles.

For example, look at this relation:

$$\texttt{Math.cos(rotation\_angle)} = \frac{adjacent\ side}{hypotenuse} = \frac{\texttt{vel\_y}}{speed}$$

In this relation, the built-in function `Math.cos()` takes the `rotation_angle` as a parameter and returns a value. That value is equal to `vel_y` divided by the speed.

So, if we have the `rotation_angle` (in our example, −12 degrees) and the speed (in our example, 5 pixels) plus the value of `Math.cos(rotation_angle)`, which is given by the `Math.package` in ActionScript 3.0, we can calculate `vel_y`.

There is just one more, small wrinkle. We gave the `rotation_angle` in degrees, but the `Math.cos()` function takes as a parameter the angle in radians. The conversion from degrees to radians is done automatically by another function in the `Math.package`:

$$\texttt{rotation\_angle}(\text{in radians}) = \texttt{rotation\_angle}(\text{in degrees}) * \frac{Math.PI}{180}$$

So the complete relation with the `Math.cos()` function is:

$$Math.\cos\left(rotation\_angle * \frac{Math.PI}{180}\right) = \frac{vel\_y}{speed}$$

So vel_y is given by

$$vel\_y = speed * Math.\cos\left(rotation\_angle * \frac{Math.PI}{180}\right)$$

Similarly `vel_x` is calculated using the `Math.sin()` function:

$$vel\_x = -speed * Math.\sin\left(rotation\_angle * \frac{Math.PI}{180}\right)$$

Note the minus sign in front of the value for `vel_x`. It is necessary to accommodate the sign convention for angles that Flash uses.

Exercise 9.3

ballVelocity. This exercise describes the ideas of speed and velocity. You will practice giving values to speed and direction and become familiar with their manipulations. That will be important in the design of the car racing game that follows. Again, we use a similar interface as in Exercise 9.1 to get user input and manipulate the ball with those values.

Activities for Frame 1.

1. Open a new Flash document. Create a movie clip symbol of a ball and name it `MC_ball`. Drag an instance of the ball to the stage. Give it the instance name `ball_mc`.
2. As in Exercise 9.1, create two instances of input text boxes and name them `getValuex` and `getValuey`. Create two instances of static text boxes and give them the captions `Angle` and `Velocity`.
3. Create a button symbol and drag it to the stage. Name it `buttonPos`. Create a static text box to identify the button. Make the caption `Submit`. Your screen should now match Figure 9.8.
4. Type the following code into the Actions pane of frame 1:

```
stop();
var speed: Number;
var angle: Number;

function buttonClick(myevent:MouseEvent): void {
      angle=Number(getValuex.text);
      speed=Number(getValuey.text);
      gotoAndStop(2);
}

btnPos.addEventListener(MouseEvent.CLICK,buttonClick);
```

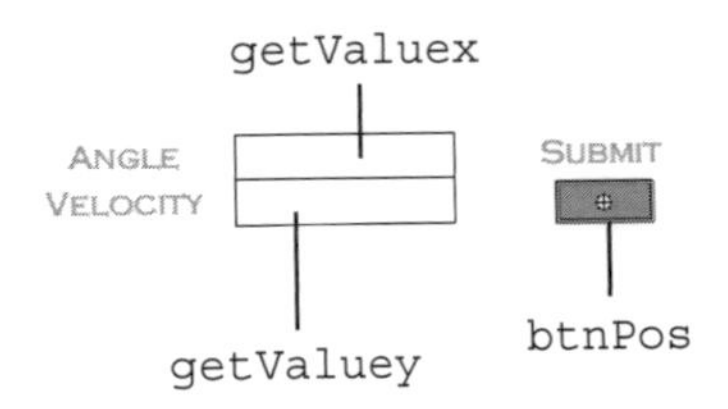

Figure 9.8
Frame 1 layout.

Activities for Frame 2

1. Right-click frame 2 and insert a keyframe.
2. Type the following code in frame 2:

```
ball_mc.addEventListener(Event.ENTER_FRAME, moveball);
function moveball(myevent:Event):void {
        ball_mc.y + = Math.cos(angle*Math.PI/180) * speed;
        ball_mc.x - = Math.sin(angle*Math.PI/180) * speed;
}
```

Explanation

Exercise 9.3 shows you how to move the ball in any direction with any speed. Exercise 9.2 only showed you how to move the ball in x and y directions. In Exercise 9.3, the program first prompts the user for input and then proceeds to frame 2. Frame 2 moves the ball by calculating the x and y displacements using trigonometry as explained earlier.

Rotating an Object

If you are moving a round object, then what we did up to now covers everything about velocity. But if you want to move an object with a shape (such as a car object) in a particular direction, you must first rotate the car so that it is facing in that direction. You saw how to rotate an object in Chapter 2. The code is simple. If you have `car1_mc` as the instance of a car object on the stage, use `car1_mc.rotation += 10;` to rotate the car clockwise through 10 degrees and `car1_mc.rotation -= 5;` to rotate it counterclockwise through 5 degrees.

The current value of `car1_mc.rotation` will give you the angle at which the car is oriented relative to the vertical. You would want to move the car precisely in that direction, so the same angle should be used to calculate `vel_x` and `vel_y`, as explained earlier.

Example Let us start with the car oriented vertically. In this orientation, its rotation angle with the vertical is 0 degrees. Now if we want the car to move 10 pixels in each frame, at an angle of 12 degrees to the vertical, we first orient the car in that direction and declare our speed:

```
car1_mc.rotation += 12;

speed: Number=10;
```

Then we calculate vel_x and vel_y using our formulas:

$$vel\_x = -speed * Math.\sin\left(car1\_mc.rotation * \frac{Math.PI}{180}\right);$$

$$vel\_y = speed * Math.\cos\left(car1\_mc.rotation * \frac{Math.PI}{180}\right);$$

Then in the Enter_Frame event, we just increment the x and y values of the position of the car:

```
car1_mc.x += vel_x;
car1_mc.y += vel_y;
```

That does the job for us.

Acceleration

Of course, we cannot always have objects moving with the same speed. We will have cases where the speed (or velocity) changes, and that is where acceleration comes into the picture.

Acceleration is a change in velocity per unit of time. Acceleration is produced by forces acting on the object. We are not interested here in explicitly dealing with the forces. We deal with acceleration, which results from the forces. On the stage, acceleration is simulated by changing the velocity in each frame. In the simplest case, if an object is moving in a straight line, acceleration results in a change in speed. But in general, acceleration, like velocity, has a direction, and so there is an x_ and a y_ component of acceleration. We will call them accel_x and accel_y. These values affect only the corresponding components of velocity.

Here, we will deal with objects moving in straight lines only, so the algorithm for accelerated motion (in a straight line) is:

1. Give current values to position, velocity (speed and direction), and acceleration.
2. The following must be done in the Enter_Frame event for the object (car or ball or any other object)
   a. Calculate vel_x, vel_y.
   b. Increment x with vel_x and y with vel_y.
   c. Increment speed with acceleration.

Friction

Friction is a force that always opposes motion. It always results in an acceleration that reduces the speed. You can simulate friction by giving a negative value to acceleration, but be careful! When the car slows down to zero speed because of friction, the acceleration due to friction should also be set to zero; otherwise the object will start speeding up in the opposite direction, which never happens with friction.

Exercise 9.4 covers the concepts of rotation, acceleration, and friction. carAccel.fla has a car object that is rotated to face the direction of movement. The angle of rotation, the speed, and the acceleration are entered as numerical values. Friction is treated as a constant value in the code, and the user can only choose between the presence and the absence of friction by entering Y/N in the input box for friction. The code in frame 1 collects the user input and advances to frame 2. The code in frame 2 follows the Algorithm for accelerated motion in a straight line to calculate and update values of position and velocity in each frame.

Note

Note that friction results in acceleration. In principle, there is no difference between acceleration due to friction or any other force, except that friction on a moving object, called *kinetic friction,* is present only when the object is moving. If friction is present, then the code simulates the presence of friction by decrementing the speed, as friction would. If the speed reduces to zero, or to a small value (we chose `0.1` in the code), there is no friction.

To clearly understand the effects of friction, first set the acceleration to `0`, set the speed to some value, say `5`, and then set friction to `Y`. You will see that the car just slows down and stops because of friction. Now, set friction to `N`, and set acceleration to a negative value, say `–0.2`. The car will again slow down, similar to what happens with friction, but when it stops, the acceleration is still there, and this results in the car starting to move and picking up speed in the opposite direction. This is the correct behavior and shows the real difference between acceleration due to friction and acceleration due to other (constant) forces.

So go ahead and have fun with the code in Exercise 9.4

Exercise 9.4

Activities for Frame 1

1. Look at Figure 9.9. Set up your stage with four input boxes, labels, a button, and a car, so that it is similar to the setup in the figure. Name the input text boxes as `getAngle`, `getAccel`, `getSpeed`, and `getFriction`.

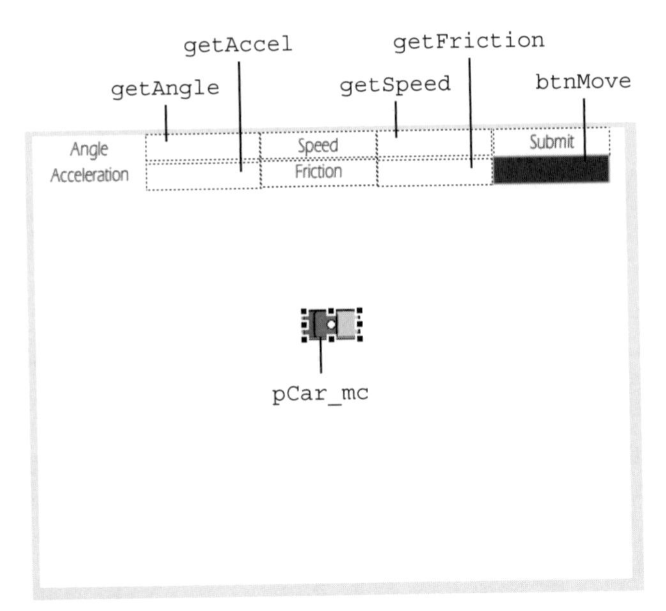

Figure 9.9
Rough layout.

2. Name the button instance btnMove.

3. Add a movie clip and name it MC_car. Drag an instance to the stage and name it pCar_mc.

4. Click on frame 1 and type the following code in the Actions frame:

```
stop();
var angle: Number;
var speed: Number;
var accel: Number;
var friction: String;
function buttonClick(myevent:MouseEvent): void {
        pCar_mc.rotation=Number(getAngle.text);
        speed=Number(getSpeed.text);
        accel=Number(getAccel.text);
        friction=getFriction.text;
        gotoAndStop(2);
}
btnMove.addEventListener(MouseEvent.CLICK,buttonClick);
```

Activities for Frame 2 Right-click on frame 2 and insert a keyframe in it. Type the following code into frame 2's Actions pane:

```
pCar_mc.addEventListener(Event.ENTER_ FRAME, moveCar);
```

```
function moveCar(myevent:Event):void {
        pCar_mc.y += Math.cos(pCar_mc.rotation*Math.PI/180) * speed;
        pCar_mc.x -= Math.sin(pCar_mc.rotation*Math.PI/180) * speed;
        speed += accel;
        if ((friction == "Y" ) && (speed > 0.1)) {
                speed -= 0.1;
        }
}
```

Exercise 9.5

Car Racing Game Car racing games are very exciting. In this exercise, we look at how to create such a game with Flash. We follow the game development process discussed in earlier chapters, starting with the design phase, followed by game development and coding and, last, the testing phase.

The new method used in this game is the `hitTestPoint()`. You have already used the `hitTestObject()` method in earlier chapters. The `hitTestObject()` method returns a true value if the two objects in the given instance collide with one another; the `hitTestPoint()` method returns a true value if the display object intersects with a specified point given by the x and y parameters. In the car racing game we use both these methods. The player car works with the `hitTestObject()` method, and the computer-controlled car works with the `hitTestPoint()` method.

Phase One: Design. The design phase consists of creating the story line, the storyboard, and the game pieces. These are discussed next.

Story Line. The car racing game does not have a formal story. The game has two cars—a player car and a computer car—that race with each other. The goal is to win against the computer car. The game displays a winning message at the end. One additional feature included in the game is the ability to set the computer car's speed at run time.

Storyboard. The storyboard for this game is that we have a racetrack on which the two cars can race against each other. The racetrack has different markers similar to laps to keep track of the lap that was completed. In this game there are four markers that must all be completed sequentially to win the game. In addition, the game also has a boundary for the racetrack to make sure that the car is on the track, not out of the track, at all times. The game allows the player car to be controlled by the arrow keys for speed and direction and introduces friction and acceleration when necessary.

Game Pieces. The game pieces (all the graphics and sound files) required for the game are:

- Game assets—pieces for the game (game design phase)
- Game assets—sound files to be played throughout the game (game design phase)
- Instructions to the user (game development phase)

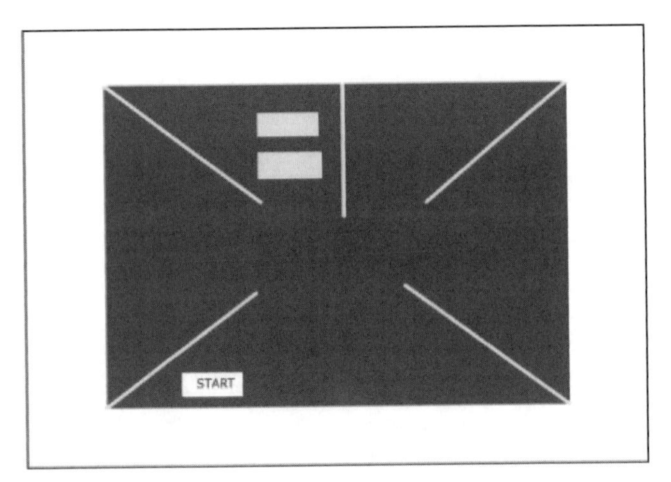

Figure 9.10
A rough layout.

- Display message (game development phase)
- Option to play again or quit (game development phase)

Figure 9.10 is a rough sketch of the game.

Phase Two: Game Development and Code. The big picture for this game is that we have a player car and a computer car. The car race starts once the Start button is pressed. The computer car has a constant speed determined by the speed entered into an input box by the player. It is also programmed to turn appropriately once it hits the marker on the race track. If the computer car reaches the finish line before the player car, then the computer car wins the race. The player car starts at a speed and accelerates if the up arrow or down arrow is pressed. The program checks to see if the speed reaches a set limit; if it does, the speed is decreased by a certain amount. The left arrow and right arrow keys are programmed to rotate the car by a certain amount to allow the player to turn the car at the lap marks on the race track. As long as the car is on the land (race track), it can move; if the car is outside the race track, the movement of the car is disabled. If the car collides with each of the four markers and reaches the finish line before the computer car, the player car wins. Figure 9.11 provides a logic flow of the game.

For this game, we have three layers: the Instructions layer, Competing Cars layer, and Game and Actions layer. Instructions to create these layers follow.

Activity for Layer 1, Frame 1: Creating the Instructions Scene. This is the introduction scene to your game. It will have the title of your game, the instructions to the user on how to play the game, the rules of the game, and a button to start the game. Here are the instructions to create this scene:

1. Open a new Flash document.

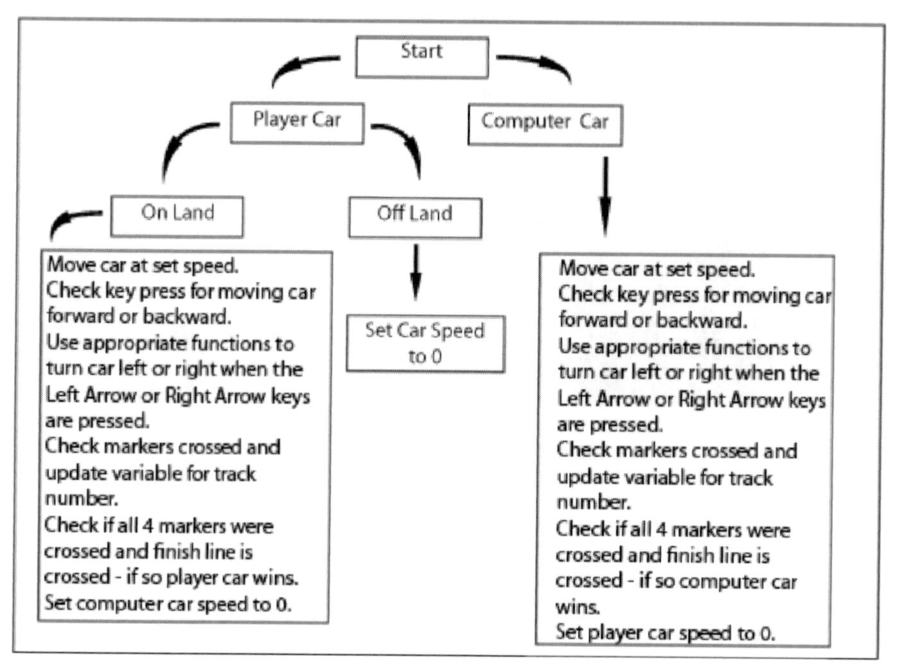

Figure 9.11
Logic flow.

2. Create a movie clip for the racetrack, similar to Figure 9.12. Name it `MC_Track`. It is important to make your track as close as possible to the figure. What we mean by this is that you should have the two black rectangles that serve as boundary markers (of course you can use what ever color you like), but these rectangles should have no fill in them. If you want to design a more attractive track, you can do that so long as you make sure that there is no fill.

3. Click on Scene 1 and drag an instance of the racetrack to the stage. Give it the instance name `land`.

4. Create a movie clip for the finish line, similar to Figure 9.13. Name it `MC_finishline`.

5. Click on Scene 1 and drag an instance of the finish line to the stage. Give it the instance name `finish`. Your stage should now be similar to Figure 9.14. This completes layer 1.

Activity for Layer 2, Frame 1: Creating the Player and Computer Cars. In this scene, the two cars—the player car and the computer car—must be designed. You can either draw your own cars or import some images that you like to the library and convert them to movie clips. To create your own cars, follow these instructions:

1. Insert a new layer and type `cars` for the layer name.

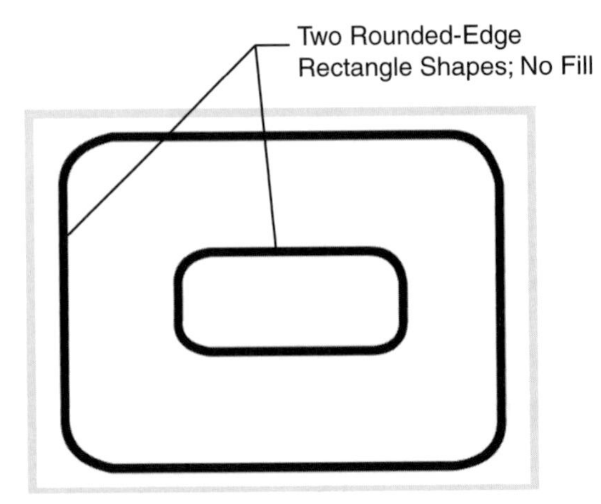

Figure 9.12
The racetrack.

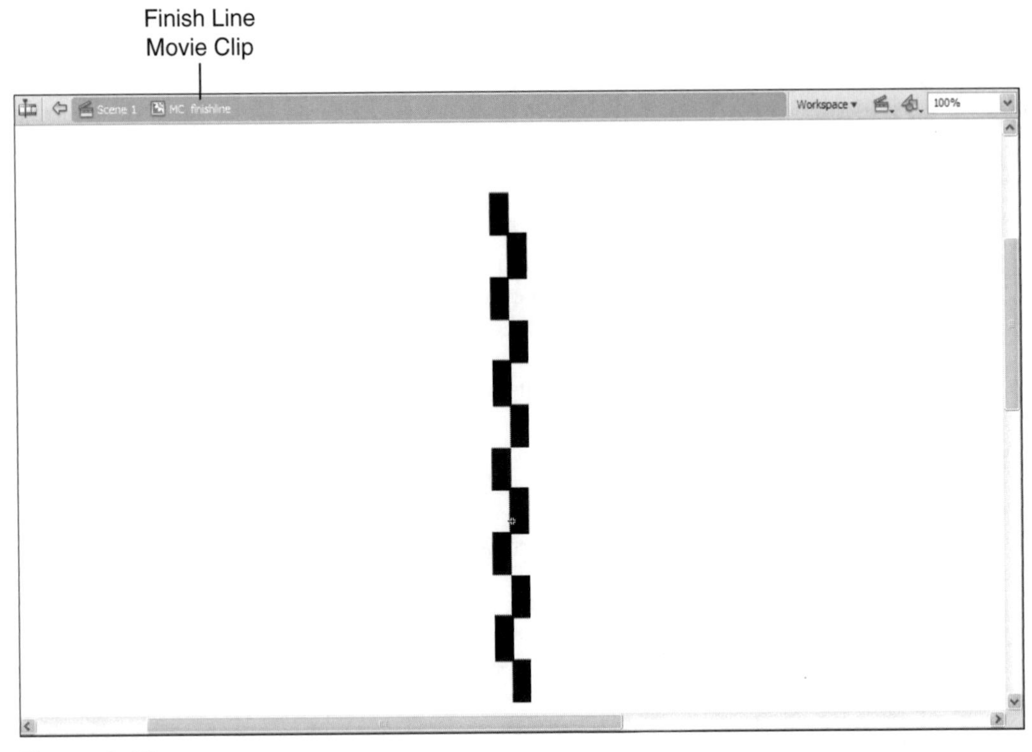

Figure 9.13
The finish line.

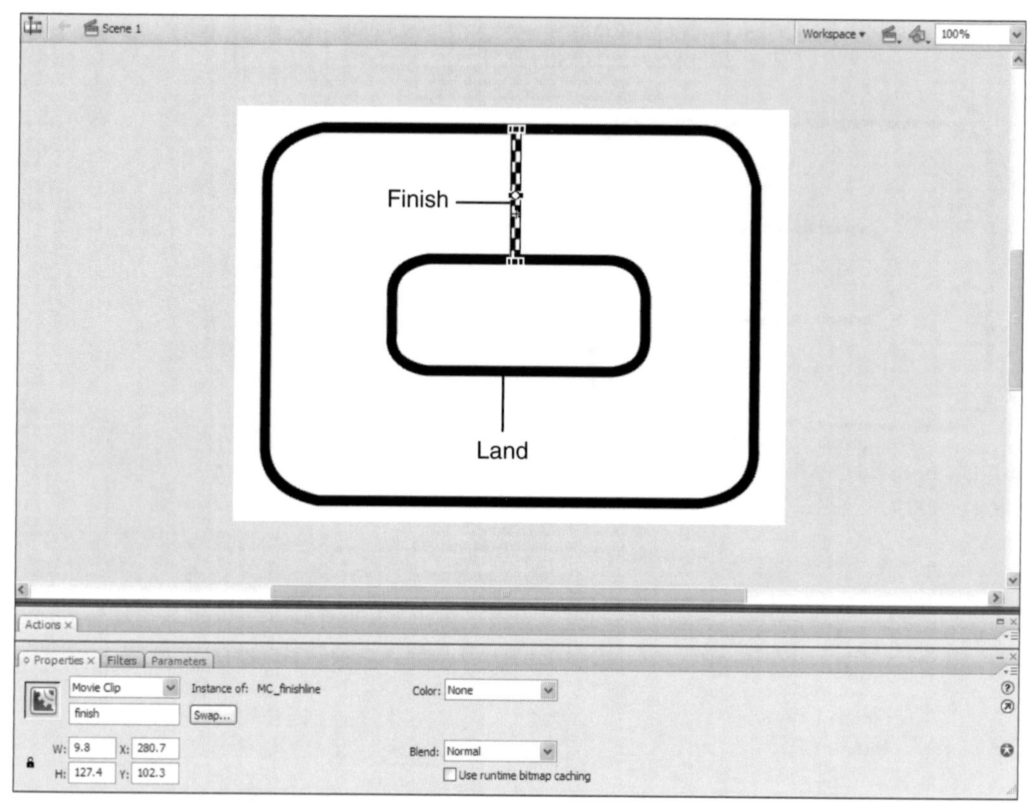

Figure 9.14
The stage with the finish line.

2. To create the computer car, click on Insert, New Symbol, choose Movie Clip, and name it `MC_CompCar`. When creating the car, you need to design it from the perspective above the car. Also, it is important that the length of the car runs vertically. See Figure 9.15 for details. Go back to Scene 1.

3. Follow the same procedure to create the player car. Name it `MC_PlayCar`. Go back to Scene 1.

4. Drag an instance of `MC_PlayCar` and `MC_CompCar` to the stage. See Figure 9.16.

5. Name the computer car instance `cCar_mc` and the player car `pCar_mc`.

6. Rotate both instances of cars 90 degrees clockwise.

7. You also need to adjust their horizontal positions. Select `cCar_mc` and in the Properties panel, set the x position to `277`. Repeat this for `pCar_mc`.

This completes the activities for the Cars layer.

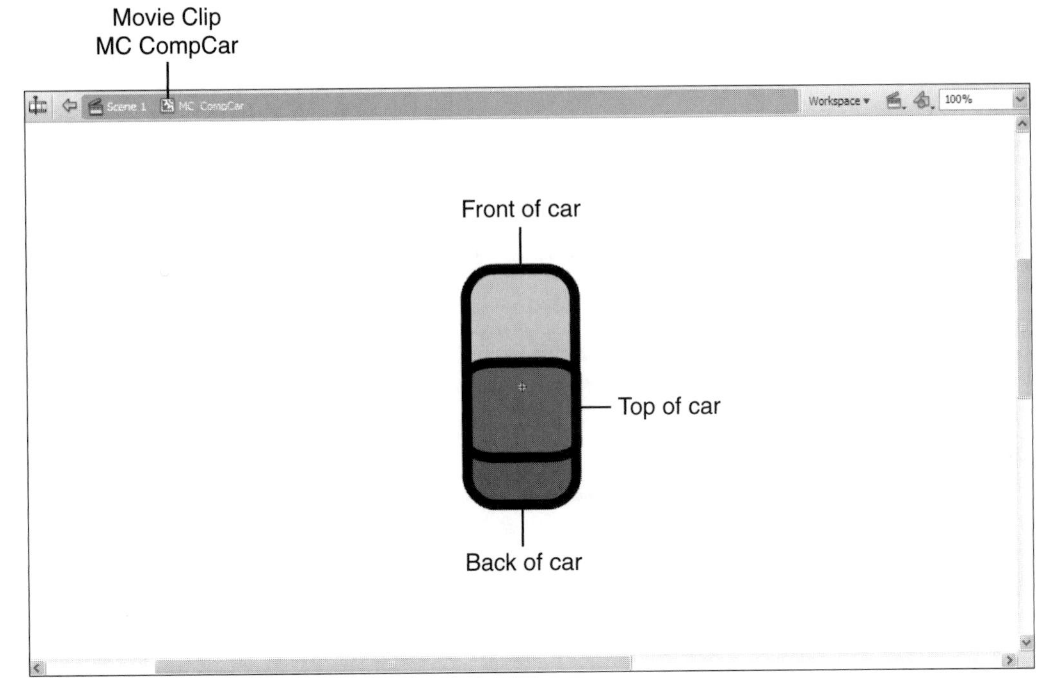

Figure 9.15
The computer car.

Activity for Layer 3, Frame 1: Creating the Laps, Buttons, Display Box, and Code. This is the crucial scene, where all the action takes place. The lap markers required for the race track, the buttons to start and restart the game, the display box, and the code are all included in this layer. So let's get started.

1. Insert a new layer and type `actions` for the layer name.

2. Click on Insert, New Symbol, choose Movie Clip as the type of the symbol, and type `lap1` as the symbol name. Draw a slanted line (see Figure 9.17). Go back to Scene 1.

3. Repeat step 2 to create three more symbols for the other three laps, which will be placed on the stage. Name these symbols `lap2`, `lap3`, and `lap4`, respectively. Make sure you go back to Scene 1.

4. Drag an instance of each of the four lap movie clips and place them on the stage, as in Figure 9.18. Provide the instance names `t1`, `t2`, `t3`, and `t4`, respectively, for each of these laps. It is important to line up the lap markers exactly as they are in the figure. A misaligned lap marker could prevent the computer car from moving.

5. Click on Insert, New Symbol and create a button. Name it `Button`. Choose any shape and color you like. Go back to Scene 1.

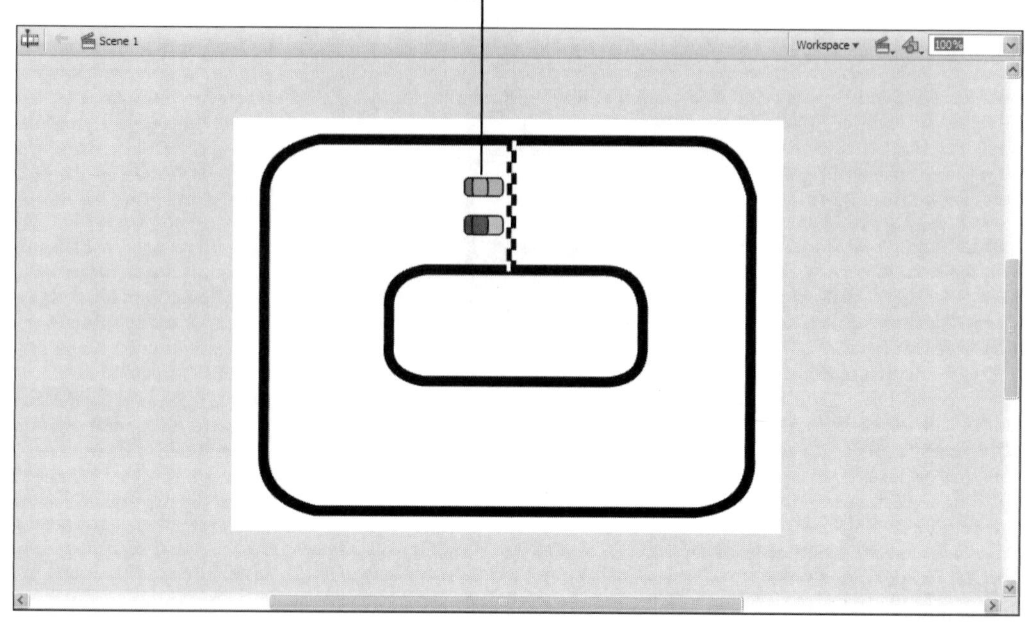

In the movie clips, the cars are vertical. In Scene 1, the instances of both cars have been rotated. That is important to remember.
Scene 1
Workspace
100%

Figure 9.16
The stage with cars.

6. Drag an instance of the button to the bottom of the stage. Give it the instance name `start_btn`. Drag an instance of a static text box next to the button. Write `Start` in it.

7. Drag another instance of this button to the stage. Give it the instance name `restart_btn`. Drag an instance of a static text box next to this button and type `Play Again` in it.

8. Drag an instance of a static text box and type `Set Computer Speed`.

9. Right next to this box, drag an instance of an input text box. Give it the instance name `compSpeed_txt`.

10. Drag an instance of a dynamic text box to the middle of the track. Give it the instance name `message_txt`. In the caption field of this text box, type `5`. This will set a default value for the computer car. When the game starts, the player can then change the speed. Your screen should now match Figure 9.19.

This completes the GUI for the game. Click on frame 1 of the Actions layer and type the following code:

```
// Declare all variables
```

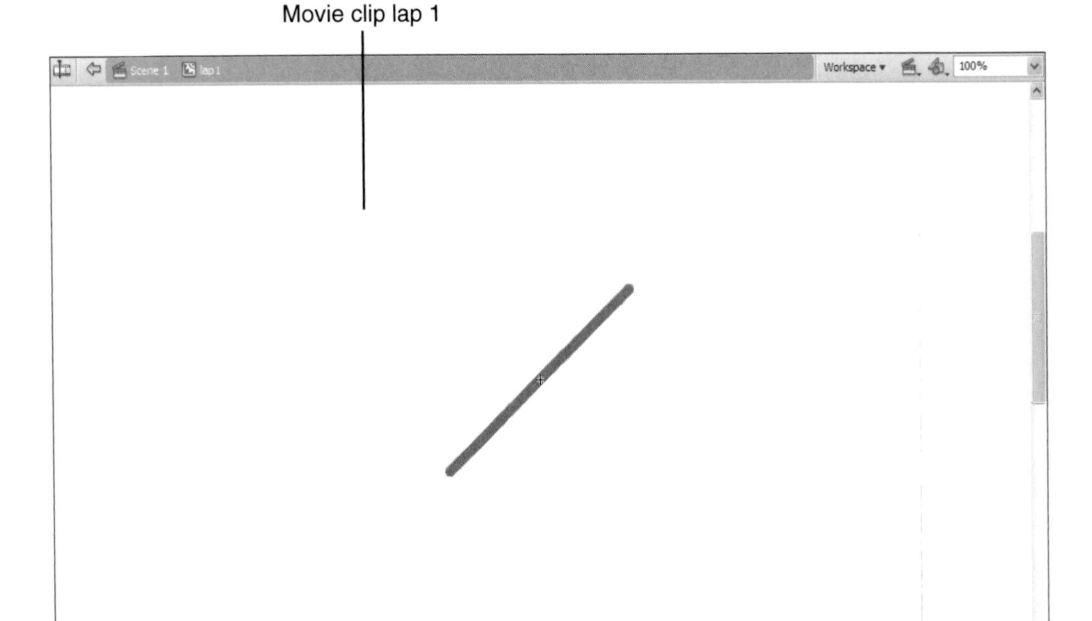

Figure 9.17
Lap movie clip.

```
var speed:Number=0;
var chkPath:Number=0;
var cchkPath:Number=0;
var finishRace:Boolean=false;
var startRace:Boolean=false;
var compCarSpeed:Number=Number(compSpeed_txt.text);
var speedDecay:Number =0.96;
var backSpeed:Number=1;
stage.addEventListener(KeyboardEvent.KEY_DOWN, keyPressed);
stage.addEventListener(KeyboardEvent.KEY_UP, keyReleased);
stage.addEventListener(Event.DEACTIVATE, clearKeys);
var keysDown:Object=new Object();

// function to record key code for key while being pressed
function isDown(keyCode:uint):Boolean {
      return Boolean(keyCode in keysDown);
}
function keyPressed(event:KeyboardEvent):void {
      // create a property in keysDown with the name of the keyCode
      keysDown[event.keyCode]=true;
```

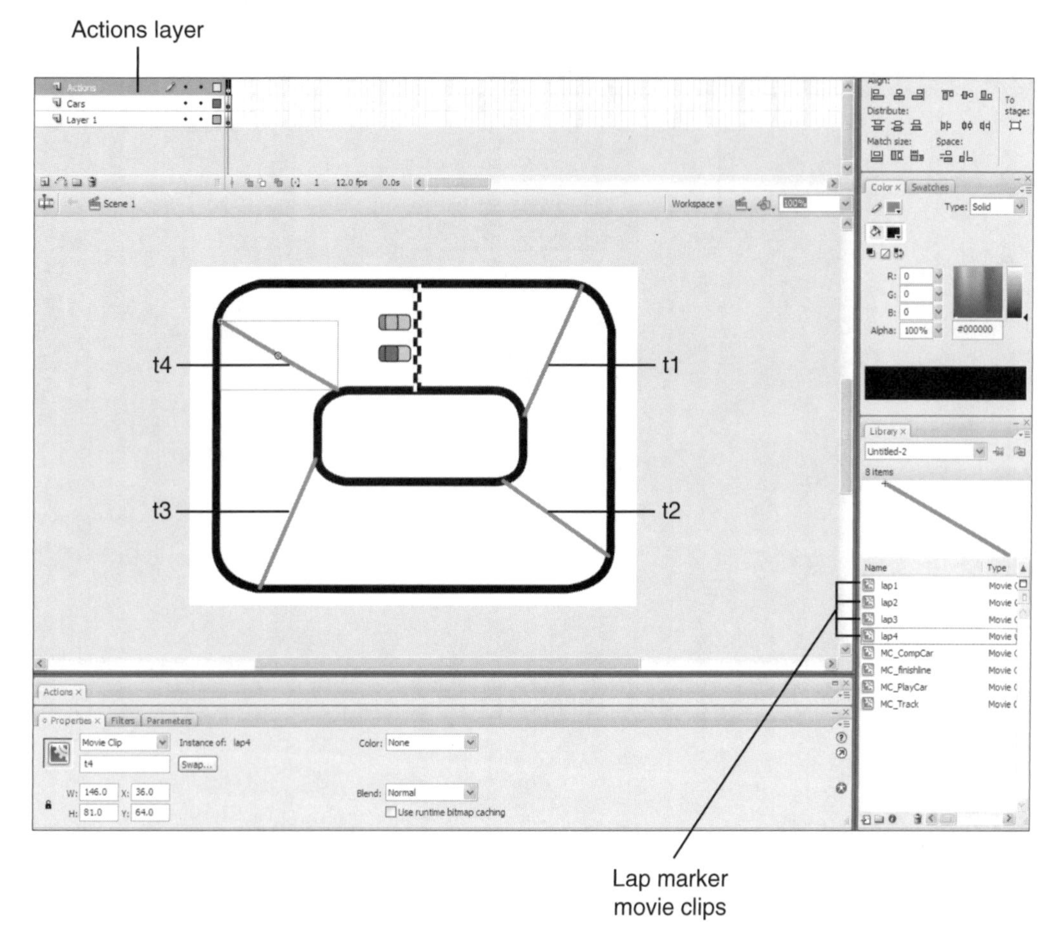

Figure 9.18
The stage with lap markers.

```
}

// Event handler for capturing keys being released
function keyReleased(event:KeyboardEvent):void {
	if (event.keyCode in keysDown) {
		// delete the property in keysDown if it exists
		delete keysDown[event.keyCode];
	}
}

//Event handler for Flash Player deactivation
function clearKeys(event:Event):void {
	// clear all keys in keysDown since the player cannot
	// detect keys being pressed or released when not focused
```

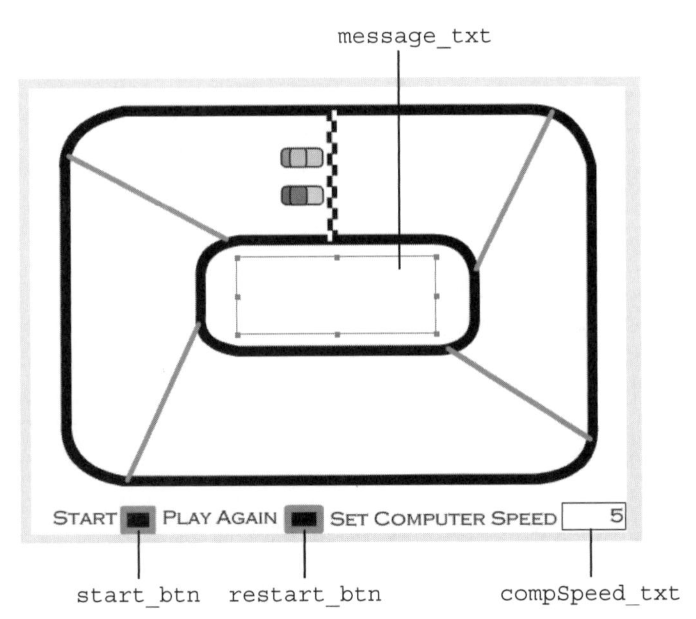

Figure 9.19
The stage with buttons.

```
        keysDown = new Object();
}

// function to move player car

//check if all laps were crossed

//check keys pressed and call function calc_xy

//update chkPath to track laps crossed
function move_pCar(event:Event):void {
        if (t1.hitTestObject(pCar_mc)==true) {
                if ( chkPath==0) {
                        chkPath=1;
                }
        }
        if (t2.hitTestObject(pCar_mc)==true) {
                if ( chkPath==1) {
                        chkPath=2;
                }
        }
        if (t3.hitTestObject(pCar_mc)==true) {
                if ( chkPath==2) {
                        chkPath=3;
```

```
            }
        }
        if (t4.hitTestObject(pCar_mc)==true) {
            if ( chkPath==3) {
                chkPath=4;
            }
        }
        if ((chkPath == 4) && (finish.hitTestObject(pCar_mc)==true) ) {
            message_txt.text="Player has Won";
            finishRace=true;
            startRace=false;
            speed=0;
            compCarSpeed=0;
        }
        // check if startRace is true, if so perform rotation

    // on left, right key press, also reset speed to new values
    if (startRace) {
            if (this.isDown(Keyboard.LEFT) && !finishRace) {
                pCar_mc.rotation -= 12;
            }
            if (this.isDown(Keyboard.RIGHT) && !finishRace) {
                pCar_mc.rotation += 12;
            }
            if (this.isDown(Keyboard.UP) && !finishRace) {
                speed += 0.2;
                speed *= .98;
                calc_xy();
            }       else {
                    if (speed>2) {
                        speed *= speedDecay;
                        calc_xy();
                    }
                }
            if (this.isDown(Keyboard.DOWN) && !finishRace) {
                speed -= backSpeed;
                calc_xy();
            }
        }

        //function calc_xy calculates x, y positions for the player car
        //with math.sin and math.cos functions
        function calc_xy():void {
```

```
        var incx:Number = Math.sin(pCar_mc.rotation*(Math.PI/180))*speed;
        var incy:Number = -Math.cos(pCar_mc.rotation*(Math.PI/180))
        *speed;
        if (!land.hitTestPoint(pCar_mc.x+incx, pCar_mc.y+incy, true)) {
                pCar_mc.x += incx;
                pCar_mc.y += incy;
        } else {
                speed =0;
            }

    }

}
this.addEventListener(Event.ENTER_FRAME, move_pCar);

///////////////// Computer Car//////////////////////

//add enter frame event listener to computer car, which calls move_cCar
cCar_mc.addEventListener(Event.ENTER_FRAME, move_cCar);

//move_cCar checks if start race is true

//if so it calculates x, y positions for the cCar

//if cCar is not on land and has not finished race

//the car's x, y positions are incremented
function move_cCar(myevent:Event):void {
    if (startRace) {
var cxincr:Number = Math.sin(cCar_mc.rotation*(Math.PI/180))*compCarSpeed;
var cyincr:Number = -Math.cos(cCar_mc.rotation*(Math.PI/180))*(compCarSpeed);
if (!land.hitTestPoint(cCar_mc.x+cxincr, cCar_mc.y+cyincr, true)
&& !finishRace) {
            cCar_mc.x += cxincr;
            cCar_mc.y += cyincr;
        //if pCar and cCar collide, compcar speed is set to 0
        // else compCar gets speed from the text box
        if (pCar_mc.hitTestObject(cCar_mc)== true) {
            compCarSpeed=0;
            speed= -1.5;
        } else {
            compCarSpeed=Number(compSpeed_txt.text);
            }
        }
```

```
        }
    }

    // Enter Frame event is added to the stage, which calls detectCollision
    stage.addEventListener(Event.ENTER_FRAME, detectCollision);

    //detectCollision checks if cCar hits the lap markers and increments
    //cchkPath after crossing each lap
    function detectCollision(myevent:Event):void {
    var cxincr:Number=Math.sin(cCar_mc.rotation*(Math.PI/180))*compCarSpeed;
    var cyincr:Number= -Math.cos(cCar_mc.rotation*(Math.PI/180))*(compCarSpeed);
    if (t1.hitTestPoint(cCar_mc.x+cxincr, cCar_mc.y+cyincr, true) && !finishRace) {
                if ( cchkPath==0) {
                      cchkPath=1;
                }
                cCar_mc.rotation=180;
        }
    if (t2.hitTestPoint(cCar_mc.x+cxincr, cCar_mc.y+cyincr, true)
    && !finishRace) {
                if ( cchkPath==1) {
                      cchkPath=2;
                }
                cCar_mc.rotation=270;
        }
    if (t3.hitTestPoint(cCar_mc.x+cxincr, cCar_mc.y+cyincr, true)
    && !finishRace) {
                if ( cchkPath==2) {
                      cchkPath=3;
                }
                cCar_mc.rotation=360;
        }
    if (t4.hitTestPoint(cCar_mc.x+cxincr, cCar_mc.y+cyincr, true)
    && !finishRace) {
                if ( cchkPath==3) {
                      cchkPath=4;
                }
                cCar_mc.rotation=90;
        }
    if ((cchkPath == 4) && (finish.hitTestPoint(cCar_mc.x+cxincr,
    cCar_mc.y+cyincr, true))) {
                message_txt.text="Computer has Won";
```

```
            finishRace = true;
            startRace = false;
            speed = 0;
            compCarSpeed=0;
      }

}

// Mouse Click event added to start_btn which calls starter
start_btn.addEventListener(MouseEvent.CLICK, starter);


// starter sets the initial values for various variables
function starter(evt:MouseEvent):void {
      if (pCar_mc.x == 277 && cCar_mc.x == 277) {
            startRace = true;
            speed = 0;
            chkPath=0;
            cchkPath=0;
            finishRace=false;
            startRace=true;
            compCarSpeed=Number(compSpeed_txt.text);
            speedDecay =0.96;
            backSpeed = 1;
            mov ="One";
      }

}

// Mouse Click event added to restart button which calls restarter
restart_btn.addEventListener(MouseEvent.CLICK, restarter);


//restarter resets values for various variables
function restarter(evt:MouseEvent):void {
      finishRace = true;
      pCar_mc.x = 277;
      pCar_mc.y=100;
      cCar_mc.x = 277;
      cCar_mc.y = 50;
      pCar_mc.rotation =cCar_mc.rotation=90;
      message_txt.text ="";

}
```

Explanation of the Code. Wow! That was a lot of code. But it is neat and fun. First, we created all the variables required for the game: `speed`; `chkPath` for the player car; `cchkPath`, for the computer car; `finishRace`, set to false to begin; `compCarSpeed`, to get the speed for the computer-controlled car; `speedDecay`, `backSpeed`, `mov`, and `keysDown`, which is a variable of object type.

Next, we added event listeners to the stage, so if at anytime there is a key pressed, it can be detected. Notice that each of the event listeners that was added to the stage is also called a function. The functions used are:

- Function `isDown()` returns a Boolean value: true if the key is down and false if the key is not down.
- Function `keyPressed()` creates a property in `keysDown` with the name of the `keyCode`.
- Function `keyReleased()` is an event handler for capturing keys being released.
- Function `clearKeys()` clears all keys in `keysDown` because the player cannot detect keys being pressed or released when not focused.

The next section of the code deals with the player car, `pCar_mc`. We add the event listener `Enter_frame` to the stage for this car, which happens when the car enters the frame. This event then calls the function `move_pCar()`. This function does the following two major tasks: It checks for collisions of the player car with the marker, and it checks if the variable `startRace` is set to true, which happens if the Start button is pressed. If true, then it checks for the keys pressed. The following are the conditions if a key is pressed:

- If the `keyPressed()` is Left and the `finishRace` variable is not true, then the car is rotated 12 degrees to the left.
- If the `keyPressed()` is Right and the `finishRace` variable is not true, then the car is rotated 12 degrees to the right.
- If the `keyPressed()` is Up and the `finishRace` variable is not true, then the speed is incremented by 0.2. The function `calc_xy()` is called to increment x, y positions of the `pCar_mc.x` and `pCar_mc.y`. Recall how we calculated these values in Exercise 9.4.
- If the `keyPressed()` is Down and the `finishRace` variable is not true, then the speed is decremented by `backSpeed`. The function `calc_xy()` is called to decrement x, y positions of `pCar_mc.x` and `pCar_mc.y`. This is similar to what we did in Exercise 9.4.

An `if` condition is used to check if the player car has collided with the lap mark `t1` on the track. We use the `hitTestObject()` method for detecting this collision. If the player car collided with the marker, then the variable `chkPath`, which was originally set at 0, is set now to 1. This process is repeated for the other lap marks, t2, t3, and t4. Once the player car crosses t4, chkPath equals 4, and the player car collides with the finish line, the following happens: The winning message is displayed in the message box, the Boolean variable finishRace is set to true, startRace is set to false, speed is set to 0, and the speed of the computer car is also set to 0.

Computer Car Code. The next section of the code is for the computer-controlled car. An event listener is added to the car when it enters the frame, which then calls the move_cCar() function. move_cCar() checks if startRace is set to true. If so, it increments the x and y positions of the car with the values given by the sine and cosine functions. Next, a hitTest-Point() function is used to check if the car collided with markers t1, t2, t3, t4, and finish, the finish line. Upon colliding with each of the markers, two things happen: First, the value of the variable mov changes from 1, to 2, to 3, etc.; and second, the angle of rotation for the car changes by 90 degrees. So when the computer car collides with the first marker, t1, the value of cchkPath changes from 1 to 2, and the angle of rotation becomes 180 degrees. The same process is repeated for the other three laps. Once the computer car completes the four laps and crosses the finish line, a message displaying that the computer car has won the race is displayed, and the variables finishRace, startRace, speed, and compCarSpeed are set as follows:

```
finishRace = true;
startRace = false;
speed = 0;
compCarSpeed=0;
```

The other two sections of code are for the Start and Restart buttons. The Start button checks to see if the cars are in the right position and sets the startRace variable to true, speed to 0, chkPath to 0, cCheckPath to 0, finishRace to false, startRace to true, speedDecay to 0.96, backSpeed to 1, mov to 1, and compCarSpeed to the values entered into the compSpeed_txt text box.

The Restart button calls the restarter() function, which does the following: It sets finishRace to true, the x position of pCar_mc to 277, the y position of pCar_mc to 40, the x position of cCar_mc to 277, the y position of cCar_mc to 70, the rotation for both cars to 90 degrees, and message_txt.text to "".

That's it for the code. Now it's time to race away and have fun!

Summary

In this chapter, we looked at some basic math and physics components to make our games more realistic. This is by no means a comprehensive treatment of these topics but just a quick introduction. We saw the application of sine and cosine functions and the ideas of speed, velocity, acceleration, and friction in games.

End-of-Chapter Exercises

1. Figure out the x and y displacements necessary to make an object move by 100 pixels in a direction of 30 degrees from the horizontal.

2. Use the code in this chapter to make an object move in a triangular path. First, let it move 100 pixels to the right; then, at an angle of –60 degrees, let it move through 100 pixels. Figure out the angle at which you should then move 100 pixels to get back to the starting point.

3. Make an object resembling a wheel and then make it rotate on the screen. Finally, try to make it roll from the left edge to the right edge of the stage.

Programming Exercises

1. Try reversing the car. Write the code to make the car go forward and then move backward.

2. How can you make an object move on a curved path instead of a straight line? One way is to change the x and y displacements by different amounts in each frame. Try this prescription:

   object.x += speed

   object.y = 100 × Math.cos (object.x) + 200

   Give some value for the speed (for example, speed = 2).

3. Rotate the object while moving it. Give any shape to the object. Then in Exercises 1 and 2, add a rotation to the object so that it twirls while moving. Add the statement `object.rotation += 5`.

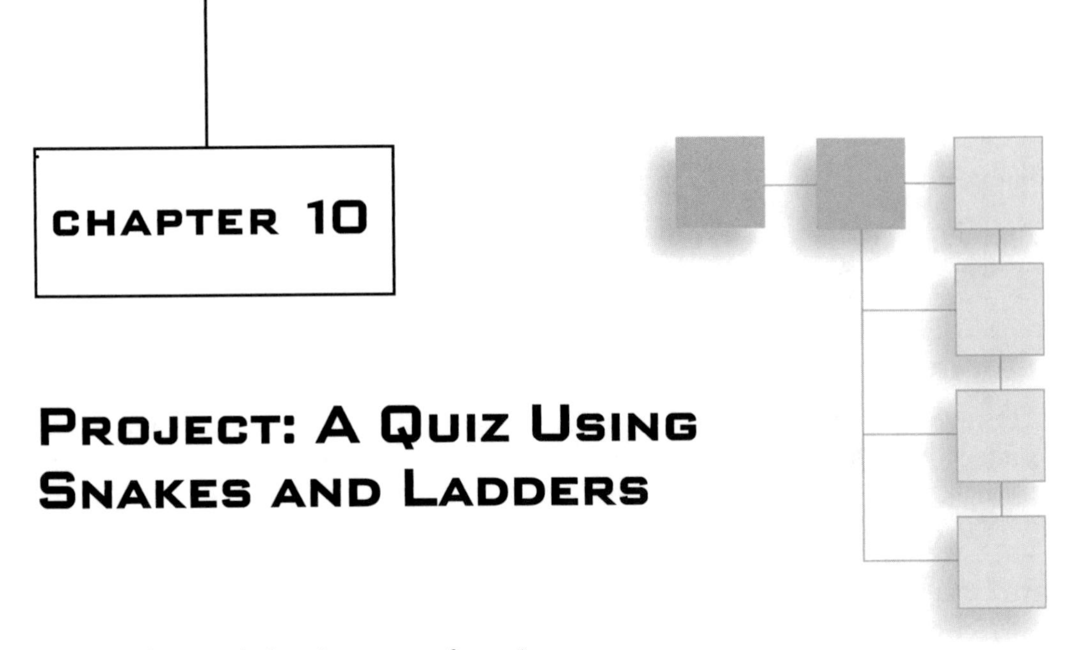

Chapter 10

Project: A Quiz Using Snakes and Ladders

- Understand the elements of a quiz
- Design a quiz
- Set up the stage with the required movie clips for Snakes and Ladders
- Create layers for the quiz
- Create Submit buttons to submit answers
- Create radio buttons for multiple-choice questions
- Incorporate the quiz into the game
- Write ActionScript for quiz logic

Elements of a Quiz

This chapter does not introduce any new topics. Instead, we will look at designing a quiz, using the game Snakes and Ladders. This chapter will combine all the concepts you have learned so far. We will use movie clips and buttons and create radio buttons and tweening. Before we design the game, let us look at the elements of a quiz.

The first thing you need to decide is the subject for your quiz. The subject we're dealing with in our game is chemistry. Within chemistry, this quiz is about photosynthesis. The quiz questions can be adapted to use with any other subject, like math, language, and so forth.

A multiple-choice quiz displays questions and answers. The correct answers are known to the program. There should be a score and a prize at the end.

Story Line

This quiz is an interactive game that can be used as a good learning tool for any subject. A Snakes and Ladders game board is set up. Figure 10.1 shows how the finished game will look.

The questions are displayed one at a time to the player. The player tries to determine which answer is correct and selects it. The computer checks the answer; if it is correct, the ball moves up the ladder. Then the next frame is displayed with the next question. If the answer is wrong, then the ball moves down the ladder and the previous frame is displayed with the previous question. A scoreboard keeps track of the number of questions that the player answers correctly. The score is incremented every time the answer is correct and decremented every time the answer is wrong. The ultimate goal is to get all the questions correct and complete the quiz.

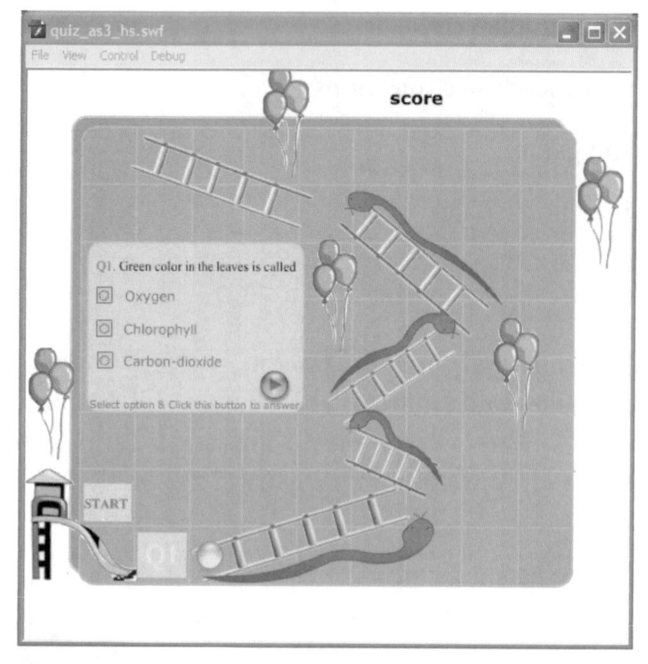

Figure 10.1
A Snakes and Ladders quiz game.

Storyboard

The stage is set up with Snakes and Ladders. You can add other props, like balloons and other attractive items, to make the playing board look appealing, as you saw in Figure 10.1.

The first step is to set up the questions you need for the quiz. We have five multiple-choice questions in our quiz game. The following list presents the questions and the corresponding answers in our quiz. The correct answers are in bold.

1. Q1 The green color in the leaves is called
   a. a1 Oxygen
   b. a2 Chlorophyll
   c. a3 Carbon dioxide
2. Q2 Plants breathe in
   a. b1 Oxygen
   b. b2 Carbon dioxide
   c. b3 Hydrogen
3. Q3 Plants breathe out
   a. c1 Oxygen
   b. c2 Carbon dioxide
   c. c3 Hydrogen
4. Q4 Plants use __________ to capture sunlight.
   a. d1 Chlorophyll
   b. d2 Carbon dioxide
   c. d3 Oxygen
5. Q5 Photosynthesis is the way plants make food.
   a. e1 True
   b. e2 False

Note

Note that the answers each have unique numbers: `a1`, `a2`, and `a3` for Q1; `b1`, `b2`, and `b3` for Q2; `c1`, `c2`, and `c3` for Q3; `d1`, `d2`, and `d3` for Q4; and `e1` and `e2` for Q5. These are the actual variable names we will use later in our code to refer to these radio buttons when we check answers in the game.

Game Development

This game will include an accompanying sound file, which reads the questions aloud to the student. Each frame consists of one question and its corresponding answer choices. Radio buttons are set up for each answer.

Exercise 10.1

For this game, we need to create several layers. Use layers to organize your work, and set up questions using text in a new layer.

Activities for the Balloons Layer

1. Open a new Flash document. Rename layer 1 `balloons`.
2. Place the image of the balloons and any other props you want to have on that layer. These are just symbols of type graphic. You can draw them or import them from the library.
3. Copy frame 1 in this layer to five additional frames.

There are no actions associated with this layer. You can just create different balloon props to decorate your game board. See Figure 10.2.

Activities for the Snakes & Ladders Layer

Here you will set up snakes and ladders to decorate your board, as you can see in Figure 10.3. Again, all these are just symbols of type graphic. Remember to keep some empty space for the questions-and-answers block.

1. Create a new layer and call it `Snakes & Ladders`.
2. Place images of ladders ascending to the top and beside each ladder place a snake.
3. Copy frame 1 of this layer to five additional frames.

Activities for the Gold Ball Indicator Layer

Here you will create the gold ball and the motion tween to make it move up the ladder.

1. Create a new layer and call it `Gold Ball Indicator`.
2. Draw a bright gold ball.
3. Right-click on the ball and convert it to a movie clip. Give it the instance name `player_mc`. Go back to the main scene by clicking Scene 1.
4. Double-click on the ball movie clip and create a motion tween for the ball for correct answers. You can increment the Timeline by 5 each time. Label the frames `c1`, `c2`, `c3`, `c4`,

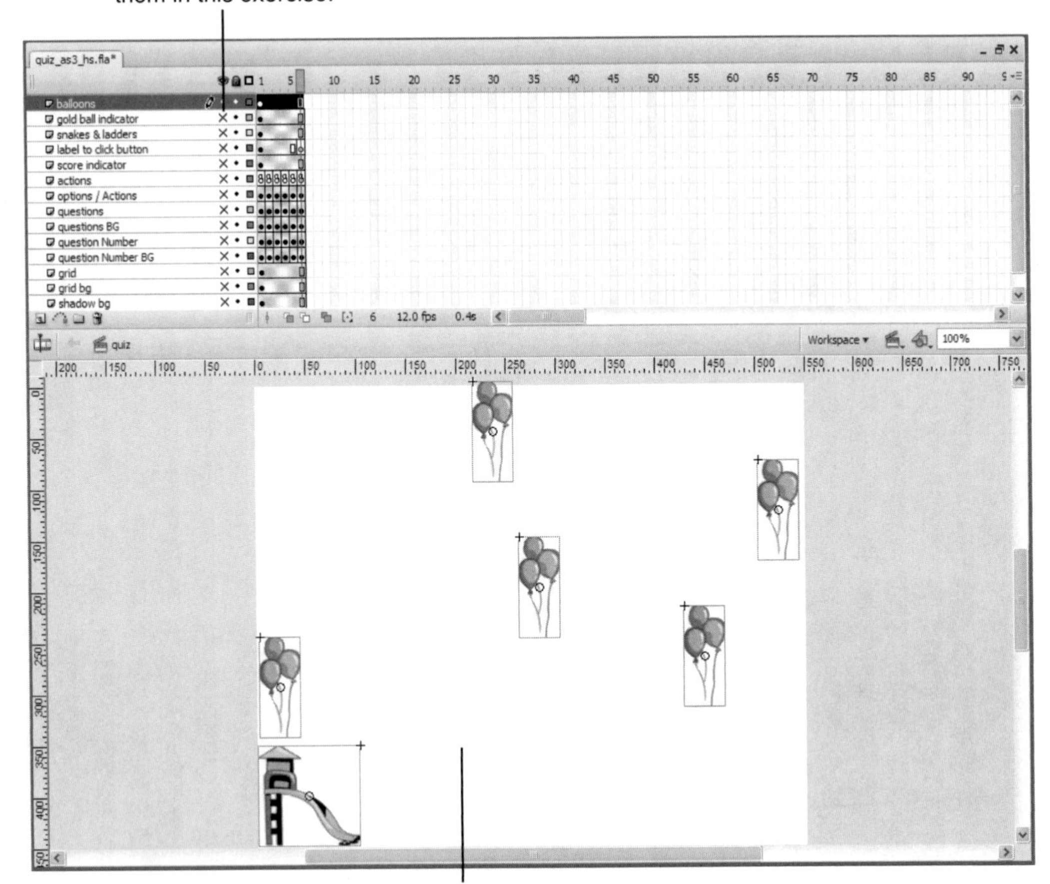

Figure 10.2
Balloons and other props.

and c5 for the five correct answer motions of the ball. Using a guide layer to guide your path, each time increment the ball up the ladder to the next slot. For the wrong answers, you can create frames starting from frame 60, again incrementing by 5 frames. Label them w5, w4, w3, w2, and w1. Use the guide layer to draw your path down from the top to the bottom using the snakes as your downward path. See Figure 10.4 on how to set up the motion tween.

5. Place the ball at the bottom of the lowest ladder. See Figure 10.5.

6. Copy frame 1 in this layer to five additional frames. Your screen should look like Figure 10.5.

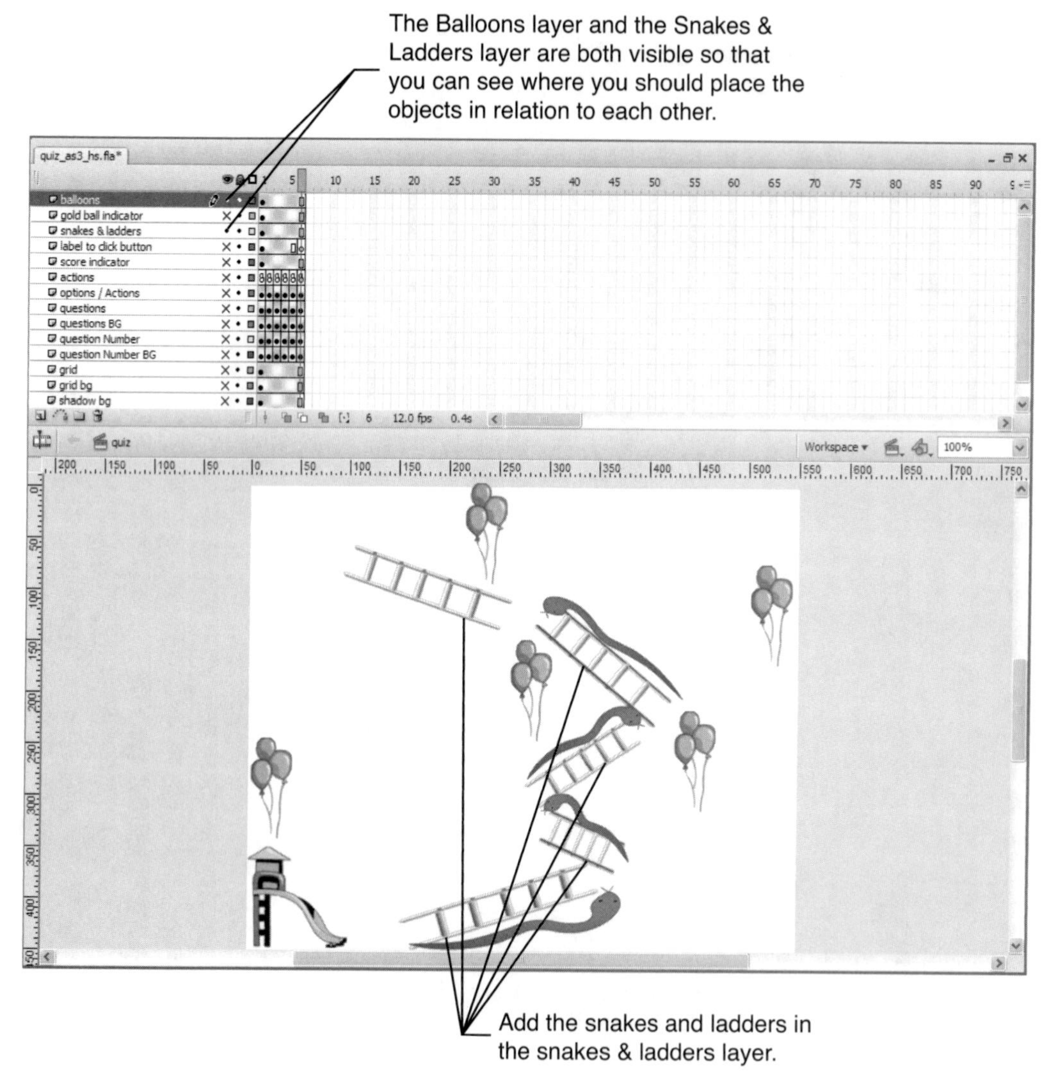

Figure 10.3
Snakes and Ladders.

Activities for the Score Indicator Layer

1. Add a new layer and name it `score indicator`. Set up the score indicator, which consists of a text box with the word `Score` in it.

2. Create a dynamic text box next to the word `Score`. Give the dynamic text box the variable name `score_txt`.

3. Position the score text box and the dynamic text box on the top right of the stage.

4. Copy frame 1 in this layer to five additional frames. See Figure 10.6.

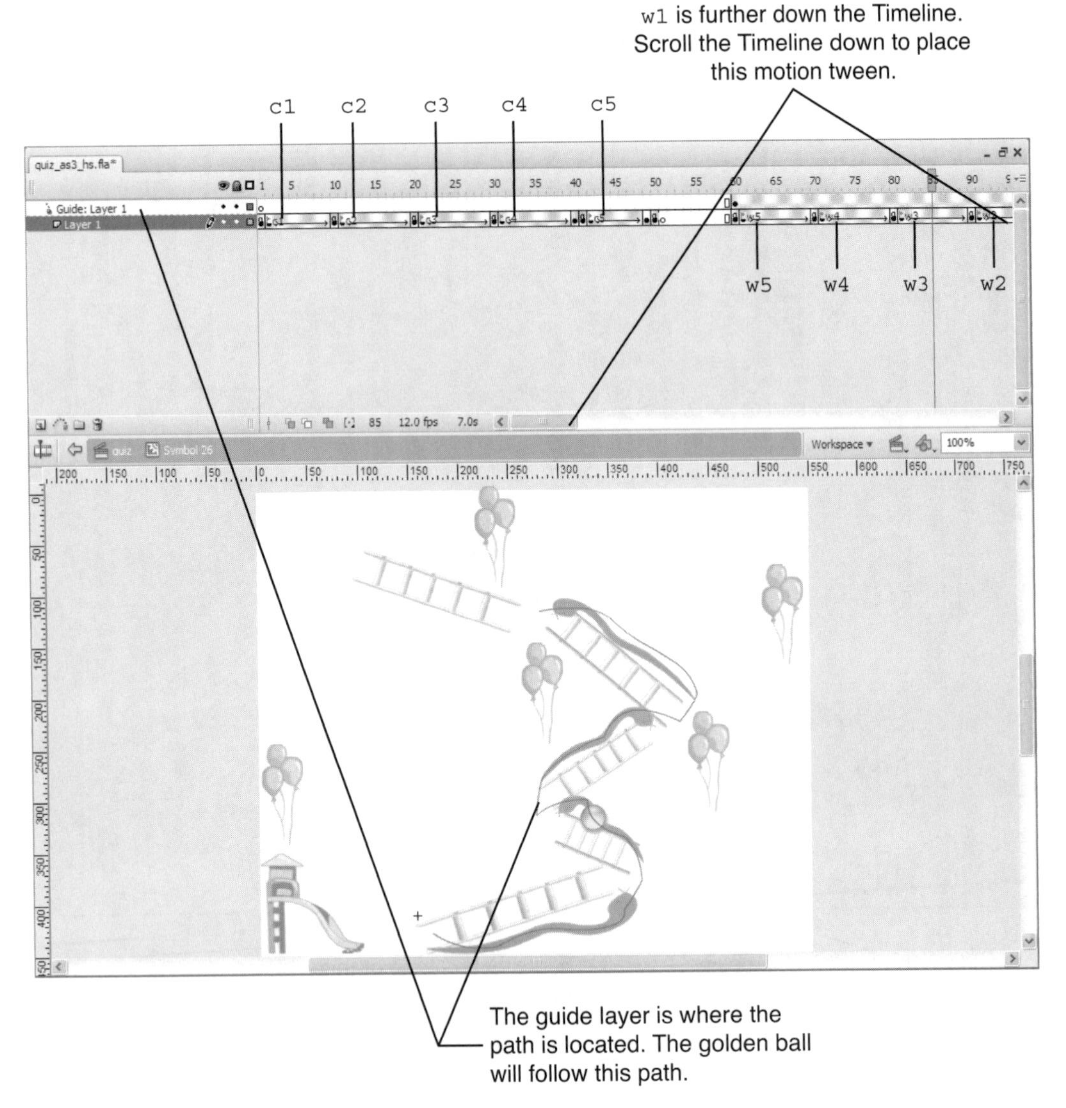

Figure 10.4
Gold ball motion tween.

Activities for the Questions BG Layer

1. Create a new layer and call it `Questions BG`.

2. Draw a box in the empty space to identify the area where the questions will appear. Color it light green.

3. Now create a button for submitting answers. First, create a green circle and give it a dark green arrow in the center. Convert this to a button symbol. In the Over state of the button,

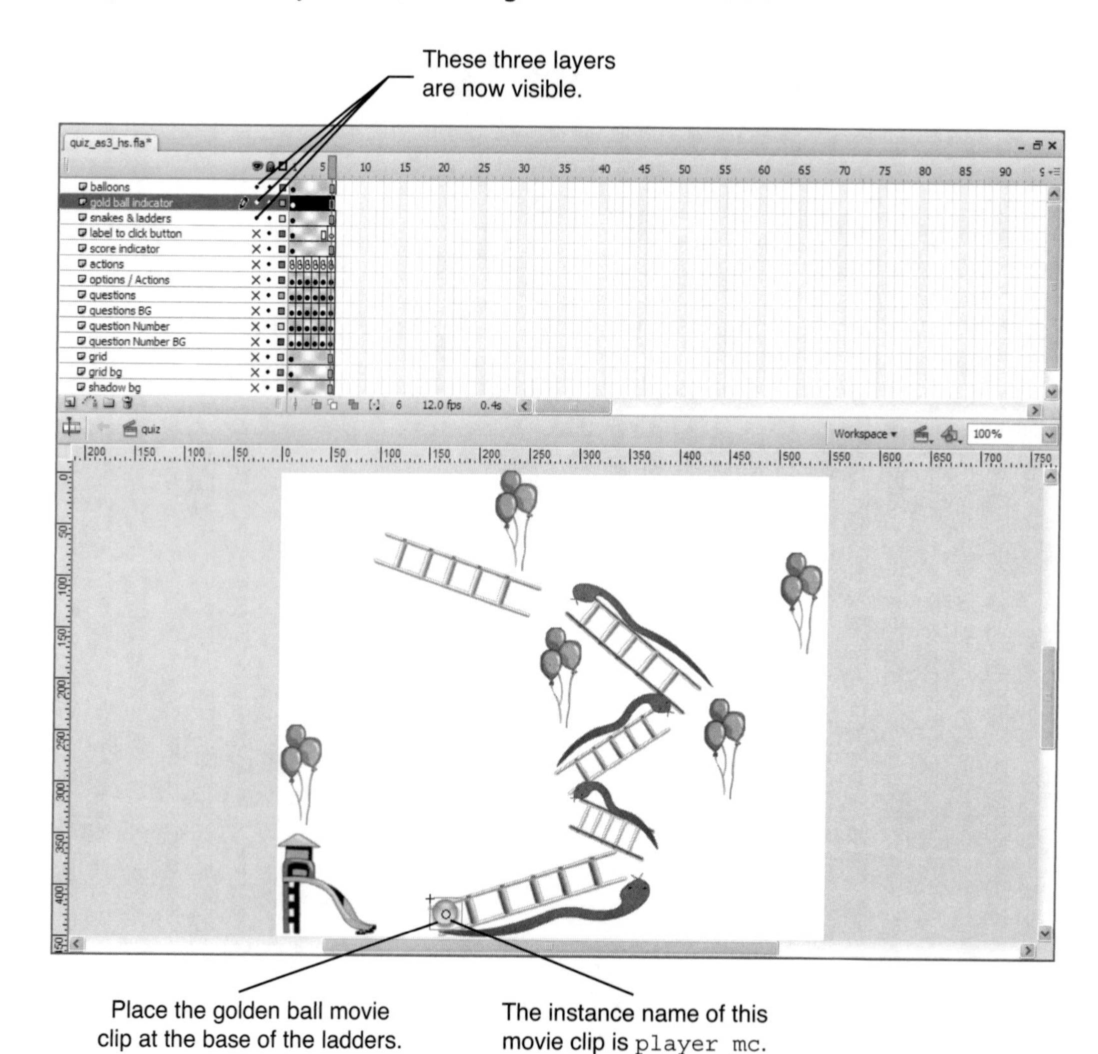

Figure 10.5
Gold ball.

make the dark green arrow white. In the Down state, make the button black and the arrow white. In the Hit state, make the entire button black.

4. Place the green button at the bottom of the box.

5. Copy frame 1 in this layer to five additional frames. In each frame change the instance name of the green button: `q1_btn` in frame 1, `q2_btn` in frame 2, `q3_btn` in frame 3, `q4_btn` in frame 4, and `q5_btn` in frame 5.

You can make your question numbers brighten or flash using motion tweening. These are all look and feel layers and can be all grouped into a single layer or kept as separate layers. You

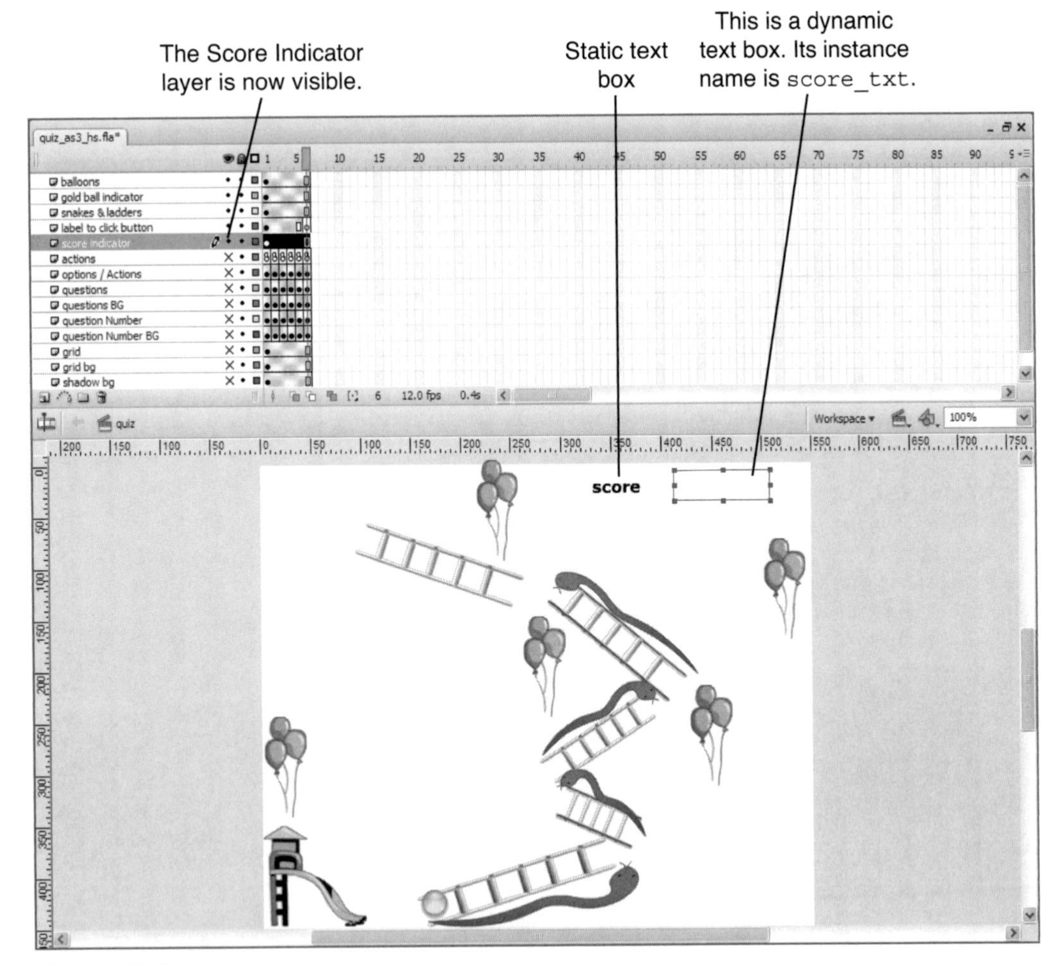

Figure 10.6
Score indicator and label for click button.

can create other layers to add more to your game. Some examples are given below, and you can see Figure 10.7 for ideas.

- A grid for the background of the game board
- A background color
- A shadow for the background
- Text boxes for the starting point (labeled Start) and for the destination (labeled Home),
- A background square box for your questions and answers
- Additional labels

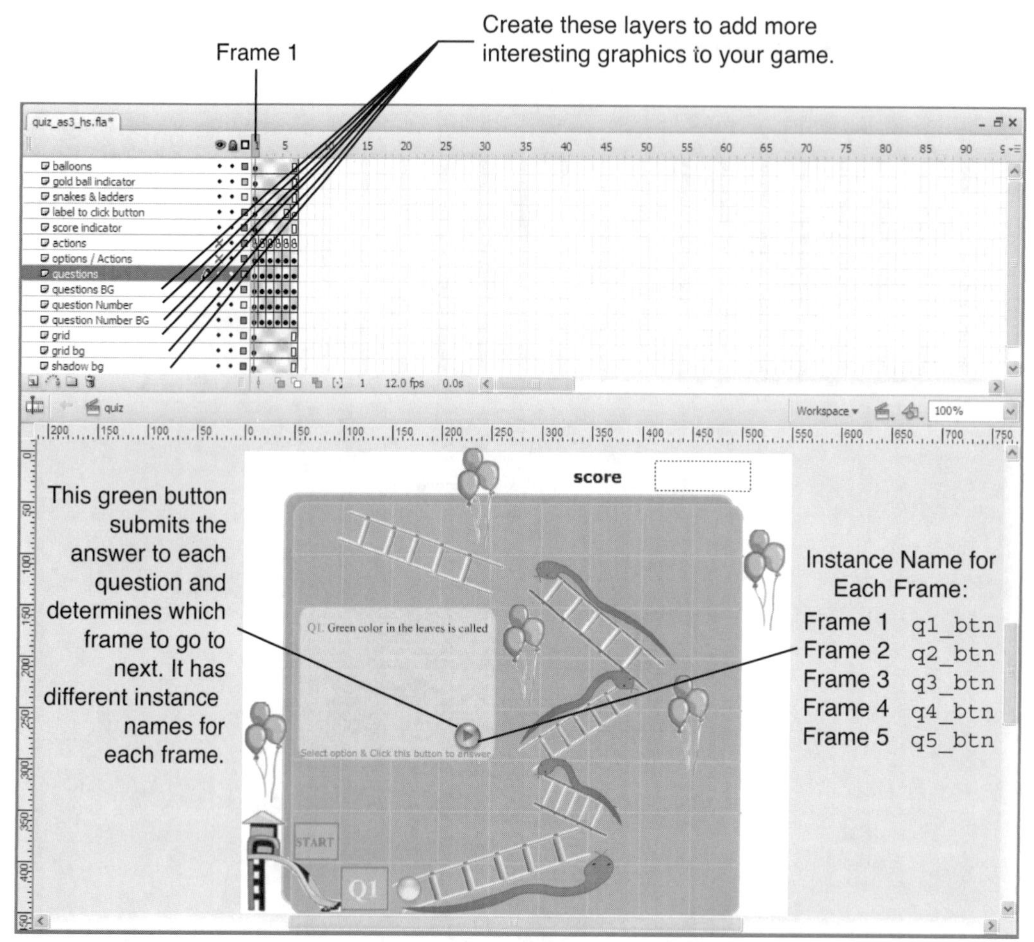

Figure 10.7
Arrow button and other decorative layers.

Activities for the Questions Layer

All of our questions will come into this layer.

1. Create a new layer and name it `Questions`.
2. In frame 1, type the first question into a static text box, as you can see in Figure 10.8. Position this text box in an appropriate location on the stage in the empty space.
3. Copy frame 1 of this layer to five additional frames.
4. Click on frame 2 and change the question number and text to create the second question. Do this for all five frames to create the five questions.

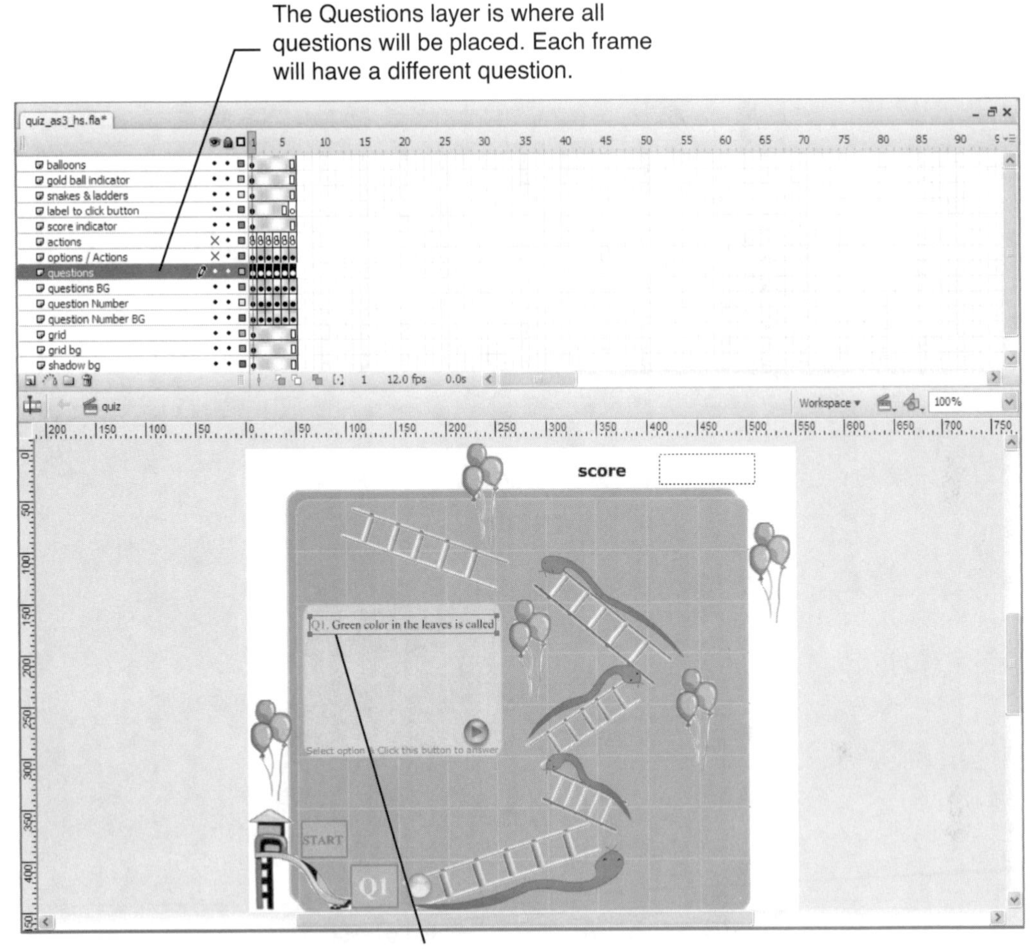

Figure 10.8
Questions layer (frames 1–5).

5. In the sixth frame, replace the question with the text `Congratulations! Winner`. Remove the answers and add a Play Again button and give it the instance name `pa_btn`, as you can see in Figure 10.9.

Activities for the Options Layer

In this layer, we will add the answers and radio buttons for each question. First, we will create a radio button movie clip and keep it ready to use. Then we will create the answers for each frame of this layer corresponding to the questions in the Questions layer.

Radio Button Creation

1. To create a radio button, draw a square with a small circle inside it.

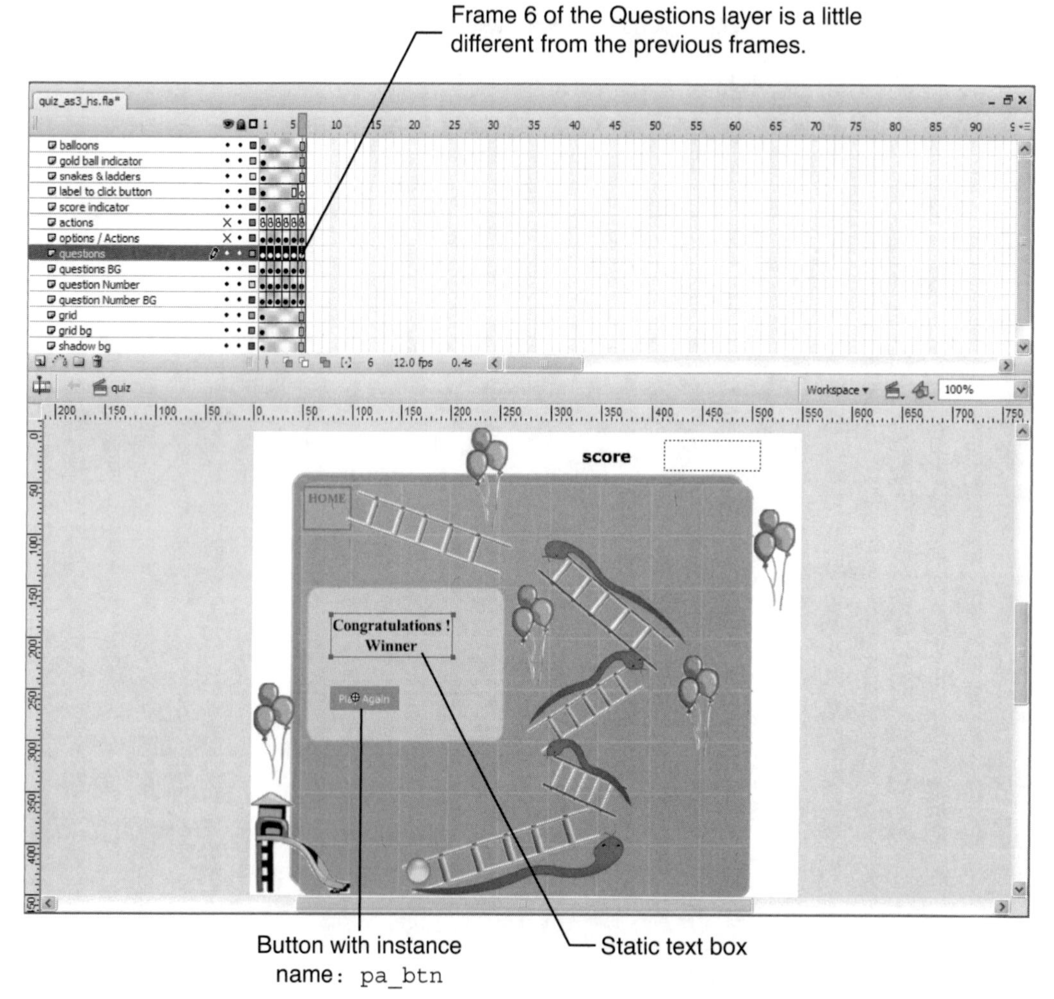

Figure 10.9
Questions layer (frame 6).

2. Fill the square and circle with a light gray color.

3. Convert this symbol to a movie clip. Name it `MC_Radio`.

4. To make it behave differently when clicked, insert a keyframe. In frame 1, leave the radio button as you created it.

5. In the actions for frame 1, just add a `stop();` so that it does not proceed automatically to the next frame of this movie clip.

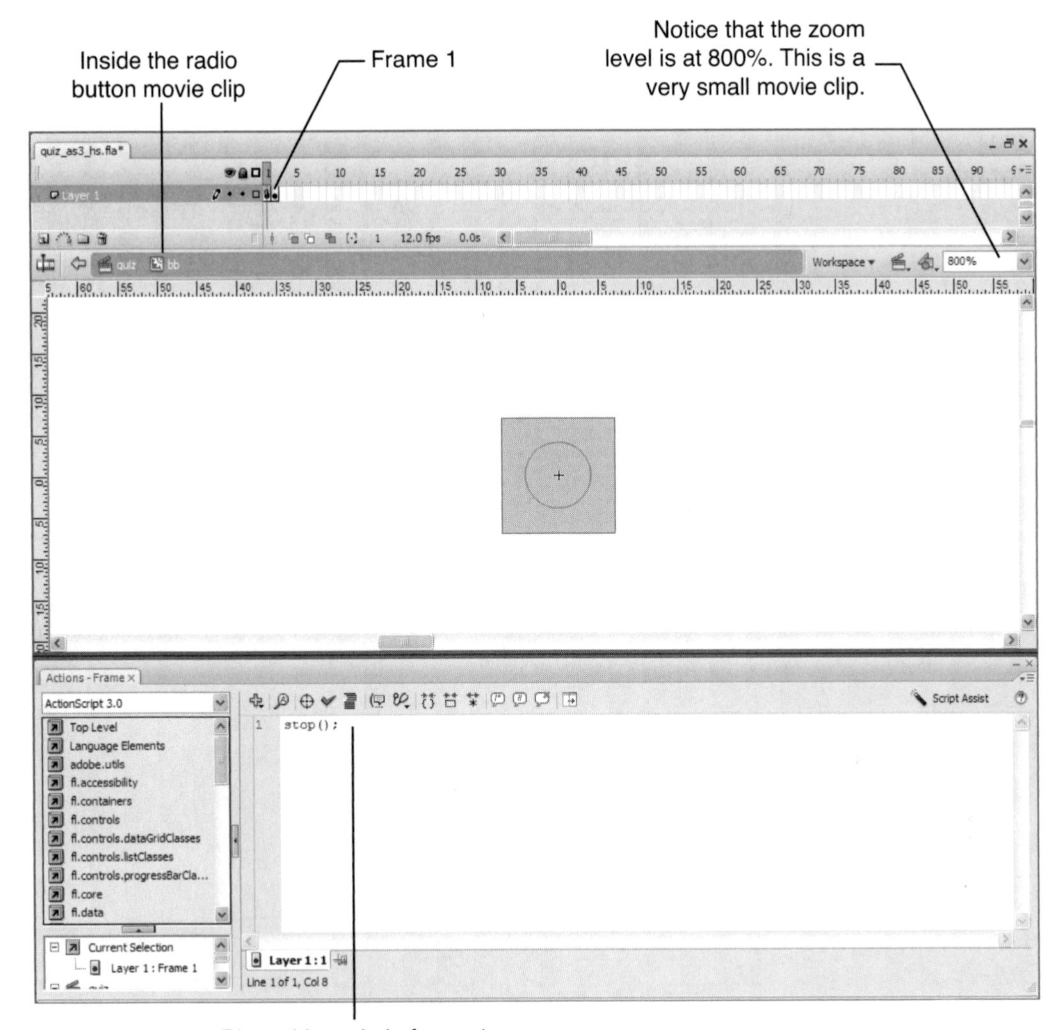

Figure 10.10
Radio button movie clip (frame 1).

6. In frame 2, fill in the circle with a black or dark gray color. Keep this movie clip for use in the Options layer. See Figures 10.10 and 10.11 for a zoomed-in view of the two frames for the radio button.

7. Return to Scene 1.

Activities for the Options/Actions Layer

1. Create a new layer and call it `Options/Actions`.

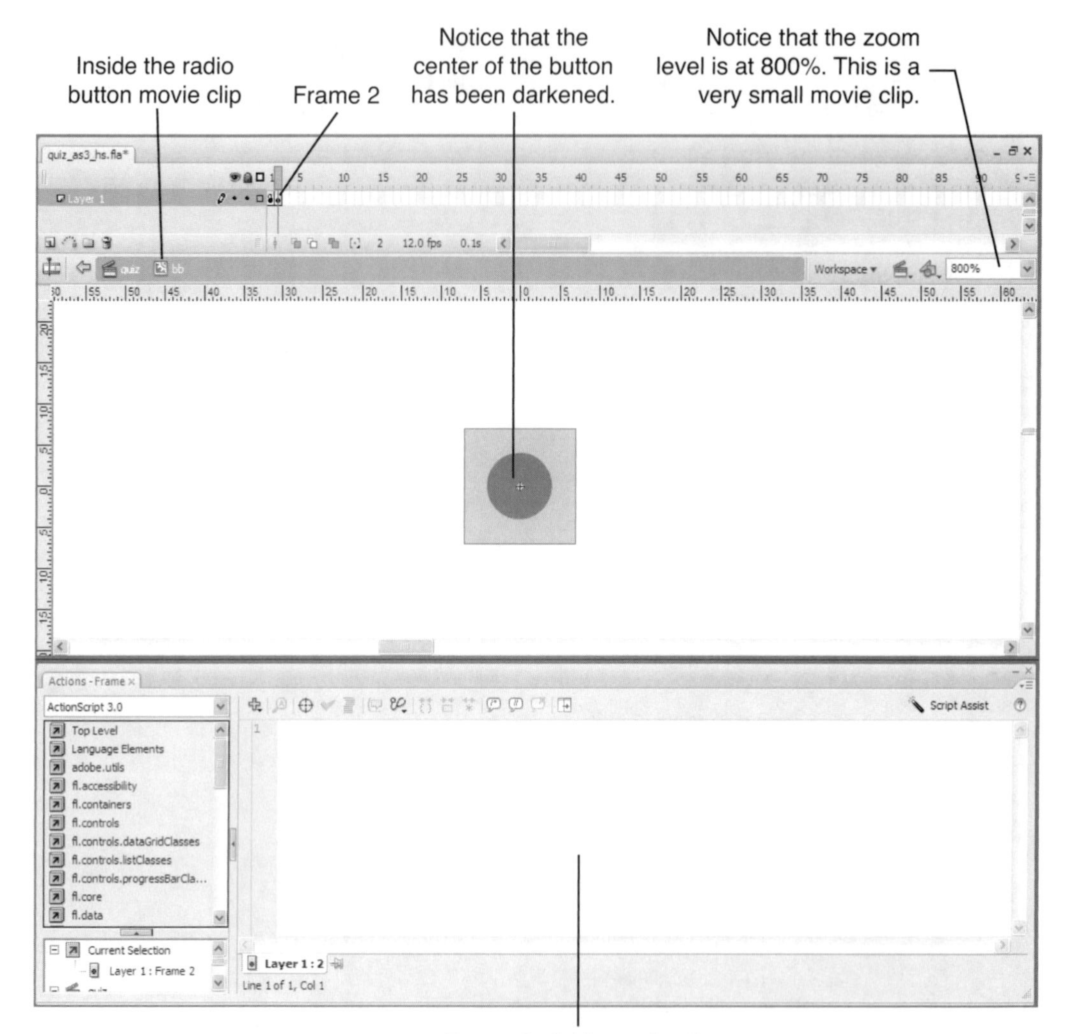

Figure 10.11
Radio button movie clip (frame 2).

2. In frame 1, create text boxes for the three answers for question 1 and place them below the question. Drag three instances of the radio button movie clip onto the stage beside the three answers. Give each radio button instance an instance name as follows: `a1` for the first answer, `a2` for the second answer, and `a3` for the third answer.

3. Create a keyframe in this layer and change the answers to the answers for the second question in frame 2. Give the radio buttons new instance names `b1`, `b2`, and `b3`.

4. Create a keyframe in this layer and change the answers and instance names for the third question to `c1`, `c2`, and `c3`.

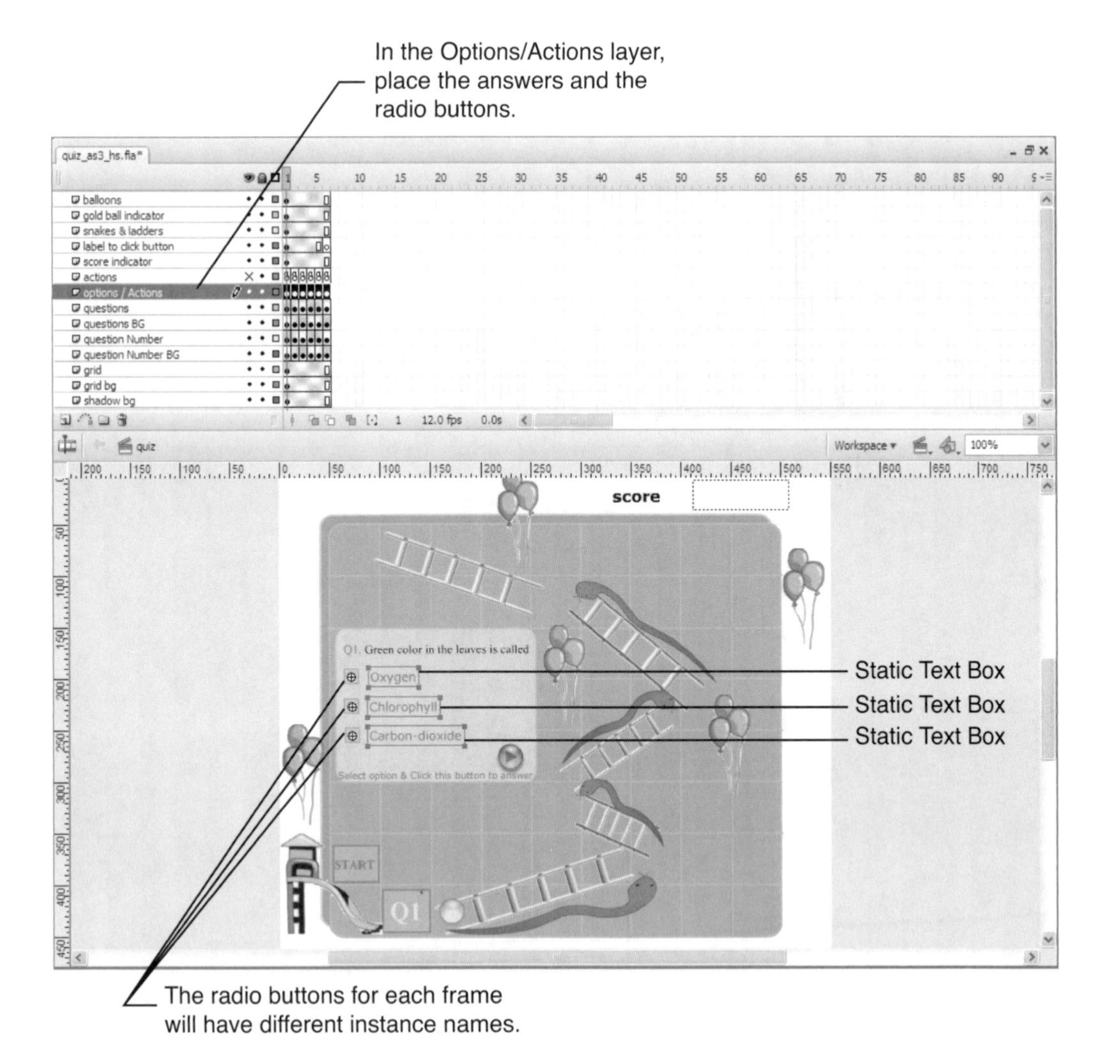

Figure 10.12
Quiz answers (frames 1–5).

5. Go on until the fifth frame, as you can see in Figure 10.12.

6. In the sixth frame, instead of the answers, drag a picture of a prize from the library or create a prize. See Figure 10.13.

Activities for the Actions Layer

Create a new layer and call it `Actions`. Here we will write ActionScript code in the Actions layer to add logic to the buttons.

Sound Files

You should create sound files in .mp3 format and import them into the library for use with your game. If you don't have sound files you should eliminate the code that includes or references sound files below.

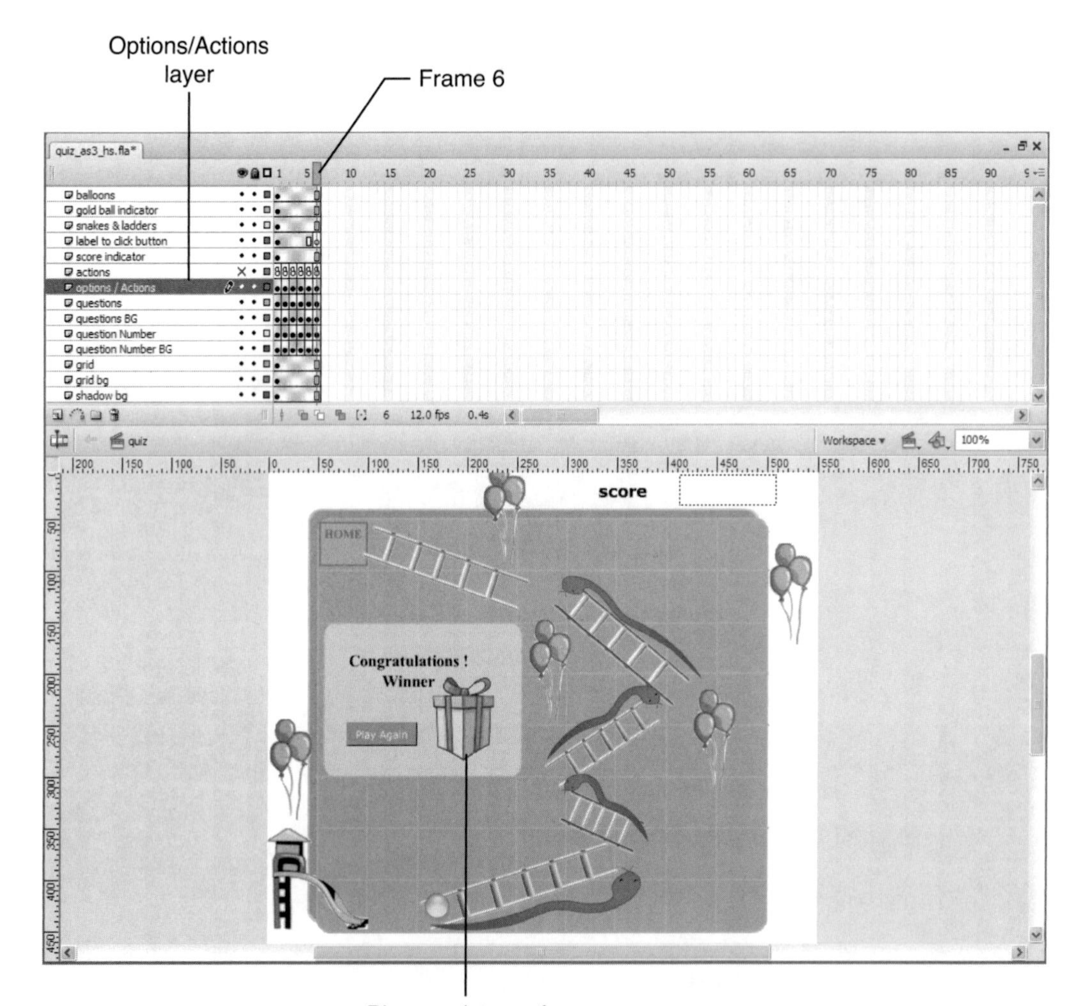

Figure 10.13
Prize (frame 6).

ActionScript for Frame 1

The ActionScript for frame 1 is given next. The explanation of the code appears in comments within the code. Place the following code into the Actions pane of the Actions layer, frame 1:

```
stop();


// initialize all answers to false
var ans1:Boolean = false;
var ans2:Boolean = false;
var ans3:Boolean = false;
```

```
var ans4:Boolean = false;
var ans5:Boolean = false;


// initialize score to 0
var score:Number = 0;


// play the voice file that reads out the first question
var q1s:q1_voice_over = new q1_voice_over();
var channel1:SoundChannel = q1s.play();

/* create a listener for the mouse click for the green button q1_btn invoke the
function chkAns1 */
q1_btn.addEventListener(MouseEvent.CLICK, chkAns1);

/* function chkAns1 checks if the answer is right or wrong. if the answer is
right, proceed to the next frame, increment the score by 20, display the score,
roll the ball up the ladder by playing the ball's c1 motion tween.*/
function chkAns1(myEvent:MouseEvent):void {
 if (ans1 == true) {
        nextFrame();
        score+=20;
        score_txt.text = String(score);
        player_mc.gotoAndPlay("c1");
 }
}

/* Create a listener for the mouse click for the first radio button a1 and
invoke the function clka1 */
a1.addEventListener(MouseEvent.CLICK, clka1);

/* function clka1 - Since a1 was clicked, for a1, go to frame 2. This will show
that the radio button was clicked because the version with the dark center will
show up. For the other radio buttons, show frame 1 which shows that they weren't
clicked. Set ans1 to false because ans1 is a2.*/
function clka1(myEvent:MouseEvent):void {
 a1.gotoAndStop(2);
 ans1 = false;
 a2.gotoAndStop(1);
 a3.gotoAndStop(1);
}

/* Create a listener for the mouse click for the second radio button a2 and
invoke the function clka2 */
```

```
a2.addEventListener(MouseEvent.CLICK, clka2);

/* function clka2 - Since a2 was clicked, for a2, go to frame 2. This will show
that the radio button was clicked. For the other radio buttons, show frame 1
which shows that they weren't clicked. Set ans1 to true because the answer to
Question 1 is a2. */
function clka2(myEvent:MouseEvent):void {
 a2.gotoAndStop(2);
 ans1 = true;
 a1.gotoAndStop(1);
 a3.gotoAndStop(1);
}

/* Create a listener for the mouse click for the third radio button a3 and
invoke the function clka3 */
a3.addEventListener(MouseEvent.CLICK, clka3);

/* function clka3 - Since a3 was clicked, for a3, go to frame 2. This will show
that the radio button was clicked. For the other radio buttons, show frame 1
which shows that they weren't clicked. Set ans1 to false because the answer to
Question 1 is a2.*/
function clka3(myEvent:MouseEvent):void {
 a3.gotoAndStop(2);
 ans1 = false;
 a1.gotoAndStop(1);
 a2.gotoAndStop(1);
}
```

ActionScript for Frame 2

Place the following code into the Actions pane of the Actions layer, frame 2:

```
// stop the first voice file
channel1.stop();

// play the voice file that reads out the second question
var q2s:q2_voice_over = new q2_voice_over();
var channel2:SoundChannel = q2s.play();

/* create a listener for the mouse click for the green button q2_btn to invoke
the function chkAns2 */
q2_btn.addEventListener(MouseEvent.CLICK, chkAns2);

/* function chkAns2 checks if the answer is right or wrong. If the answer is
right, proceed to the next frame, increment the score by 20, display the score
```

```
and roll the ball up the ladder by playing the ball's c2 motion tween. If the
answer is wrong, stop the current sound file, then move to the previous frame,
decrement the score by 20, display the score and roll the ball down the ladder
by playing the ball's w2 motion tween.*/
function chkAns2(myEvent:MouseEvent):void {
 if (ans2 == true) {
        nextFrame();
        score+=20;
        score_txt.text = String(score);
        player_mc.gotoAndPlay("c2");
 } else if (ans2 == false) {
        channel2.stop();
        prevFrame();
        score-=20;
        score_txt.text = String(score);
        player_mc.gotoAndPlay("w2");
 }
}

/* create a listener for the mouse click for the first radio button b1 and
invoke the function clkb1. */
b1.addEventListener(MouseEvent.CLICK, clkb1);

/* function clkb1 - Since b1 was clicked, for b1, go to frame 2. This will show
that the radio button was clicked. For the other radio buttons, show frame 1
which shows that they weren't clicked. Set ans2 to false because ans2 is b2.*/
function clkb1(myEvent:MouseEvent):void {
  b1.gotoAndStop(2);
  b2.gotoAndStop(1);
  b3.gotoAndStop(1);
  ans2 = false;
}

/* Create a listener for the mouse click for the first radio button and invoke
the function clkb2 */
b2.addEventListener(MouseEvent.CLICK, clkb2);

/* function clkb2 - Since b2 was clicked, for b2, go to frame 2. This will show
that the radio button was clicked. For the other radio buttons, show frame 1
which shows that they weren't clicked. Set ans2 to true because answer is b2.*/
function clkb2(myEvent:MouseEvent):void {
  b2.gotoAndStop(2);
  b1.gotoAndStop(1);
```

```
 b3.gotoAndStop(1);
 ans2 = true;
}

/* Create a listener for the mouse click for the first radio button and invoke
the function clkb3 */
b3.addEventListener(MouseEvent.CLICK, clkb3);

/* function clkb3 - Since b3 was clicked, for b3, go to frame 2. This will show that
the radio button was clicked. For the other radio buttons, show frame 1 which
shows that they weren't clicked. Set ans2 to false because answer is b2. */
function clkb3(myEvent:MouseEvent):void {
 b3.gotoAndStop(2);
 ans2 = false;
 b1.gotoAndStop(1);
 b2.gotoAndStop(1);
}
```

ActionScript for Frame 3

Place the following code into the Actions pane of the Actions layer, frame 3:

```
// stop the second voice file
channel2.stop();


// play the voice file that reads out the third question
var q3s:q3_voice_over = new q3_voice_over();
var channel3:SoundChannel = q3s.play();

/* create a listener for the mouse click for the green button and invoke the
function chkAns3 */
q3_btn.addEventListener(MouseEvent.CLICK, chkAns3);

/* function chkAns3 checks if the answer is right or wrong. If the answer is
right, proceed to the next frame, increment the score by 20, display the score
and roll the ball up the ladder by playing the ball's c3 motion tween. If the
answer is wrong, stop the music, move to the previous frame, decrement the
score by 20, display the score, and roll the ball down the snake by playing the
ball's w3 motion tween. */
function chkAns3(myEvent:MouseEvent):void {
 if (ans3 == true) {
       nextFrame();
       score+=20;
       score_txt.text = String(score);
```

```
        player_mc.gotoAndPlay("c3");
    } else if (ans3 == false) {
        channel3.stop();
        prevFrame();
        score-=20;
        score_txt.text = String(score);
        player_mc.gotoAndPlay("w3");
    }
}
/* create a listener for the mouse click for the first radio button and invoke
the function clkc1 */
c1.addEventListener(MouseEvent.CLICK, clkc1);

/* function clkc1 - Since c1 was clicked, for c1, go to frame 2. This will show
that the radio button was clicked. For the other radio buttons, show frame 1
which shows that they weren't clicked. Set ans3 to true because answer is c1. */
function clkc1(myEvent:MouseEvent):void {
 c1.gotoAndStop(2);
 ans3 = true;
 c2.gotoAndStop(1);
 c3.gotoAndStop(1);
}

/* Create a listener for the mouse click for the second radio button c2 and
invoke the function clkc2 */
c2.addEventListener(MouseEvent.CLICK, clkc2);

/* function clkc2 - Since c2 was clicked, for c2, go to frame 2. This will show
that the radio button was clicked. For the other radio buttons, show frame 1
which shows that they weren't clicked. Set ans3 to false because answer is c1. */
function clkc2(myEvent:MouseEvent):void {
 c2.gotoAndStop(2);
 ans3 = false;
 c1.gotoAndStop(1);
 c3.gotoAndStop(1);
}
/* Create a listener for the mouse click for the third radio button c3 and
invoke the function clkc3 */
c3.addEventListener(MouseEvent.CLICK, clkc3);

/* function clkc3 - Since c3 was clicked, for c3, go to frame 2. This will show
that the radio button was clicked. For the other radio buttons, show frame 1
which shows that they weren't clicked. Set ans3 to false because ans3 is c1.*/
function clkc3(myEvent:MouseEvent):void {
```

```
  c3.gotoAndStop(2);
  ans3 = false;
  c1.gotoAndStop(1);
  c2.gotoAndStop(1);
 }
```

ActionScript for Frame 4

Place the following code into the Actions pane of the Actions layer, frame 4:

```
// stop the third voice file
channel3.stop();


// play the voice file that reads out the fourth question
var q4s:q4_voice_over = new q4_voice_over();
var channel4:SoundChannel = q4s.play();

/* Create a listener for the mouse click for the green button and invoke the
function chkAns4 */
q4_btn.addEventListener(MouseEvent.CLICK, chkAns4);

/* function chkAns4 checks if the answer is right or wrong. If the answer is
right, proceed to the next frame, increment the score by 20, display the score
and roll the ball up the ladder by playing the ball's c4 motion tween. If the
answer is wrong, stop the sound, move to the previous frame, decrement the
score by 20, display the score, and roll the ball down the snakes by playing the
ball's w4 motion tween. */
function chkAns4(myEvent:MouseEvent):void {
 if (ans4 == true) {
       nextFrame();
       score+=20;
       score_txt.text = String(score);
       player_mc.gotoAndPlay("c4");
 } else if (ans4 == false) {
       channel4.stop();
       prevFrame();
       score-=20;
       score_txt.text = String(score);
       player_mc.gotoAndPlay("w4");
 }
}

/* create a listener for the mouse click for the first radio button d1 and
invoke the function clkd1 */
```

```
d1.addEventListener(MouseEvent.CLICK, clkd1);

/* function clkd1 - Since d1 was clicked, for d1, go to frame 2. This will show
that the radio button was clicked. For the other radio buttons, show frame 1
which shows that they weren't clicked. Set ans4 to true because answer is d1.*/
function clkd1(myEvent:MouseEvent):void {
 d1.gotoAndStop(2);
 ans4 = true;
 d2.gotoAndStop(1);
 d3.gotoAndStop(1);
}

/* Create a listener for the mouse click for the second radio button d2 and
invoke the function clkd2 */
d2.addEventListener(MouseEvent.CLICK, clkd2);

/* function clkd2 - Since d2 was clicked, for d2, go to frame 2. This will show
that the radio button was clicked. For the other radio buttons, show frame 1
which shows that they weren't clicked. Set ans4 to false because answer is d1.*/
function clkd2(myEvent:MouseEvent):void {
 d2.gotoAndStop(2);
 ans4 = false;
 d1.gotoAndStop(1);
 d3.gotoAndStop(1);
}

/* Create a listener for the mouse click for the third radio button d3 and
invoke the function clkd3 */
d3.addEventListener(MouseEvent.CLICK, clkd3);

/* function clkd3 - Since d3 was clicked, for d3, go to frame 2. This will show
that the radio button was clicked. For the other radio buttons, show frame 1
which shows that they weren't clicked. Set ans4 to false because ans4 is d1.*/
function clkd3(myEvent:MouseEvent):void {
 d3.gotoAndStop(2);
 ans4 = false;
 d1.gotoAndStop(1);
 d2.gotoAndStop(1);
}
```

ActionScript for Frame 5

Place the following code into the Actions pane of the Actions layer, frame 5:

```
// stop the fourth voice file
channel4.stop();

// play the voice file that reads out the fifth question
var q5s:q5_voice_over = new q5_voice_over();
var channel5:SoundChannel = q5s.play();

/* create a listener for the mouse click for the green button and invoke the
function chkAns5 */
q5_btn.addEventListener(MouseEvent.CLICK, chkAns5);

/* function chkAns5 checks if the answer is right or wrong. If the answer is
right, proceed to the next frame, increment the score by 20, display the score
and roll the ball up the ladder by playing the ball's c5 motion tween. If the
answer is wrong, move to the previous frame, decrement the score by 20, display
the score, and roll the ball down the snake by playing the ball's w5 motion
tween. */
function chkAns5(myEvent:MouseEvent):void {
 if (ans5 == true) {
        nextFrame();
        score+=20;
        score_txt.text = String(score);
        player_mc.gotoAndPlay("c5");
 } else if (ans5 == false) {
        channel5.stop();
        prevFrame();
        score-=20;
        score_txt.text = String(score);
        player_mc.gotoAndPlay("w5");
 }
}

/* Create a listener for the mouse click for the first radio button e1 and
invoke the function clke1*/
e1.addEventListener(MouseEvent.CLICK, clke1);

/* function clke1 - Since e1 was clicked, for e1, go to frame 2. This will show
that the radio button was clicked. For the other radio buttons, show frame 1
which shows that they weren't clicked. Set ans5 to true because answer is e1.*/
function clke1(myEvent:MouseEvent):void {
 e1.gotoAndStop(2);
 ans5 = true;
 e2.gotoAndStop(1);
}
```

```
/* Create a listener for the mouse click for the second radio button e2 and
invoke the function clke2 */
e2.addEventListener(MouseEvent.CLICK, clke2);

/* function clke2 - Since e1 was clicked, for e1, go to frame 2. This will show
that the radio button was clicked. For the other radio buttons, show frame 1
which shows that they weren't clicked. Set ans5 to true because answer is e1.*/
function clke2(myEvent:MouseEvent):void {
 e2.gotoAndStop(2);
 ans5 = false;
 e1.gotoAndStop(1);
}
```

ActionScript for Frame 6

Place the following code into the Actions pane of the Actions layer, frame 6:

```
// stop the fifth voice file
channel5.stop();

// play the congratulations voice file
var q6s:Congrats = new Congrats();
var channel6:SoundChannel = q6s.play();

// create a listener for the mouse click for the play again button
pa_btn.addEventListener(MouseEvent.CLICK, playAgain);

/* function playAgain - Go to frame 1 to start the game over, initialize the
score to 0, initialize the score display and stop the congratulations sound
file.*/
function playAgain(myEvent:MouseEvent):void {
 gotoAndStop(1);
 score = 0;
 score_txt.text = "";
 channel6.stop();
}
```

Summary

In this chapter, we developed a complete quiz. You can enhance this quiz by adding more props and more questions and by expanding it to other subjects.

Project

Create a math quiz game on any topic you like.

1. Design the game board using your imagination.
2. Develop five questions with their answers.
3. When the player clicks on Start, pop up the first question in a square on the stage with three answer choices with radio buttons.
4. Put a small Submit button in the square.
5. When the Submit button is clicked, check if the answer is correct. If the selected answer is correct, increment the score and pop up the second question; if the selected answer is incorrect, supply a message telling the user the correct answer and don't increment the score.
6. In the end, give the user a final score for this quiz with the number of questions answered correctly and number of questions answered incorrectly.

INDEX

Symbols

// (parallel lines), 16

A

acceleration
- due to friction, 198
- objects, 197

ActionScript
- arrays in, 119–120
- assignments, 14
- data types, 14
- expressions, 17–18
- keyframe code, 14–16
- overview of, 13–14
- Simple Simon Piano game, 154–160
- Snakes and Ladders game, 232–241
- variables, 14
- Visual Built-in Classes, 18–41

ActionScript panel, 5

Actions-Frame, 27

Actions layer, Simple Simon Piano game, 153–154

`addEventListener()` method, 48

adding
- buttons, 24, 26, 31
- code
  - Frame 1 (sample adventure game), 52
  - Frame 2 (sample adventure game), 54
  - Frame 3 (sample adventure game), 55
  - Frame 4 (sample adventure game), 57–58
  - Frame 5 (sample adventure game), 59–60
  - Frame 6 (sample adventure game), 60
- sound, 101–102
- text animations, 82–85

`addNewChild()` method, 137

algorithms, accelerated motion, 197

alien spaceships, creating, 97–98

Alpha property, 132

angles, finding, 192

animations, 65
- cel, 72–74
- overview of, 65–66
- stars, 88
- text, 82–85
- tweened, 66–72
- types of, 66

answers, quiz, 231

applying
- arrays
  - constructors, 144
  - literals, 144
- SharedObject class, 163–182

arguments, 17

Array class, 144

arrays, 117, 118
- in ActionScript, 119–120
- constructors, applying, 144
- creating, 144
- elements
  - deleting, 146
  - inserting, 145
- literals, applying, 144
- methods, 145–149
- overview of, 143–144
- querying, 148
- sorting, 148
- `tempSeq`, 160
- truncating, 148

Arrow button, 226

Arrow tool, 7
assets, High Scores game, 164
assignments, ActionScript, 14

B

backgrounds
  images, 78
  keyframes, inserting, 80
ballDisp.fla, 188
`ball1` **event listener, 122**
`ballVelocity`**, 195**
blank keyframes, 5
breaking images, 127
built-in functions, game-design process, 46–48
`buttonClickexplore()` **event handler, 58**
`buttonClickLeft()` **event handler, 54**
`buttonClickRight()` **event handler, 54**
`buttonClickSearch()` **event handler, 58**
`buttonmove()` **function, 186**
`buttonPlayagain()` **event handler, 56, 59, 60**
buttons, 9
  adding, 24, 26, 31
  Arrow, 226
  Clear Scores, 175
  clicking, 28–35
  creating, 23, 30, 40
  Play Again, 174
  radio, 227–229, 230
  sample adventure game, 49–51
  Start, 168
  states, 19, 24, 39–41
  Visual Built-in Classes, 19–20
Buttons layer, Simple Simon Piano game, 152

C

calculating
  displacements, 196
  trigonometry, 192–196
  velocity, 191
calling functions, 45
Car Racing game
  game development, 201–215
Car Racing games, 200
cars
  code, 215
  creating, 202
cel animation, 72–74
`checkClick` **function, 160**
classes
  Array, 144
  SharedObject, 163–182
  timer, 103
  Visual Built-in Classes, 18–41
Clear Scores button, 175
`CLICK`**, 39**
`clickHandler()` **function, 48**
clicking buttons, 28–35
code
  adding
    Frame 1 (sample adventure game), 52
    Frame 2 (sample adventure game), 54
    Frame 3 (sample adventure game), 55
    Frame 4 (sample adventure game), 57–58
    Frame 5 (sample adventure game), 59–60
    Frame 6 (sample adventure game), 60
  Car Racing game, 201–215
  cars, 215
  game development phase, 103–114
  game over scene, 112–114
  game pieces, 105–112
  High Scores game, 166–168
  instructions scene, 104
  keyframes, 14–16
Color Mixer, 5, 8, 9
components of documents, 2–5
`concat()` **method, 148**
conditional statements, 142
conditions, `while` **loops, 142**
constant forces, acceleration due to, 198
constructors, applying arrays, 144
conventions, sign, 194
Convert to Symbol dialog box, 128
copying instances, 89
correctness, 43
counters
  loops, 123
  variables, 142
creating. ***See*** **formatting**
creation tools, 6
cursors, customizing, 79–82

D

data types, ActionScript, 14
`delete()` **operator, 147–148**
deleting arrays, 146
design, 124
  Car Racing game, 200
  game-design process, 44–49
  game development, 93–103
  OOD (object-oriented design), 44
  Simple Simon Piano game, 153

dialog boxes
Convert to Symbol, 128
Linkage Properties, 120
direction, moving objects, 189–190
displacements
calculating, 196
objects, 186–189
distance, finding, 191
documents
components of, 2–5
keyframes, 5
stage, 2–3
Timeline, 4–5
`do...while` loops, 143
drag and drop methods, 120–123
drawing
flowers, 76
text boxes, 29
Drawing tools panel, 5, 6
dynamic text, modifying, 29
dynamic text boxes, 20, 134
High Scores game, 171, 172, 173

E

ease of use, 43
elements
arrays, 144
deleting, 146
inserting, 145
of a quiz, 217–241
`Enter_Frame` event, 197
Eraser, 7
errors, game development, 114–115
event handlers
`buttonClickexplore()`, 58
`buttonClickRight()`, 54
`buttonClickSearch()`, 58
`buttonPlayagain()`, 56, 59, 60
game-design process, 48–49
event listeners, `ball1`, 122
events
`Enter_Frame`, 197
game-design process, 48–49
mouse, 19–20, 35–39
`mouseDown`, 122
`mouseUp`, 122
expressions, 17–18, 142

F

fields, text, 20–41
files, adding sound, 101–102
fills, types of, 8
finding
angles, 192
distance, 191
Flash, overview of, 1–2
`flash.utils` package, 111
flowcharts, storyboards
High Scores game, 165
sample adventure game, 50
flowers, drawing, 76
`for` loops, 123, 142
formatting
alien spaceships, 97–98
arrays, 144
buttons, 23, 30, 40
game pieces, 96–102
hovercrafts, 98–99
input boxes, 25
missiles, 99–100
movie clips
sample adventure game, 49
target, 130
objects, arrays, 119
radio buttons, 227–229
sample adventure game, 49–51
Simple Simon Piano game, 150
stopwatches, 100–101
tanks, 99–100
fps (frames per second), 66
object speed, relation to, 190
frame-by-frame animation, 72–74
frames, 4
motion tweening, 68
rates, 65
frames per second (fps), 66
object speed, relation to, 190
Free Transform tool, 7, 30
friction
kinetic, 198
objects, 198
functions
built-in, 46–48
`buttonmove()`, 186
calling, 45
`checkClick`, 160
`clickHandler()`, 48
game-design process, 45–46
`gotoAndPlay`, 47–48
`gotoAndStop`, 46–47, 54, 61
`Math.cos()`, 194
`paClk`, 114

functions *(continued)*
- `pieceMove`, 138
- `startDrag()`, 81
- `stop()`, 26, 34, 46
- `tc`, 111
- `trace`, 17

G

game-design process, 44–49
- built-in functions, 46–48
- event handlers, 48–49
- events, 48–49
- functions, 45–46
- storyboards, 44–45

game development, 93
- Car Racing game, 201–215
- coding phase, 103–114
- design phase, 93–103
- game pieces, creating, 96–102
- Layer 1 activities, 124–126
- Layer 2 activities, 126–129
- Layer 3 activities, 129–132
- phases, 124–126
- roles for game pieces, 102–103
- Snakes and Ladders game, 220–241
- storyboards, 94–96
- story lines, 94
- testing phase, 114
- troubleshooting, 114–115

games
- Car Racing, 200
- High Scores, 163–182
- math and physics for, 183
- realistic movement, 183–215
- sample adventure, 49–62. *See also* sample adventure game
- Simple Simon Piano, 149–160
- Snakes and Ladders
  - ActionScript, 232–241
  - elements of a quiz, 217–218
  - game development, 220–241
  - storyboards, 219
  - story lines, 218

`gotoAndPlay` function, 47–48
`gotoAndStop` function, 46–47, 54, 61
Gradient Transform tool, 7
graphics, 9

H

High Scores game, 163–182
- game pieces scene, 168–182
- instructions scene, 166–168

`hitTestObject()` method, 200, 214
`hitTestPoint()` method, 200
`hitTextObject()` method, 103
hovercrafts, creating, 98–99
hypotenuse, 193

I

identifiers, linkage, 120–122
images
- backgrounds, 78
- breaking, 127
- separating, 128

indentation, 16
indexes, arrays, 144
initialization of variables, 144
Ink Bottle, 7
input boxes, creating, 25
input text box, 20
inserting. *See also* adding
- array elements, 145
- images, 78
- keyframes, 80
- layers, 77–79, 126
- symbols, 173

instances
- copying, 89
- dynamic text boxes, 172
- naming, 129, 151

instructions scene, 104, 125
- High Scores game, 166–168

J

`join()` method, 149

K

keyframes
- code, 14–16
- documents, 5
- inserting, 80
- types of, 4

keywords, new, 144
kinetic friction, 198

L

laps
- creating, 205
- movie clip, 207

Lasso tool, 7
layers, 4
- inserting, 77–79, 126
- linking, 70
- Lock, 130
- renaming, 77–79
- Simple Simon Piano game
  - Action, 153–154
  - Buttons, 152
  - MovieClip, 150–152

libraries, symbols, 24
Library panel, 5, 6
limitations of SharedObject class, 164
lines, object acceleration, 197
Line tool, 7
linkage identifiers, 120–122
Linkage Properties dialog box, 120
linking layers, 70
lists, scores, 178
literals, applying arrays, 144
Lock layer, 130
logic
- explanation, Simple Simon Piano game, 152–154
- flow, Car Racing game, 202

loops, 123–138
- `for`, 123, 142
- counter variables, 123
- `do...while`, 143
- overview of, 141
- `while`, 123, 142–143

M

maintainability, 43
masking, 76–79
- text animations, 83

`Math.cos()` function, 194
math for games, 183
- objects. *See* objects
- realistic movement, 183–215
- trigonometry, 192–196

measurements of object speed, 190
menus, creating Motion tween, 69
methods
- `addEventListener()`, 48
- `addNewChild()`, 137
- arrays, 145–149
- `concat()`, 148
- `hitTestObject()`, 200, 214
- `hitTestPoint()`, 200
- `hitTextObject()`, 103
- `join()`, 149
- movie clips, 117, 120–123
  - `startDrag()`, 120
  - `stopDrag()`, 120
- `myTime.start()`, 111
- `pop()`, 146
- `push()`, 145, 152
- `reverse()`, 148
- `shift()`, 146
- `slice()`, 149, 152
- `sort()`, 148
- `splice()`, 145–146, 146–147
- `toString()`, 149
- `unshift()`, 145

missiles, creating, 99–100
modification
- dynamic text, 29
- objects, displacement, 186–189
- tools, 6

motion
- accelerated objects algorithm, 197
- Motion Guide, linking/unlinking layers, 70
- tweening, 67

`mouseDown` event, 122
mouse events, 19–20, 35–39
`MOUSE_OUT`, 39
`mouseUp` events, 122
movement
- objects, moving on stage, 184–215
- realistic, 183–215
- slanted, 189

MovieClip layer, Simple Simon Piano game, 150–152
movie clips, 9
- laps, 207
- linkage identifiers, 120–122
- methods, 117, 120–123
  - `startDrag()`, 120
  - `stopDrag()`, 120
- properties, 18–19

movie clips *(continued)*
radio buttons, 230
sample adventure game, 49
target, creating, 130
testing, 114
Visual Built-in Classes, 18–19
moving
objects, 184–215, 189–190
panels, 5
multidimensional arrays, 118, 143–144. *See also* **arrays**
`myTime.start()` **method, 111**

N

naming
instances, 129, 151
layers, 77–79
players, 176
navigating documents, 2–5
new keyword, 144
numbers, positioning objects, 184–186

O

object-oriented design (OOD), 44
objects
acceleration, 197
arrays, creating, 119
displacement, 186–189
friction, 198
moving, 189–190
moving on stage, 184–215
positioning, 184–186
rotating, 196–197
SharedObject class, 163–182
speed, 190
symbols. *See* symbols
target, 179
velocity, 190–196
Onion Skin feature, 74–76, 77
OOD (object-oriented design), 44
operators, `delete()`**, 147–148**
Oval tool, 7

P

packages, `flash.utils`**, 111**
`paClk` **function, 114**
Paint Bucket, 7
panels, 5–9
parallel lines (//), 16
parameters, `scene`**, 47**
paths, motion tweening, 67–70
persistent data, 163
phases of game development, 93–115, 124–126
physics for games, 183
objects. *See* objects
realistic movement, 183–215
`pieceMove` **function, 138**
pixels per second (pps), 190
planning, 44. *See also* **design**
Play Again button, 174
players
creating, 202
names and scores, 176
`pop()`**method, 146**
portability, 43
positioning objects, 184–186
pps (pixels per second), 190
properties
Alpha, 132
Linkage Properties dialog box, 120
movie clips, 18–19
Properties window, 24
Property Inspector, 66
`push()` **method, 145, 152**

Q

querying arrays, 148
quiz, elements of, 217–241

R

radians, 194
radio buttons
creating, 227–229
movie clips, 230
realistic movement, 183–215
objects, moving on stage, 184–215
Rectangle tool, 7
renaming layers, 77–79
reusability, 43
`reverse()` **method, 148**
right triangles, 192
robustness, 43
roles for game pieces, 102–103

Text tool, 7, 25
Timeline, 4–5
 keyframe code, 14–16
timer class, 103
tools, 5–9
 Arrow, 7
 creation, 6
 Eraser, 7
 Free Transform, 7, 30
 Gradient Transform, 7
 Ink Bottle, 7
 Lasso, 7
 Line, 7
 modification, 6
 Oval, 7
 Paint Bucket, 7
 Rectangle, 7
 selection, 6
 Sub Selection, 7
 Text, 7, 25
`toString()` **method, 149**
`trace` **function, 17**
transitions, 86
triangles
 hypotenuse, 193
 right, 192
trigonometry, 192–196
troubleshooting game development, 114–115
truncating arrays, 148
tweened animations, 66–72
two-dimensional arrays, 118. ***See also*** **arrays**
types
 of animations, 66
 of arrays, 118
 data, 14
 of fills, 8
 of keyframes, 4
 of symbols, 9
 of text boxes, 20
 of tweened animations, 66

U

unlinking layers, 70
`unshift()` **method, 145**

V

validation, 43
values of speed, 195. ***See also*** **speed**
variables
 ActionScript, 14
 counters, 142
 initialization, 144
 loops, 123
vectors, right triangles, 193
velocity of objects, 190–196
`vel_y`**, 190**
Visual Built-in Classes, 18–41
 buttons, 19–20
 movie clips, 18–19
 text fields, 20–41
visual effects, 65–66. ***See also*** **animations**
 custom cursors, 79–82
 masking, 76–79
 Onion Skin feature, 74–76
 rollover effects, 85–88

W

`while` **loops, 123, 142–143**
windows, Properties, 24
work area, 3

X

X, position, 186
x_displacement, 186

Y

Y, position, 186
y_displacement, 186

`ROLL_OVER`, 39
rollover effects, 85–88
rotating objects, 196–197

S

sample adventure game, 49–62
  buttons, creating, 49–51
  Layer 1, Frame 1, 51–52
  Layer 1, Frame 2, 53–54
  Layer 1, Frame 3, 55–56
  Layer 1, Frame 4, 56–58
  Layer 1, Frame 5, 58–60
  Layer 1, Frame 6, 60–62
  movie clips, creating, 49
  storyboards, 50
scalability, 43
`scene` parameter, 47
scores
  High Scores game, 176. *See also* High Scores game
  lists, 178
  Snakes and Ladders game, 225
selection tools, 6
separating images, 128
shapes, tweening, 71–72, 75
SharedObject class, 163–182
`shift()` method, 146
sign conventions, 194
Simple Simon Piano game, 149–160
  ActionScript, 154–160
  Actions layer, 153–154
  activities for MovieClip layer, 150–152
  creating, 150
  design, 153
  logic explanation, 152–154
single-dimensional arrays, 118, 143. *See also* **arrays**
slanted movement, 189
`slice()` method, 149, 152
Snakes and Ladders game
  ActionScript, 232–241
  elements of a quiz, 217–218
  game development, 220–241
  storyboards, 219
  story lines, 218
software-engineering principles, 43–44
sorting arrays, 148
`sort()` method, 148
sound, adding, 101–102
speed of objects, 190. *See also* **velocity**
`splice()` method, 145–146, 146–147
stages
  Flash document, 2–3
  objects, moving on, 184–215
star animations, 88
Start button, 168
`startDrag()` function, 81
`startDrag()` method, 120
statements, conditional, 142
states, buttons, 19, 24, 39–41
static text boxes, 20, 135
`stopDrag()` method, 120
`stop()` function, 26, 34, 46
stopwatches, creating, 100–101
storyboards, 44–45, 124
  Car Racing game, 200
  flowcharts, High Scores game, 165
  game development, 94–96
  High Scores game, 164
  sample adventure game, 50
  Snakes and Ladders game, 219
story lines, 94, 124
  Car Racing game, 200
  High Scores game, 164
  Snakes and Ladders game, 218
straight lines, object acceleration, 197
Sub Selection tool, 7
symbols, 9–11
  inserting, 173, 204
  libraries, 24

T

tanks, creating, 99–100
target movie clips, creating, 130
target objects, 179
`tc` function, 111
`tempSeq` array, 160
testing game development, 114
text
  animations, 82–85
  dynamic, modifying, 29
  fields, 20–41
text boxes
  drawing, 29
  dynamic, 134
  High Scores game, 171, 172, 173
  static, 135

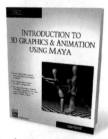

License Agreement/Notice of Limited Warranty

By opening the sealed disc container in this book, you agree to the following terms and conditions. If, upon reading the following license agreement and notice of limited warranty, you cannot agree to the terms and conditions set forth, return the unused book with unopened disc to the place where you purchased it for a refund.

License

The enclosed software is copyrighted by the copyright holder(s) indicated on the software disc. You are licensed to copy the software onto a single computer for use by a single user and to a backup disc. You may not reproduce, make copies, or distribute copies or rent or lease the software in whole or in part, except with written permission of the copyright holder(s). You may transfer the enclosed disc only together with this license, and only if you destroy all other copies of the software and the transferee agrees to the terms of the license. You may not decompile, reverse assemble, or reverse engineer the software.

Notice of Limited Warranty

The enclosed disc is warranted by Thomson Course Technology PTR to be free of physical defects in materials and workmanship for a period of sixty (60) days from end user's purchase of the book/disc combination. During the sixty-day term of the limited warranty, Thomson Course Technology PTR will provide a replacement disc upon the return of a defective disc.

Limited Liability

THE SOLE REMEDY FOR BREACH OF THIS LIMITED WARRANTY SHALL CONSIST ENTIRELY OF REPLACEMENT OF THE DEFECTIVE DISC. IN NO EVENT SHALL THOMSON COURSE TECHNOLOGY PTR OR THE AUTHOR BE LIABLE FOR ANY OTHER DAMAGES, INCLUDING LOSS OR CORRUPTION OF DATA, CHANGES IN THE FUNCTIONAL CHARACTERISTICS OF THE HARDWARE OR OPERATING SYSTEM, DELETERIOUS INTERACTION WITH OTHER SOFTWARE, OR ANY OTHER SPECIAL, INCIDENTAL, OR CONSEQUENTIAL DAMAGES THAT MAY ARISE, EVEN IF THOMSON COURSE TECHNOLOGY PTR AND/OR THE AUTHOR HAS PREVIOUSLY BEEN NOTIFIED THAT THE POSSIBILITY OF SUCH DAMAGES EXISTS.

Disclaimer of Warranties

THOMSON COURSE TECHNOLOGY PTR AND THE AUTHOR SPECIFICALLY DISCLAIM ANY AND ALL OTHER WARRANTIES, EITHER EXPRESS OR IMPLIED, INCLUDING WARRANTIES OF MERCHANTABILITY, SUITABILITY TO A PARTICULAR TASK OR PURPOSE, OR FREEDOM FROM ERRORS. SOME STATES DO NOT ALLOW FOR EXCLUSION OF IMPLIED WARRANTIES OR LIMITATION OF INCIDENTAL OR CONSEQUENTIAL DAMAGES, SO THESE LIMITATIONS MIGHT NOT APPLY TO YOU.

Other

This Agreement is governed by the laws of the State of Massachusetts without regard to choice of law principles. The United Convention of Contracts for the International Sale of Goods is specifically disclaimed. This Agreement constitutes the entire agreement between you and Thomson Course Technology PTR regarding use of the software.